Dear F~~r~~

I'd like to take this opportunity to personally thank you for visiting one of our many offices to pick up this cook book. May it provide you, your family and friends many hours of pleasant dining.

We hope this book will always remind you that there is ALWAYS something "cooking" at American Savings. We can provide you with the highest quality ingredients available to anyone, including:

★ **SAFETY SINCE 1885**

★ **CAPITAL AND RESERVES <u>OVER TWICE</u> LEGAL REQUIREMENTS**

★ **ASSETS OVER 4¼ <u>BILLION</u> DOLLARS STRONG**

★ **NATION'S <u>HIGHEST INTEREST</u> ON INSURED SAVINGS**

★ **MANY FREE SERVICES WITH SPECIFIED MINIMUM BALANCES**

★ **CONVENIENT LOCATIONS**

★ **PLEASANT AND HELPFUL COUNSELORS TO SERVE YOU**

We know you will find these ingredients to your liking, and that is why American Savings is one of the NATION'S LARGEST financial institutions.

Remember, at American Savings YOU <u>*NEVER*</u> LOSE, YOU <u>*ALWAYS*</u> GAIN! And, Bon Appétit!

Sincerely,

S. Mark Taper

S. Mark Taper, Chairman of the Board

AMERICAN SAVINGS AND LOAN ASSOCIATION

HUNDREDS OF
THE BEST RECIPES FROM

The Art of
Fish Cookery

Milo Miloradovich

BANTAM BOOKS · TORONTO · NEW YORK · LONDON

Hundreds of the
best recipes from
THE ART OF FISH COOKERY

A Bantam Book / *published by arrangement with*
Doubleday and Company, Inc.

PRINTING HISTORY

Doubleday edition published March 1949
2nd printing ..... March 1949
3rd printing ... February 1959
4th printing .. December 1961
5th printing ... September 1962
6th printing ... February 1963

Bantam Reference Library edition published March 1963
Bantam Cookbook Shelf edition published October 1965

3rd printing .... June 1966	7th printing .... July 1970
4th printing ... November 1967	8th printing .... June 1971
5th printing .... April 1969	9th printing ... February 1972
6th printing .... February 1970	10th printing .... June 1972

11th printing

12th printing

13th printing

Bantam Books are published by Bantam Books, Inc., a National
General company. Its trade-mark, consisting of the words "Bantam
Books" and the portrayal of a bantam, is registered in the United
States Patent Office and in other countries. Marca Registrada.
Bantam Books, Inc., 666 Fifth Avenue, New York, N.Y. 10019.

PRINTED IN THE UNITED STATES OF AMERICA

To ELLYN H. BRUSH

EVER A WISE TEACHER AND INSPIRING FRIEND

PREFACE

This book has been written in the hope that it will stimulate the interest and imagination of many who have missed the undreamed-of goodness in the taste of fish and shellfish *cooked at home*. It may have been because they knew of too few ways in which to prepare these most delicious and nutritious foods, or perhaps because they were unfamiliar with the many kinds which can be quickly and easily prepared. But whatever the reasons, may these suggestions assist and encourage everyone who enjoys eating tasty, delicious food to increase their enjoyment by using many more kinds of sea foods.

The *fish* and *shellfish* have been arranged separately in the volume for the sake of convenience and clarity; especially since each of these sea foods has a distinct and separate method of preparation as well as its own individual appeal.

The wide choice of the many kinds of *fish* and *shellfish* we may enjoy, in all sections of the country, is almost breath-taking as we stop to count the varieties. Approximately 160 kinds of fresh fish pass through the Fulton Market, New York, during the year; and with our improved shipping and *quick-freezing methods*, these varieties are now widely distributed. In addition to this number, the North, South, East, West, and Middle West have their own particular seasonal species of fish and shellfish.

Whether cooked quite simply or prepared with an elaborate sauce, real "home-cooked" fish and shellfish have an indescribable flavor when they are carefully and correctly handled. With just a little patience and practice, the preparation of even a complicated recipe can be quick and easy and the results delicious and satisfying. I believe more people would eat more fish and shellfish if they only knew more varieties and a greater number of tempting and interesting ways in which to prepare them.

CONTENTS

〜〜〜〜〜〜〜〜〜〜〜〜〜〜〜〜〜〜〜〜〜〜〜〜

Part Two: SHELLFISH

PART ONE

❧ FISH ❧

1. How to Purchase Fish

~~~~~~

If there is one suggestion which may take preference over all others when purchasing fish, it is this: *always be sure that the fish is fresh.* The fresher, the better. From the time fish is caught until it is received it should always be packed in ice. From the time it is delivered to you until it is cooked the *fish should be kept in the coolest part of the refrigerator.*

Absolutely fresh fish may be identified by observing five very important features:

1. The *eyes* should be full and bulging, with their surfaces bright and clear.

2. The *gills* should be reddish-pink, entirely free from any slime or unnatural odor.

3. The *scales* should retain their brightly colored sheen and adhere tightly to the skin.

4. The *meat* should cling closely to the bones; be firm and elastic to the touch. If pressed, it should come back to its original shape.

5. All fish have a more or less characteristic odor; but *all fresh fish have no objectionable odors.*

❧ FROZEN FISH   As distinguished from fresh, refrigerated fish, it is becoming more and more popular as the frozen-food industry develops and compares favorably with fresh fish in food value and appearance. *It may be used and prepared in the same manner as fresh fish.* However, additional cooking time should be allowed unless the fish has been thoroughly thawed immediately prior to cooking. Like other frozen foods, the fish should be delivered frozen and kept frozen until ready for use. It should *never be refrozen.*

◄§ HOW TO IDENTIFY MARKET FORMS AND CUTS OF FIN FISH Both freshly refrigerated and frozen fish may be purchased in a number of forms, depending upon the most usual market size. The small and medium-sized fish are usually marketed whole or round, drawn, dressed, and pan-dressed. Other varieties are filleted in either single or butterfly forms; while still larger fish are sold as steaks and sticks.

1. WHOLE OR ROUND: Fish as they come from the water. These are usually small fish, or small sizes of certain varieties and types that keep fresher without dressing.

2 DRAWN: Entrails only removed.

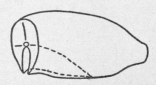

3. DRESSED: Entrails, head, tail, and fins removed. Very large dressed fish sometimes are marketed in chunks.

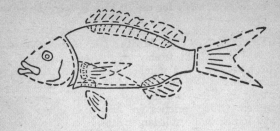

4. PAN-DRESSED: Usually these are the smaller varieties. Entrails, head, tail, and fins removed. Fish may be split along belly or back and the backbone removed.

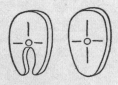

5. STEAKS: Steaks are the cross-sections of the large-sized dressed fish. Usually cut an inch or more thick, the only bone is the small section of the backbone in the center of the steak.

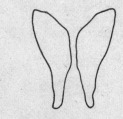

6. FILLETS: *Single fillets* are the meaty sides of the fish which are cut lengthwise away from the backbone. Their thickness and weight depend upon the original plumpness and weight of the fish. Fillets may weigh from several ounces to several pounds.

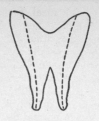

7. FILLETS: *Butterfly fillets* are fillets held together by the uncut belly skin of the fish. *All* fillets are practically boneless.

8 STICKS: Sticks are cut either crosswise or lengthwise into uniform portions *with* the backbone left in after the head, fins, entrails, and skin have been removed.

❧ HOW MUCH TO PURCHASE   The allowance for serving one person is generally considered to be ⅓ to ½ pound of the edible part of the fish. Therefore, when serving steaks, fillets, or sticks, purchase ⅓ to ½ pound for each person.

When purchasing dressed fish, calculate ½ pound for each serving. If whole or round fish is purchased, it is necessary to allow one pound for each person, or as shown here:

STEAKS, FILLETS, STICKS: One serving, ⅓ lb.

DRESSED FISH: One serving, ½ lb.

WHOLE OR ROUND   One serving, 1 lb.

❧ FOOD VALUES OF FISH   When you serve fish to your family you are not only giving them a new taste thrill but a rich combination of vitamins, minerals, and proteins found in few foods; there is no other one food which supplies so great a degree of these essentials of the daily diet.

An average portion at a meal, for example, will provide 10 per cent of the daily allowance of Vitamin A, more than all of Vitamin D, 15 per cent of thiamin, and from 20 to 70 per cent of the necessary riboflavin and nicotinic acids. Some fish also contain Vitamin C. The fillets of fatty fish, such as mackerel and salmon, contain 200 units of Vitamin A in 100 grams (about ¼ lb. of fish) and 600 units of Vitamin D. The energy value of fat fish is also high.

Minerals, so necessary to normal development and growth, and to the maintenance of healthy teeth and bones, are found in rich quantities in all fish products. For example: calcium and phosphorous, iron, copper, iodine, and magnesium, which are so essential for the proper metabolism of the tissues. All salt-water fish contain from 50 to 200 times as much iodine as is found in other foods. In the coastal communities, where fish is eaten as a good proportion of the diet, anemia and goiter are almost unheard of.

The food value of the proteins in fish is also unusually high and the digestibility is exceptional, ranging from 85 to 95 per cent. For all interested in valuable as well as delicious food it is well to remember that proteins are the foundation of all diets and a necessity for the maintenance of life itself.

2. Basic Instructions

~~~~~~

How to Clean and Dress Fish

The next time your enthusiastic young son or your amateur-fisherman husband brings in a beautiful brook trout or a string of deep-sea bass, or flounders, don't hold up your hands in frantic frustration and tell him to give "the horrible dead things away." It's quite easy and not at all unpleasant to scale, clean, and dress a fish. In fact, it can be done quickly and pleasantly and the only necessary tool is a very sharp, thin knife. If you want to scale your fish like a professional, use a regular fish scaler; though this isn't a "must," because a knife, held in a vertical position, will do the trick just as well.

As an illustration, suppose we use the *flounder* since, in addition to cleaning and dressing, this fish is often filleted. Here are the easy steps:

1. Wash fish thoroughly but quickly in cold, salted water; 1 tbs. salt to each quart of water.

2. Lay *wet* fish on wooden table top or board; grasp head firmly with one hand.

3. Holding sharp knife almost vertical, scrape scales off from the tail toward the head.

4. Remove entrails by cutting the entire length of the belly from the vent to the head.

5. Cut around pelvic fins (near head); remove them.

6. Remove head, including pectoral fin, by cutting above collarbone and through backbone. If backbone is very large, cut down to it on each side of the head and then snap bone over edge of table.

7. Cut any remaining flesh which holds head to body; cut off tail.

8. Remove back fin by cutting flesh along each side of fin, then give quick pull forward toward the head, which re-

moves the fin with root bones. Remove other fins in same manner. *Never trim fins off with shears.*

9. Dip fish quickly in cold salted water to remove any blood or remaining membranes.

10. Fish is now *dressed* or *pan-dressed,* ready for cooking.

◄§ HOW TO FILLET FISH If instead of cleaning and dressing the fish you wish to prepare it in fillets, you can do it in less than 5 minutes. Your single tool is the same sharp, thin knife. To *fillet* a fish:

1. Cut down through flesh along back from tail to just behind the head.

2. Cut down the backbone just above collarbone.

3. Turn the knife flat and cut flesh along backbone to the tail; the knife runs along rib bones and fillet comes off in one piece.

4. Turn the fish and repeat the same process on the other side.

If you wish to *skin* the fillets, then continue with the fifth step:

5. Lay fillet flat on wooden table top or board, skin side down.

6. Grasp tail end with fingers; cut through the flesh to the skin (about ½ inch from end of the fillet).

7. Flatten the knife on the skin and cut flesh away by pushing knife forward; fillet is then skinned.

8. Always hold free end of skin firmly with fingers.

9. Wipe fillet with damp cloth only; do not wash.

How to Cook Fish

Raw, fresh fish is always tender and juicy. If the cooked fish is tough and dry and has become shrunken in appearance, then the fish is overcooked. There is only one easy hint to remember if you are to become an expert in cooking fish. It is simply this: *fish needs no tenderizing.* Fish is cooked to *bring out* and develop its natural, individual, and distinctive flavor and to hold together its valuable proteins. Have everything prepared before beginning a recipe, for the secret of serving delicious sea food lies in the speed and lightness with which the fish is handled. Fish cooked at home can be as superior in flavor to restaurant-cooked fish as other home-cooked food can be.

◆§ BAKING   Any size or market form of fresh- or salt-water fish may be baked. Fillets, steaks, pan-dressed, drawn or dressed, cut portions, or split fish may be used.

Marinating fish in blended herbs and wine vinegar, or in French dressing before baking, adds an extra tanginess to the flavor. As a change from basting with butter, try a white wine or fish stock instead. The result is delightful.

Baking fish is a quick, easy way to cook it, for fish takes less time than any other meat. It is no longer necessary to poke at baking fish, and lose the tasty, natural juices, if these suggestions are remembered:

1. Have fish cleaned and dressed ready for baking. If fish must be washed, dip it quickly in cold salted water; wipe fish dry with damp cloth. Also be sure that blood line under backbone has been scraped and removed.

2. Have fish weighed *with or without head* as you intend to bake it.

3. Head may be left on or taken off as desired. Leaving the head on seals in the juices. The head may be removed before fish is served if preferred.

4. If fish is to be stuffed, never fill cavity more than ⅔ full.

5. Keep stuffing inside fish by closing cavity with skewers, or lace with white thread.

6. Place fish in shallow baking pan over a layer of buttered brown or waxed paper.

7. Always preheat oven moderately hot only—400° F.

8. Bake exact time as directed. Overbaking dries out natural flavor and juices.

9. Serve as soon as taken from oven; standing makes fish soggy.

◆§ BOILING   When fish is boiled with herbs, or in a broth, and is to be served with a sauce, the process must be more like a gentle simmering. Fillets and steaks are sometimes simmered or boiled in *Court Bouillon;* and fish trimmings are boiled with herbs and vegetables to make a fish stock. These are the few pointers to remember:

1. If whole fish is boiled, have fish cleaned and dressed at market.

2. Wipe dressed fish, fillets, or steaks with damp cloth.

3. Tie fish securely in cheesecloth. If fish trimmings are being boiled to make fish stock, *do not tie* in cheesecloth.

4. Bring to boiling point; lower flame and simmer gently. (See time in individual recipes.)

5. Drain; then prepare and serve fish as desired.

BROILING Sizzling broiled fish, whether it's a fillet, a steak, a split fish, or a whole dressed fish, is one of the most tempting and tasty dishes you can prepare. But it should always be served *sizzling hot* at the very moment it is taken from the broiler. Nothing is quite so discouraging to an expectant appetite as a piece of lukewarm fish. Work quickly and lightly when broiling, and take great care not to burn or overcook the fish.

Fillets vary in thickness from about ¼ to 1 inch, depending upon the species of fish: whether the fillet was prepared from a plump or a thin fish. Steaks may be cut to any thickness preferred, but a good average thickness is 1 inch.

Fillets and steaks are placed on the broiler rack 2 inches from the flame while the distance from the source of heat for the split fish and whole dressed fish varies from 2 to 6 inches.

When split fish is broiled, it is best to have the backbone left in, as the fish is juicier and has much more flavor. The whole dressed fish is cleaned and prepared as for baking.

Fish, properly broiled, should always be juicy and a light, golden brown. These hints will help you attain the desired results:

1. Preheat broiling compartment and pan for at least 10 minutes to broiling heat as directed by the range manufacturer. (Approximately 550° F.)

2. If fish must be washed, do so quickly in cold salted water.

3. Dust fish lightly with flour.

4. Brush top of fish with butter and seasonings as directed. If whole fish is used, brush entire fish.

5. Place on preheated broiling rack the distance below flame as directed.

6. Do *not* turn *fillets* and *split* fish during broiling period; *baste* as directed; season at end of broiling time.

7. *Fish steaks* and *whole fish* are broiled on one side, then *turned* and *broiled* on the second side as *directed*.

8. *Fish steaks* and *whole fish* are basted *after* turning; *seasoned* at end of broiling time.

9. Serve all broiled fish *immediately*.

❧ DEEP FRYING   Fish in its filleted form is more adaptable to deep frying than other forms. It is quick, easy, and odorless when care is taken so that the butter or fat is never allowed to smoke. To deep-fry fillets or very small whole fish such as smelt:

1. Wipe fish with damp cloth.

2. Dip fillets in milk, then in cracker crumbs.

3. Place *one layer only* of fish in wire frying basket.

4. Heat butter or fat in deep kettle to 350°–385° F.

5. Fry quickly as directed until golden brown. (3 to 5 minutes is an average.)

6. Serve *immediately* with preferred sauce or garnish.

❧ PAN FRYING   Small, whole game fish of many varieties as well as local salt-water fish are often prepared *pan-fried*. Care should be taken not to overcook. The juices of the fish are sealed in when the fish is dropped quickly into very hot butter or vegetable fat. For thin fish, use a regular frying pan; for the plumper species, a skillet is better. All other forms of fish may be pan-fried if desired, but broiling is preferable.

To pan-fry fillets, steaks, pan-dressed, drawn, or dressed fish, split or cut into serving portions:

1. Wipe fish with damp cloth.

2. Dip fish into milk, then in cracker crumbs or flour.

3. Use sufficient fat or butter to cover bottom of pan from ¼ to ½ inch deep, depending upon thickness of fish. For example: if steak is 1 inch thick, melted butter should be ½ inch deep.

4. Heat butter but do not allow to smoke.

5. Fry fish at moderate heat 3 to 5 minutes, or until light brown.

6. Turn fish carefully with spatula; brown second side as directed. (Average, 3 minutes.)

7. Garnish; *serve fish immediately*.

◆§ PLANKING   A planked fish can be a work of art as well as an epicurean repast. Any variety of fish, suitable for baking or broiling, may be prepared in this attractive manner. A whole planked fish, with three or four of the season's most decorative vegetables, makes a festive appearance on any table. Care should always be taken not to overcook the vegetables before they are arranged on the plank, otherwise the time in the oven will wreck not only their appearance but their flavor.

To plank fish or fish steak of your choice:

1. If possible, use a *wooden* plank made from well-seasoned hickory, ash, or oak. Plank should be 1½ inches thick. Oven glass may be used if wooden plank is not available; but it, too, should be grooved around the edge, with several additional grooves cut into the surface to hold the juices.

2. Put cold plank in *cold* oven. Preheat oven as directed (usually 10 minutes).

3. Remove hot plank; oil or butter thoroughly.

4. Arrange fish in center of plank.

5. Proceed as directed on page 10. Vegetables are parboiled; potatoes mashed; fish garnished; return to oven to finish baking.

6. Serve piping hot on plank at table.

◆§ SAUTÉING   A great treat lies in store for all those who have never been introduced to the piquant flavor surprises of fish fillets and steaks which have been gently sautéed in rare spices, or simmered in white and red wines.

When the Europeans sauté fish, they usually select a firm, sweet, white-meated fish which is then cut into cubes or serving pieces as preferred. For example: in the recipe for "Cod Carcassonne," as cod is prepared in the ancient French walled city of that name, the fish is simmered with parsley, olive oil, and a little water until the liquid has practically evaporated and given the fish an unusual herb flavor. Or fish sautéed with a generous amount of wine, as in "Carp Hilda with Burgundy," is something of a taste thrill you can never forget.

It isn't necessary to cut the fish into cubes, for whole fillets and steaks are equally delicious when sautéed. Select the fish and the form you prefer and use your favorite red or white wine, then:

1. Wipe fillets or steaks with damp cloth.
2. Melt generous quantity of butter in saucepan over medium flame.
3. Add herbs and seasonings sparingly as directed.
4. Add liquid as directed (usually fish stock and wine).
5. Simmer gently over low flame as directed. (Time varies with species of fish.)
6. Serve fish piping hot, with liquid in which it was cooked.

◄§ STEAMING There are those who say that fish never tastes so delicate as when it has been steamed. Perhaps this is because a steamed fish can't possibly become shriveled and dried. The juices and flavor remain in the fish when it is cooked over moisture and the pan is tightly covered. Any deep pan will be all right, and if a steaming rack is not available, anything may be used that prevents the fish from touching the water. Both fresh and frozen fish may be easily steamed by observing these instructions:

1. Wipe fish with damp cloth.
2. Tie fish carefully in cheesecloth so it may be lifted out of pot easily in one piece.
3. Use any deep pot with a tight cover.
4. Fill pot with 2 inches water, not more.
5. Place metal rack in bottom of pot; or place fish in wire basket which does not touch water.
6. When water boils rapidly, place fish on rack; cover pot tightly.
7. Steam any fish (less than 2 inches thick) 1 minute for each ounce of weight when fish is ready for steaming.
8. Salt fish only after steaming.
9. Water may be seasoned with any desired seasoning, such as garlic, onion, cloves, parsley, wine, celery, or vinegar. Herbs and wine should be added to water as soon as it is poured into pot so that the flavors of the herbs will blend well and permeate the fish.
10. Serve steamed fish with preferred mild sauce; or flaked as recipe directs.

How to Reduce Natural Frying Odors

To keep all natural frying odors at a minimum when cooking either deep-fried or pan-fried fish, remember these two simple suggestions:

1. Heat fat or butter TO SMOKING POINT ONLY, because *hot fat or butter absorbs most of natural odors; smoking fat or butter does not.*

2. So *never allow heated fat or butter to smoke.*

How to Store Fish in Refrigerator

All fish should always be kept as cold as possible: *before* cooking and *after* cooking, whenever it is stored. *Raw* fish should be placed near the freezing unit of the refrigerator or in the freezing compartment itself. But wherever you place it, be sure to take these precautionary steps:

1. *Fish must be clean before it is stored.* Remove the congealed blood pocket which lies under the backbone if this has not been done by the dealer at the market. Simply scrape the cavity with a sharp knife and wipe the fish clean with absorbent paper.

2. Wrap fish tightly in waxed paper; place in freezing compartment. Fish may be kept in this manner as long as refrigerator is not allowed to defrost.

3. Or place fish in glass dish which can be tightly covered. Fish stored carefully in this manner will keep several days.

4. *Cooked, leftover fish* should be stored in tightly covered dish and placed in refrigerator as soon as you realize it is to be left over.

How to Sweeten Pans and Hands

Your hands may be kept sweet and free from any natural, raw-fish odor if you CHILL YOUR HANDS THOROUGHLY IN COLD WATER BEFORE TOUCHING RAW FISH.

To cleanse your hands AFTER cooking fish, remember these four simple steps:

1. *Do not use soap at first.*
2. Rub hands well with moistened salt.
3. Rinse off all salt with hot water.
4. Finally, cleanse hands with soap.

To neutralize any natural odors and to sweeten dishes and utensils used in preparing and serving fish, DO NOT USE SOAP *until after all utensils have been rinsed off thoroughly and cleansed in a strong, warm salt-water solution.* Cooled oven pans should be *soaked* in *hot* salted water.

3. FISH CHOWDERS AND STEWS

~~~~~~

Chowders

CONEY ISLAND FISH CHOWDER
TIME: 45 MINUTES; SERVES 6

1½ lbs. halibut	¼ lb. salt pork, diced
1 cup water	1 No. 2 can tomatoes
1 cup Fish Stock (page 21)	1 onion, chopped
2 medium potatoes, diced	2 tbs. flour
2 stalks celery, diced	¼ tsp. salt
½ green pepper, chopped	⅛ tsp. pepper

Place water and fish stock in deep pot; add potatoes; cook 10 minutes; add fish and celery; cover; simmer 5 minutes, or until potatoes are tender.

Meanwhile, place pork in skillet; fry 5 minutes, or until golden brown. Remove from fat; cook onion and green pepper in fat 5 minutes, or until tender; gradually add flour, stirring constantly until very smooth; add tomatoes, salt, and pepper; heat thoroughly.

Remove fish from stock; flake into large pieces. Combine all ingredients with fish stock; heat thoroughly. Serve piping hot in preheated bowls.

HADDOCK CHOWDER
TIME: 45 MINUTES; SERVES 6 TO 8

1½ lbs. haddock fillets	2 large potatoes, diced
1 large onion, chopped	4 tbs. flour
3 stalks celery, chopped	1 tsp. Worcestershire sauce
4 tbs. butter	¼ tsp. pepper
3 cups water	½ tsp. salt
1 qt. milk	

Place fillets in deep kettle; cover with 1½ cups cold water; simmer over medium flame 10 minutes, or until haddock is

15

easily flaked with fork. When done, place fish in large bowl; flake fish; save fish stock for use later.

Place butter in deep kettle over medium flame; add onion; sauté 5 minutes, or until golden brown; add potatoes, celery, add 1½ cups water; cover; cook 15 minutes, or until potatoes and celery are tender.

Blend flour in small mixing bowl with one half milk; when smooth, add other half milk; then add to cooked potatoes and celery; add fish and fish stock; heat to boiling point but do not boil. Season with salt and pepper. Serve piping hot in preheated chowder bowls. Garnish each serving with chopped parsley if desired.

VARIATION: Use *any variety white-meated fish.*

NEW ENGLAND FISH CHOWDER
TIME: 40 MINUTES; SERVES 6 TO 8

2 lbs. cod fillets	1 qt. rich milk
4 slices bacon, diced	2 cups hot water
1 large onion, diced	1 bay leaf
2 large potatoes, diced	1 tsp. salt
2 tbs. chopped parsley	⅛ tsp. pepper

Cut fish fillets into 1½ inch cubes.

Place bacon in deep kettle over low flame; fry 5 minutes, or until golden brown; add onions; sauté 3 minutes; add water, bay leaf, and potatoes; cover; cook 10 minutes, or until potatoes are partially tender; add fish; simmer 10 minutes, or until fish is easily flaked with fork; add milk, salt, and pepper; heat to boiling point but do not boil. Serve piping hot in preheated chowder bowls. Sprinkle each serving with chopped parsley or favorite green herbs.

VARIATION: Use *any preferred white-meated fish.*

SALMON CHOWDER WITH MILK
TIME: 45 MINUTES: SERVES 6 TO 8

3 lbs. salmon (1 thick slice)	¼ lb. salt pork, diced
1 bay leaf	2 large onions, sliced
1 sprig parsley	3 large potatoes, diced
3 peppercorns	Salt and pepper
3 pints milk	

Place salmon carefully in deep pot; cover with water (no more than that amount); add bay leaf, parsley, peppercorns, and salt to taste (¼ teaspoon); boil 15 minutes, or until salmon can be flaked with fork and broth is cooked down.

While salmon is cooking boil diced potatoes and prepare diced pork and onions as follows: place pork in skillet; fry over medium flame 15 minutes, or until golden brown and well done; add onions; brown 5 minutes, stirring constantly.

Remove cooked salmon; flake in large pieces.

Heat deep soup tureen by letting it stand in very hot water. Place salmon, potatoes, onions, and salt pork in heated tureen; cover to keep hot.

In separate pot heat milk to boiling but do not boil; pour milk over hot ingredients; add salt and pepper to taste. Serve piping hot in preheated chowder bowls.

SCROD CHOWDER WITH CREAM
TIME: 45 MINUTES; SERVES 6

1 scrod (2½ lbs.)	*1 pt. milk*
4 potatoes, diced	*2 tbs. butter*
4 medium onions, sliced	*Salt and pepper*
¼ lb. salt pork, diced	*6 large chowder crackers,*
1 pt. water	*buttered*
1 pt. cream	*Paprika*

Place whole cleaned scrod in deep kettle; cover with 1 pint water; simmer 15 minutes, or until fish flakes easily when tested with fork. Remove from stock; set aside.

Place onions and potatoes in fish stock; boil 10 minutes, or until potatoes are tender. While vegetables are cooking, place salt pork in skillet over low flame; fry 15 minutes, or until golden brown.

Remove bones and skin from scrod; flake fish with fork. Add fish and salt pork to onions and potatoes in fish stock.

In separate saucepan heat milk and cream to boiling point but do not boil; add heated liquid to chowder; season with salt and pepper to taste.

Pour piping hot chowder over buttered chowder crackers placed in preheated chowder bowls. Sprinkle with paprika.

VARIATION: Use *2 pounds lake trout, salmon, cod,* or *haddock.* Garnish with chopped parsley.

Stews

CODFISH STEW AU LAIT
TIME: 30 MINUTES; SERVES 6

1 lb. fresh cod fillets	1 bay leaf
1 pt. oysters, in liquor	Pinch of paprika
1 tbs. butter	1/8 tsp. pepper
1 slice of onion	Salt
1 qt. rich milk	

Wipe fillets with damp cloth; salt fillets lightly on both sides; place in well-greased steamer pan; steam over boiling water 10 minutes. Remove fish; flake into small pieces with fork; set aside.

Pour milk into deep saucepan; add bay leaf, onion slice, pepper, and paprika; heat over medium flame but do not boil; add flaked cod and oysters in their liquor. When edges of oysters begin to curl (in 3 minutes), stew is ready to serve. Serve piping hot in preheated soup plates. Garnish with chopped chives or parsley.

VARIATION: *Oysters may be omitted*; serves 4.

HADDOCK STEW WITH TOMATOES
TIME: 30 MINUTES; SERVES 4 TO 6

2 lbs. haddock fillets	2 cloves garlic, minced
1 large can tomatoes	1/8 tsp. pepper
1/4 tsp. marjoram	3 stalks celery, chopped
1/8 tsp. basil	4 sprigs parsley
Salt to taste	4 slices buttered toast
1/4 cup olive oil	

Pour olive oil into deep saucepan; place over medium flame; add marjoram, basil, salt, pepper, and tomatoes; cover; simmer 20 minutes.

Meanwhile, wipe fillets with damp cloth; salt fillets lightly on both sides; place in well-greased steamer pan; steam over boiling water 10 minutes, or until fish flakes easily when tested with fork. Remove fish carefully to preheated deep vegetable dish or tureen.

Pour piping hot tomato sauce over fish. Garnish with

parsley sprigs. Serve piping hot, over buttered toast placed in preheated soup plates.

VARIATION: Use *cod, hake, halibut,* or *whitefish.*

POLLOCK STEW WITH SAUTERNE
TIME: 45 MINUTES; SERVES 4

1½ lbs. pollock fillets	½ cup dry sauterne wine
1 cup canned tomatoes	½ cup olive oil
2 medium onions, sliced	1 stalk celery, chopped
1 small carrot	1 sprig parsley
3 medium potatoes	2 cloves garlic
Juice of ½ lemon	Salt and pepper

Wipe fillets with damp cloth; cut fillets into serving pieces; sprinkle with lemon juice; season with salt and pepper to taste.

Pour 2 cups water in saucepan; parboil carrot and potatoes 10 minutes.

Pour olive oil in skillet over medium flame; sauté onions 3 minutes, or until light brown. Remove onions and save oil.

Slice potatoes; place in an earthenware pot or casserole a layer of onions and a layer of potatoes; next add the fish, then the parsley, celery, and garlic; finally add balance of onions and potatoes.

Pour olive oil, tomatoes, and sauterne wine over top. Bake in preheated moderate oven (375° F.) 30 minutes. Serve piping hot from casserole.

VARIATION: Use also *halibut, lingcod,* or *swordfish.*

SWORDFISH STEW WITH VEGETABLES
TIME: 1¼ HOURS; SERVES 6

1½ lbs. swordfish steak	2 slices bacon
3 stalks celery, diced	2 small potatoes
4 cups Fish Stock (page 21)	1 medium onion, minced
1 tbs. butter	1 small carrot, diced
1 No. 2 can tomatoes	½ green pepper, minced
½ tsp. thyme	Salt and pepper
⅛ tsp. basil	2 tbs. chopped chives

Wipe swordfish steak with damp cloth; cut into 2-inch cubes; set aside. Into deep kettle pour fish stock; add celery, butter, tomatoes, thyme, basil, onion, green pepper, salt and pepper to taste. Cover; simmer gently 30 minutes.

Meanwhile, place bacon in skillet over low flame; brown

3 minutes; add browned bacon to Fish Stock, then add swordfish cubes; simmer 15 minutes. Add potatoes and carrot; simmer 15 minutes more, or until potatoes and carrot are tender. Serve stew piping hot in preheated bowls. Garnish each serving with chopped chives or preferred green herbs.

Stocks and Fumets

COURT BOUILLON PROVENÇALE
TIME: 1½ HOURS; YIELD: 3 PINTS

2 lbs. fish trimmings	8 peppercorns
2 qts. water	2 tsp. salt
1 bay leaf	1 large onion, minced
¼ lb. butter	⅛ tsp. thyme
2 carrots, chopped	3 sprigs parsley
3 stalks celery	Juice of 1 lemon
1 qt. sweet cider	

Purchase fish trimmings of firm-meated fish, such as cod, haddock, halibut, or salmon; wipe with damp cloth; place fish trimmings in deep pot; add all ingredients; bring to boiling point over high flame; lower flame; cover, simmer gently 1 hour.

Remove fish from liquid; strain; set aside for use as directed in cooking fish and preparing sauces.

VARIATION: Use any *variety dry white wine*, such as *sauterne* or *rhine wine*, instead of cider; omit lemon juice.

COURT BOUILLON WITHOUT WINE
TIME: 45 MINUTES; YIELD: 3 PINTS

2 qts. water	2 tbs. vinegar
2 tbs. butter	2 sprigs parsley
6 whole black peppercorns	1 large onion, chopped
2 whole cloves	1 large carrot, chopped
1 bay leaf	3 stalks celery, chopped

Peel and chop vegetables. Melt butter in deep saucepan over medium flame; add chopped vegetables; sauté 5 minutes, or until golden brown; add water, peppercorns, cloves, bay leaf, vinegar, and parsley; cover tightly; simmer 30 minutes. Strain and set aside for use in boiling fish.

FISH STOCK PLAIN

TIME: 30 MINUTES; YIELD: 3 PINTS

2 lbs. fish trimmings   1 bay leaf
(heads, bones, tails)   1 tbs. salt
2 qts. water

Wash fish trimmings thoroughly in salted water. Pour water into deep saucepan; add fish, salt, and bay leaf; cover; simmer 30 minutes. Strain and set aside for use in preparing fish recipes.

FISH STOCK WITH SPICES

TIME: 45 MINUTES; YIELD: 3 PINTS

2 lbs. haddock tails   1 parsley root
2 cloves   1 bay leaf
½ tsp. mace   6 whole peppercorns
3 stalks celery, with tops   1 tbs. salt
2 qts. water

Wash haddock tails thoroughly in salted water.

Place all ingredients in deep saucepan; cover tightly and bring to a boil; lower flame; simmer gently 45 minutes. Strain and cool. Use stock as directed with fish.

FUMET*

TIME: 40 MINUTES; YIELD: APPROXIMATELY 1 PINT

1½ lbs. fish trimmings   1 carrot, sliced
2 cups water   2 stalks celery
1 bay leaf   2 tbs. chopped parsley
1 onion, sliced   Salt and pepper
2 cups sauterne wine

Purchase tail and bones of cod, haddock, or any variety firm-meated fish; wash thoroughly under cold running water.

Place all ingredients in deep kettle; bring to boiling point; cover; simmer gently 30 minutes, or until liquid is reduced half. Strain liquid through fine sieve. Set *fumet* aside for use as directed.

* A *fumet* differs from *court bouillon* in that it is more concentrated and contains equal parts of water and wine. It is a fish broth greatly reduced in cooking and is indispensable in fine fish cookery. When ready, it should always be set aside an hour or two, then used to poach the fish; or in the place of water in making fish sauces.

4. FRESH-WATER FISH

~~~~~~

◆§ BASS   CALICO BASS, native of the Great Lakes region and the Mississippi Valley, is well adapted to cultivation in ponds. The name *calico* is suggested by the markings, and the fish is easily distinguishable by its seven or eight dorsal spines. The average market weight is a pound, though larger ones may weigh as much as 2 pounds. Especially delicious when pan-fried.

ROCK BASS is a thick-bodied, meaty fish which grows to about the same size as the *calico bass.*

CALICO BASS AMERICAN INDIAN STYLE
TIME: 15 MINUTES; SERVES 6

2 lbs. calico bass, whole	½ cup yellow corn meal
1 tbs. chopped chives	½ cup white flour
2 tsp. salt	3 tbs. butter or shortening
¼ tsp. pepper	1 lemon, sliced

Pan-dress bass by removing heads, tails, fins, and entrails. (If preferred, do not remove heads.) Wipe fish with damp cloth. Sift flour, salt, and pepper into long oblong dish or on mixing board; blend in corn meal by stirring vigorously. Roll fish in flour-corn-meal mixture.

Heat butter or shortening in frying pan; brown fish quickly about 4 minutes on each side, being careful not to overcook. Garnish with chopped chives and lemon slices. Serve piping hot on preheated plates.

VARIATION: Use 3 pounds *rock bass*, whole; fry 15 minutes. *Similar tender and white-meated fish* or *fillets* may be prepared in same manner.

◆§ CARP   A European fish widely introduced into the lakes and ponds of North America. The flavor is better when the fish is taken from cold waters, therefore the best season is from October to the end of March. A firm-fleshed, lean-meated fish of real delicacy when properly prepared. Marketed in sizes 2 to 7 pounds; also as fillets, steaks, fresh, frozen, smoked, and alive.

CARP HILDA WITH BURGUNDY

TIME: 45 MINUTES; SERVES 4

1 carp (3 lbs.)	½ onion, minced
3 tbs. butter	¼ lb. mushrooms, chopped
2 tbs. flour	⅛ tsp. pepper
Salt	2 tbs. chopped parsley
3 cups burgundy wine	

Purchase live carp; have it cleaned and cut into serving pieces; wipe with damp cloth; rub salt gently into each piece of fish. Place fish pieces in deep saucepan; add burgundy wine, onion, and pepper; bring to boiling point over medium flame; cover; simmer gently 20 minutes, or until fish flakes when tested with fork.

Meanwhile, place 1 tablespoon butter in small saucepan over medium flame; add mushrooms; salt lightly; simmer mushrooms gently 15 minutes. Set aside.

When fish is done, lift out carefully; strain wine through fine sieve. Mix flour with small quantity warm wine until very smooth; add to balance of wine; add butter and sautéed mushrooms; cook sauce gently 10 minutes over medium flame, stirring constantly. Sauce should not be too thick. Add fish pieces; heat gently 5 minutes. Serve piping hot; garnish each serving with chopped parsley.

VARIATION: Use *any preferred tart red wine. Halibut, trout* or *haddock* may be substituted.

CARP SAUTÉED À LA SUISSE

TIME: 1 HOUR; SERVES 4 TO 6

1 carp (3 to 4 lbs.)	¼ lb. butter
½ cup flour	1 tbs. grated horse-radish
½ tsp. salt	1 egg yolk, beaten
⅛ tsp. pepper	1 tbs. chopped chives
1 cup rhine wine	

Have carp cleaned; wash carefully in 2 cups cold water and ½ cup vinegar; wipe with damp cloth; cut carp into serving pieces. Set aside.

Blend salt, pepper, and flour. Roll carp pieces in seasoned

flour. Melt butter in saucepan over medium flame; add carp pieces; pour rhine wine over carp; cover; simmer gently 30 minutes; stir carefully occasionally.

With spatula remove fish from sauce; arrange fish on preheated platter; keep hot over steam. Quickly stir horse-radish into sauce; remove from flame; cool 5 minutes; gradually add beaten egg yolk; stir well; return to flame; heat 1 minute.

Pour steaming hot sauce over sautéed carp; garnish with chopped chives or parsley. Serve immediately.

◄§ CATFISH   The annual catch for market has exceeded 14,000,000 pounds. The BLUE CATFISH, native of the Great Lakes and the Mississippi Valley, is considered the best of all as a food fish. Season is all year; the best months from April to September. It often attains a weight of more than 100 pounds, but the average ranges from 1 pound to 20 pounds; round, dressed, and skinned ready for cooking. The meat is firm, flaky, highly nutritious, and delicately flavored.

The BULLHEAD inhabits streams, lakes, and ponds of the eastern and middle states and is found as far westward as the Dakotas and Texas. It has a broom-shaped tail, and is seldom more than a foot and a half long. The meat is firm, flaky, and deliciously flavored; best when broiled or pan-fried.

CATFISH IN BROWN BUTTER
TIME: 20 MINUTES; SERVES 6

3 *lbs. catfish*	2 *tsp. salt*
12 *sprigs parsley*	¼ *tsp. pepper*
2 *tsp. chopped fresh mint*	2 *tbs. flour*
¼ *lb. butter*	

If fish is purchased, have it cleaned and skinned, otherwise, handle carefully to avoid painful stings caused by a fluid secreted at the base of spine. A safe, easy way is to use a heavy cloth or canvas working glove to grasp fish by its head. Turn the fish on back, slit throat through *to* the back skin but not *through* it. Bend head backward and pull down to peel off skin as you would turn a glove inside out. Split fish; wipe with damp cloth; dust lightly with flour.

Melt butter in saucepan; brush fish lightly with part of melted butter; sprinkle with chopped mint. Place on preheated broiling pan 2 inches below flame; broil 4 minutes; baste with more melted butter; broil 4 minutes more.

Meanwhile, fry parsley sprigs 4 minutes in butter over low flame. Place broiled fish on preheated platter; salt and pepper. Garnish with hot parsley sprigs and butter. Serve immediately on preheated plates.

VARIATION: Catfish may also be *pan-fried plain* or "American Indian Style" (page 22). If so, *never cover*, otherwise fish becomes soggy.

•§ CRAPPIE   The meat of the BLACK CRAPPIE, known also as the STRAWBERRY BASS is white, tender, and of excellent flavor. Average weight, 2 pounds, but it often reaches 4 pounds. The WHITE CRAPPIE, reared successfully in thousands of fish ponds, is considered among the best pan-fishes, but seldom weighs more than a pound and is truly delicious when prepared as soon as it is taken from the water. *Commercial fishing is prohibited in most states* to reserve the species for for the angler.

•§ LAKE HERRING   Native of the Great Lakes, the LAKE HERRING is not to be confused with the sea herring, for *lake herring is related to the whitefish*. These fat herring are in great demand as fresh fish since they are somewhat similar to the whitefish. Average weight, when fresh, is 5 to 6 ounces. Also marketed smoked, salted, and frozen.

(*See also* "Smoked, Salted, and Canned Fish" chapter.)

LAKE HERRING DEEP-FRIED
TIME: 10 MINUTES; SERVES 4

2 *lbs. lake herring*	1 *cup oil*
1 *cup flour*	1 *large lemon, quartered*
2 *tbs. chopped parsley*	*Salt and pepper*

Lake herring taste best when fried a golden color in deep oil or shortening. They must not be drawn or washed (also, do not cut off the heads). Wipe with damp cloth only.

Heat oil in large skillet; do not allow to smoke. Salt and pepper fish lightly; dip in flour. Brown quickly in oil about 5 minutes, or until a golden color; remove carefully with spatula to prevent breaking. Garnish with chopped parsley and lemon. Serve very hot.

•§ LAKE TROUT   Largest of all the trouts, this ranks next

to the whitefish in commercial importance. It is found in most of the lakes of the northern United States, and beyond the Arctic Circle. In Maine they are called TOGUE. The average market size is less than 10 pounds; fish caught by anglers average about half that size. The color varies, they are usually a pale green covered by small pale-yellowish spots. Like the meat of the many game trout, its flavor is sweet and delicate.

LAKE TROUT ALGONAC
TIME: 1¼ HOURS; SERVES 6 TO 8

1 lake trout (4 lbs.)	1 tsp. salt
⅛ tsp. paprika	¼ tsp. pepper

Have trout dressed; wipe with damp cloth. Blend salt, pepper, and paprika well in small dish; rub trout inside and out with this mixture.

HERB STUFFING WITH EGG

2 slices salt pork, chopped	1 egg, well beaten
2 cups soft bread crumbs	⅛ tsp. thyme
1 small onion, minced	⅛ tsp. pepper
1 tbs. chopped parsley	Pinch of nutmeg
¼ tsp. grated lemon rind	2 tbs. milk

Place salt pork and onion in skillet over low flame; brown 15 minutes, or until pork is almost crisp.

Put bread crumbs into deep mixing bowl; add all seasonings; blend well; add beaten egg; blend again.

Stuff trout lightly, about ¾ full. Arrange in shallow, well-greased baking dish; place balance of stuffing over fish; bake in preheated moderate oven (375° F.) 40 minutes. Place baked fish on preheated platter. Garnish with parsley sprigs, fresh mint, or lemon wedges. Serve immediately.

VARIATION: Try *royal planked. See* pages 62-63, "Shad Royal Planked."

◄§ LANDLOCKED SALMON Sometimes called LAKE SALMON, a landlocked form of the Atlantic salmon, the color on its back varies from a black to a blue-green, while the underpart of the body is a rather light silvery shade. Marked with black spots like the sea-run salmon, it can be easily distinguished because the spots are much larger and irregular in shape. A much smaller fish than the Atlantic salmon, its average weight is from 4 to 5 pounds, though many 35-pounders have been taken. Its flaky texture is delicious when baked and served with a rich sauce, or planked with several attractive vegetables.

LANDLOCKED SALMON BOILED SUPRÊME
TIME: 45 MINUTES; SERVES 4 TO 6

1 *landlocked salmon (4 lbs.)*	½ *cup dry sauterne wine*
1 *qt. Court Bouillon*	2 *cups Parsley Sauce*
(page 20)	*(page 81)*

Have fish drawn only; wipe with damp cloth; tie fish in cheesecloth; place in large, wide kettle. Pour Court Bouillon and wine over. (Liquid should cover entire fish.) Bring to boiling point over high flame; lower flame; cover; simmer gently 30 minutes, or until fish flakes easily when tested with fork.

Carefully remove fish from liquid; arrange on preheated platter. Serve piping hot with Parsley Sauce or preferred cream sauce. Garnish.

VARIATION: May also be *served with melted butter and sprinkled with chopped parsley.* Use *any variety firm-meated fish steaks* or *fillets.* Boil 10 to 12 minutes *only.* Do *not* overcook.

◄§ FRESH-WATER MULLET   Also known as the WHITE SUCKER, it is found in small streams and lakes all over the United States. The color varies from very dark to a fairly light olive. During the spawning season the males have two longitudinal stripes on the side: one black and a lower pinkish one. When the mullets come from the deep, cold waters or from clear running streams, as most of the commercially important ones do, the meat is firm, sweet, and flaky. The dusky flesh contains a highly palatable, delicately flavored, nutritious oil. The fish are marketed in sizes from 2 to 5 pounds; whole, drawn, dressed, filleted, fresh or frozen, salted, and smoked. The smaller sizes are best royal broiled or fried, while the 5-pound sizes are excellent for stuffing and baking.

MULLET SPICY MARINATED
TIME: 1¼ HOURS; SERVES 6

2½ lbs. mullet fillets,
  skinned
¼ tsp. thyme
½ tsp. tarragon herb
1 bay leaf, crumbled
1 small onion, minced
½ cup flour

⅓ cup olive oil
⅓ cup wine vinegar
2 tsp. salt
¼ tsp. pepper
3 tbs. shortening or fat
Water cress

Wipe fillets with damp cloth; cut into serving portions.

Pour olive oil and vinegar into large mixing bowl; add all seasonings; blend well. Marinate fish in this mixture 1 hour. Drain; dry slightly; roll in flour. Melt shortening or fat in skillet; heat but do not allow to smoke; fry fish 10 minutes; turn carefully with spatula; fry 5 minutes more, or until golden brown.

Serve immediately on preheated plates; garnish with water cress.

VARIATION: for "Baked Spiced Mullet" prepare as for "Spicy Marinated" but do not roll in flour; mince 1 extra onion. When fillets have marinated 1 hour, place them in shallow greased baking dish; sprinkle with minced onion; smother with bread crumbs; top with 3 slices bacon; bake in preheated moderate oven (375° F.) for 30 minutes.

◄§ PIKE   Has acquired several individual common names: JACK PIKE or JACKS in Canada; LAKE PIKE or LAKE PICKEREL, MUSKELLUNGE, and NORTHERN PIKE. Pike weighing from 25 to 30 pounds have been taken in the Great Lakes; the average market size, about 3 to 4 pounds, are marketed whole; larger ones are filleted, both fresh and frozen. The meat of all the pike is lean, white, firm, flaky, and has a sweet, delicate flavor.

PIKE PARMESAN
TIME: 1 HOUR; SERVES 6 TO 8

3 lbs. pike, whole
1 cup sour cream
¼ cup butter
Water cress

½ cup grated Parmesan
  cheese
½ tsp. salt
¼ tsp. pepper

Have fish cleaned but leave in backbone; wipe with damp cloth; place in shallow baking dish.

Combine all ingredients except water cress in large mixing bowl; blend well. Spread mixture over fish, which should be completely covered. Bake in preheated moderate oven (350° F.) 30 minutes, or until completely brown. Serve very hot on preheated individual plates. Garnish each serving with water cress or other green herb, as desired.

VARIATION: Use any *white-meated fillets.*

❦ SMELT   The SMELT was introduced into Great Lakes waters from its native New England in 1906 to provide food for the landlocked salmon which were being planted simultaneously in Michigan. The salmon failed but the smelt succeeded far beyond the dreams of those who carried out the project. Like the smelt that live in the ocean and ascend streams and rivers to spawn, the fresh-water smelt leave the large lakes and throng into the tributary streams. Coming up the rivers in unbelievable numbers, their slender, green, silvery bodies darken the waters and form easy prey for the hundreds of people who line the banks waiting to scoop them up. Average size, 7 to 8 inches, it takes ten or eleven to make a pound. Marketed fresh and frozen. The meat is lean and very sweet, with a particularly delicate flavor. A gourmet eats feathery bones and all.

SMELT AU GOURMET
TIME: 15 MINUTES; SERVES 4

24 medium-sized smelt	¼ lb. butter
1 cup cracker meal	2 tbs. bacon grease
Salt and pepper	Parsley sprigs

Have smelt cleaned only; do not remove heads; wipe smelt with damp cloth; sprinkle lightly with salt and pepper; roll in cracker meal.

Melt butter and bacon grease in frying pan; heat but do not allow fat to smoke. Fry smelt quickly 3 minutes on one side, or until golden brown; turn with spatula; if necessary, add more butter, since fish should be fried in plenty of fat; brown quickly another 2 minutes, or until crisp on outside but juicy when opened with fork.

Place on preheated platter. Garnish with parsley sprigs. Serve immediately on individual perheated plates.

◈§ TROUT   Also known as SPECKLED and MOUNTAIN TROUT, it thrives in rapid streams or lakes and cold torrents. The usual length is from 10 to 12 inches, weight from 1 pound to 2 pounds. The brilliance varies with the watershed. Trout on the south side of Long Island, N.Y., for instance, are very showy; those on the north, very dark. The BROWN and LOCH LEVEN trout often weigh 7 or 8 pounds and their brown color varies greatly, though they usually can be distinguished by red spots on the side.

When the CUT-THROAT migrate to salt water they are called *steelhead cut-throats* locally. From 7 to 12 inches long, some weigh as much as 8 pounds. Some fish have small golden spots and sometimes the ground color is yellowish-pink with a pink stripe. The DOLLY VARDEN's color also varies greatly but it resembles the brook trout. In small streams it is rarely over 2 pounds in weight but in lakes and rivers it may average as much as 20 pounds. The beautifully colored mountain species called GOLDEN TROUT, like the rainbow, is distinguished by its brilliant orange and yellow markings. It rarely averages more than 1 pound. The RAINBOW TROUT, sometimes called the SALMON TROUT, is much heavier than the cut-throat of the same length, its average weight is from 2 to 8 pounds; many often weigh from 30 to 40 pounds. *When the rainbow trout goes to sea it is called a "steelhead."* Next time you serve trout to your family don't forget to *sprinkle it ever so lightly with rosemary,* which isn't quite as Izaak Walton suggested when he advised: "Dress a trout with a handful of sliced horse-radish root and a handsome faggot of rosemary."

STEELHEAD EN PAPILLOTTE
TIME: 1 HOUR; SERVES 4 TO 6
1 steelhead trout (4 to 5 lbs.)
Salt and pepper
¼ lb. butter
1 tbs. chopped fresh mint
Heavy wax paper

Have trout cleaned but do not remove head; wipe with damp cloth; sprinkle lightly inside and out with salt and pepper.

Arrange large sheet of heavy wax paper in bottom of shallow baking dish. (Paper should be large enough to wrap fish around securely.) Spread butter over wax paper; arrange fish on paper; sprinkle with chopped mint; roll in paper; tie both ends of paper securely with string.

Bake wrapped fish in preheated moderately hot oven (400° F.) 50 minutes. Carefully lift fish from baking pan; place on preheated platter.

Serve while still *en papillotte* (in paper). Cut or untie ends of paper. Cut portions with sharp knife through bones and all. Serve with cream sauce and garnish.

VARIATION: Use *any variety small fish;* wrap each fish separately; bake only 30 minutes. Each person unwraps his individual fish; strings should be cut before fish is brought to table.

RAINBOW TROUT ROCKY MOUNTAIN
TIME: 30 MINUTES; SERVES 4

4 rainbow trout (1 lb. each)	1½ tsp. salt
½ tsp. paprika	½ tsp. pepper
½ cup yellow corn meal	¾ cup water
2 tbs. chopped parsley	Water cress

Clean trout thoroughly; wash in cold salted water; wipe with damp cloth. Blend paprika, salt, and pepper in small dish; rub trout inside and out with this mixture. Spread corn meal on mixing board; roll seasoned trout in it.

Melt butter in large skillet (fat should be 1 inch deep); heat but do not allow to smoke; brown fish 10 minutes; turn and fry other side 5 minutes, or until golden brown.

Arrange trout on preheated platter; surround with water cress. Garnish top with chopped parsley. Serve immediately.

VARIATION: Serve with tangy sauce such as

SHERRY-ALMOND SAUCE

¼ lb. shelled almonds
¼ lb. butter
½ cup dry sherry wine
¼ tsp. tarragon herb

Blanch almonds by dipping quickly in boiling water, then peel; shave with sharp knife. Melt butter in deep saucepan; add almonds; brown 3 minutes, stirring constantly. Blend in tarragon herb; add sherry wine. When thoroughly heated, pour over trout. Serve piping hot. Use brook, brown, cutthroat, Dolly Varden, golden, or Loch Leven trout.

❧ WHITEFISH   A native of the clear lakes and streams of the northern part of North America. A fat fish, the average weight is 2 pounds, but it often weighs more and reaches a length of 2 feet. Pale green and a bluish-silver predominate. The fins are almost white. Serve with a tangy sauce. CHUB inhabits the deeper waters of the Great Lakes, every one of the several varieties lends itself to smoking but only the BLACKFIN, is used extensively as a fresh fish; the marketed size is only 6 ounces.

WHITEFISH WITH SAUTERNE WINE SAUCE
TIME: 40 MINUTES; SERVES 4

1½ lbs. whitefish	1 bay leaf
1 clove garlic	2 cups water

Have whitefish dressed; wipe with damp cloth. Place fish in wire steaming basket; add garlic and bay leaf. Pour water in saucepan; boil; place wire basket in pan; do not allow fish to touch water; cover; steam 15 minutes. Meanwhile, prepare

SAUTERNE WINE SAUCE

¼ cup dry sauterne wine	2 cups milk
4 tbs. flour	¾ tsp. salt
4 tbs. butter	⅛ tsp. pepper
¼ tsp. dry mustard	4 hard-boiled eggs, diced
½ tsp. Worcestershire sauce	4 parsley sprigs

Melt butter in deep saucepan; blend in flour and mustard; cook 1 minute, stirring constantly; gradually add milk; continue stirring until sauce is thick (about 5 minutes). Add diced eggs, Worcestershire sauce, salt, and pepper; blend in wine; heat thoroughly.

Place steamed fish on preheated platter; pour piping hot sauce over. Garnish with parsley sprigs. Serve immediately.

VARIATION: Use *rock bass* and *lake trout*. Time approximately same.

WHITEFISH FILLED RUSSIAN STYLE:
"GEFILTE FISH"
TIME: 2 HOURS; SERVES 4 TO 6

½ lb. whitefish	4 small onions
½ lb. fluke	1 tsp. salt
1 egg	¼ tsp. pepper
2 cups cracker crumbs	Dash of cayenne
1 carrot, sliced	⅛ tsp. basil
1 bay leaf	6 tsp. grated horse-radish
6 small potatoes	3 cups boiling water

It is good to blend two or three varieties of white-meated fish. Have fish filleted but be sure to save the clean, raw skin. Wipe fillets with damp cloth; place in wooden bowl; chop into small pieces.

Break egg into large mixing bowl; beat lightly with fork; add 3 small onions finely minced; mix well; add fish, salt, pepper, basil, and cracker crumbs; blend thoroughly. Mold mixture into small balls.

Cut fish skin into 2-inch strips; wrap each ball carefully and fasten skin with toothpicks or tie with string.

Pour boiling water into saucepan; add 1 onion, carrot, and bay leaf; drop fish balls into boiling water; lower flame; cover; simmer gently 1½ hours; remove fish balls with spatula; preserve bouillon in which fish was cooked. Place fish balls in refrigerator until ready to be served cold. (Fish may be prepared day before serving.)

Boil potatoes in fish bouillon 20 minutes, or until done. Serve *hot* potatoes with *cold* fish. Garnish with horse-radish.

5. SALT-WATER FISH

~~~~~~

◄§ BASS   The BLACK SEA BASS caught off the Atlantic coast, bluish with black stripes. WHITE SEA BASS, of California coast, is lighter in color. Both are marketed in sizes of from 1 to 4 pounds. STRIPED BASS, sometimes called BLACK ROCK-FISH, is marketed up to 20 pounds, whole and filleted. Season is all year.

STRIPED BASS WITH HERB STUFFING
TIME: 1 HOUR; SERVES 6

1 striped bass (4 lbs.)	*3 slices bacon*
2 tbs. butter or margarine	*½ tsp. salt*

Have bass cleaned and boned; wipe with damp cloth; sprinkle lightly inside and out with salt. Stuff bass loosely; close with skewers; brush with melted butter; place bacon strip over top. Place in greased baking pan; bake in moderate oven (350° F.) 45 minutes, or until fish flakes easily when tested with fork. When done, remove skewers. Arrange fish on preheated platter. Serve piping hot with Lemon Butter Sauce (page 83).

HERB STUFFING WITH MUSHROOMS

4 cups dry bread crumbs	*6 tbs. butter or margarine*
1 large onion, minced	*4 large mushrooms, minced*
2 stalks celery, minced	*¼ tsp. thyme*
1 tsp. salt	*⅛ tsp. tarragon*
⅛ tsp. pepper	*⅛ tsp. rosemary*

Melt butter in saucepan over medium flame; sauté onion, celery, and mushrooms 10 minutes, or until almost tender.

Place bread crumbs in large mixing bowl; add cooked vegetables and all seasonings; mix thoroughly. (If stuffing seems dry, moisten with 2 tablespoons milk.)

VARIATION: Use *whole lake trout* or *shad*.

BLACK SEA BASS BAKED WITH FRESH MINT
TIME: 45 MINUTES; SERVES 4

1 *black sea bass (4 lbs.)*	6 *sprigs of mint*
½ *cup olive oil*	½ *cup dry sauterne wine*
½ *cup dry bread crumbs*	2 *cloves garlic, minced*
1 *sprig parsley, minced*	⅛ *tsp. pepper*
1 *tsp. salt*	⅛ *tsp. basil*

Have bass cleaned, split, and boned; wipe with damp cloth.

Put bread crumbs in large mixing bowl; add parsley, salt, pepper, and basil; mix well; add 2 tablespoons oil and half of minced garlic; blend well.

Place half bass in greased baking dish; spread mixture over the half; pour half wine over and arrange 3 sprigs mint on top; place other half bass over top; tie or skewer fish at both ends; pour balance oil over fish; bake in preheated moderate oven (350° F.) 25 minutes.

Meanwhile, chop remaining mint sprigs fine; blend in small bowl with other half of sauterne wine; add balance of minced garlic; season carefully with salt and pepper to taste. Use half of this mixture to baste fish occasionally.

When fish is done, arrange on preheated platter; remove skewers; pour remaining wine and mint mixture over fish. Serve piping hot on preheated plates.

VARIATION: Arrange 8 *mushroom caps, sautéed in 2 tablespoons butter 15 minutes,* or until tender, over top of bass just before last mixture is poured over fish at serving time.

◅§ BLOWFISH Popular commercial names for this delicious delicate fish are "sea squab" and "ocean squab," perhaps because of its juicy, chickenlike flavor. When frightened by any natural enemies it swells up to the size of a large grapefruit. Usually marketed dressed ready for cooking, its plump, meaty little body measures about 2½ inches wide and 4 or 5 inches long. Its flavor is best brought out when the fish is rolled in cracker crumbs and quickly deep-fried to a crispy golden brown. Any mild, creamy sauce adds to the taste and a fresh, green-herb garnish gives an extra touch.

BLOWFISH GOLDEN FRIED
TIME: 20 MINUTES; SERVES 4

8 blowfish	1 cup cracker crumbs
½ tsp. salt	½ cup milk
⅛ tsp. pepper	Mushroom Sauce (page 81)
1 cup peanut oil	Water cress
½ cup yellow corn meal	

Purchase dressed blowfish; wipe with damp cloth; salt and pepper lightly.

Blend yellow corn meal and cracker crumbs in mixing bowl. Dip fish in milk, then in blended cracker crumbs.

Pour oil in frying pan; heat but do not allow to smoke. Fry fish quickly 3 minutes on one side; fry 2 minutes on other side, or until golden brown; don't overcook.

Place hot fish on preheated platter; pour Mushroom Sauce over. Garnish edges of platter with water cress.

BLOWFISH WITH SAUCE RAVIGOTE
TIME: 45 MINUTES; SERVES 4

2 lbs. blowfish	½ cup milk
1 cup cracker crumbs	Salt and pepper
¼ lb. butter	

Prepare sauce before frying fish.

Purchase cleaned blowfish or sea squab; wipe with damp cloth. Dip fish in milk; season lightly with salt and pepper; roll in cracker crumbs.

Melt butter in frying pan over medium flame; heat but do not allow to smoke. Fry blowfish quickly 5 minutes on one side; turn carefully with spatula; fry fish 3 minutes on other side, or until it flakes when tested with fork. Serve piping hot on preheated plates. Cover fish with generous helping of Sauce Ravigote.

SAUCE RAVIGOTE

4 shallots, minced	½ tsp. sugar
2 tbs. butter	1 small can tomato paste
½ tsp. dry mustard	Salt
1 cup sauterne wine	

Melt butter in saucepan over medium flame; add shallots; sauté 10 minutes, or until golden brown; add mustard, wine, and sugar; blend well. Add tomato paste; salt to taste; cover; simmer gently 20 minutes.

Serve piping hot sauce over fish.

VARIATION: *Sweet cider* may be used instead of wine.

◆§ BLUEFISH   Migrates up and down the Atlantic coast from Florida to Maine. The average weight is 10 pounds, but bluefish are usually marketed whole in sizes from 1 to 7 pounds. In the same class with its widely known relative the pompano, it is excellent eating and especially delicious when baked and stuffed with a tart dressing.

BLUEFISH WITH CAPER DRESSING

TIME: 1 HOUR; SERVES 6

1 bluefish (5 lbs.)	*1 tbs. melted butter*
½ tsp. salt	*⅛ tsp. pepper*
½ cup hot water	*1 slice of onion*

Have fish cleaned and dressed; wipe with damp cloth; rub inside and out lightly with salt and pepper.

Stuff bluefish with *caper dressing* loosely; close with skewers. Brush fish with 1 tablespoon melted butter; place in baking pan with ½ cup hot water and 1 slice onion; bake in preheated moderate oven (350° F.) 50 minutes, or until fish can be flaked from bone with fork. When done, remove skewers. Arrange fish on preheated platter. Garnish with green celery leaves. Serve piping hot.

CAPER DRESSING

2 tbs. capers	*2 cups bread crumbs*
1 small sour pickle, chopped	*½ cup hot water*
1 tbs. chopped parsley	*¼ onion, grated*
1 tbs. butter, melted	*Salt and pepper to taste*

Place bread crumbs in large mixing bowl. Add all ingredients except water; blend well. Add water, blend again.

VARIATION: *Grated onion* may be omitted, if preferred.

◆§ BUTTERFISH   Most butterfish are from 6 to 8 inches long and average about ½ pound each, though some run to 10 inches.

In Maine the butterfish is often called the DOLLARFISH,

and in Connecticut the PUMPKIN SEED. An ideal fish for pan broiling, it turns golden brown so easily; its meat is rather fat and its soft texture melts in the mouth.

BUTTERFISH NORFOLK
TIME: 15 MINUTES; SERVES 6
6 butterfish (½ lb. each)
1½ tsp. salt   ¼ cup white flour
⅛ tsp. pepper   3 tbs. butter or shortening
½ cup white corn meal   6 sprigs fresh mint

Have butterfish drawn only; wipe with damp cloth. Sift flour, salt, and pepper into oblong dish or on mixing board; blend in white corn meal by stirring vigorously. Roll butterfish in flour-corn-meal mixture.

Heat butter or shortening in frying pan; brown fish quickly about 4 minutes on each side, being careful not to overcook. Serve piping hot on preheated plates. Garnish with sprigs of mint.

VARIATION: Use *other fat fish*, such as *lake herring, mackerel,* and *tuna.*

৺ COD   Native of the North Atlantic and North Pacific, the average market size of this lean flaky fish is about 10 pounds, though the fish reaches a maximum weight of 100 pounds. These large sizes are prepared and shipped as attractively packaged fillets. Other market forms are whole, steaks, sticks, fresh, salt, pickled, flaked, smoked, and shredded. *Haddock, hake, pollock,* and *whiting* are all related to the cod. SCROD is the young cod weighing 1½ to 2½ pounds.

COD CARCASSONNE
TIME: 45 MINUTES; SERVES 6
3 lbs. cod steaks   1 tbs. walnuts, minced
½ cup olive oil   1 tbs. hazel nuts, minced
2 onions, chopped   1 tbs. almonds, minced
2 tbs. chopped parsley   2 tbs. bread crumbs
½ cup water   1 cup Fish Stock (page 21)
Croutons   6 sprigs parsley

Wipe cod steaks with damp cloth; cut into 6 serving pieces. Pour oil into saucepan; add onions and chopped parsley; heat over low flame; carefully add cod steaks, then water; simmer gently 15 minutes, or until water has evaporated.

Meanwhile, mince nuts; place in separate saucepan; brown 3 minutes over low flame, stirring constantly. Add bread crumbs; blend well; continue stirring 3 minutes more, or until crumbs are golden brown. Add fish stock; stir constantly until sauce begins to boil.

Pour boiling sauce over sautéed cod steaks (which may have broken into smaller pieces since the fish flakes so readily). Place several croutons on preheated plate; arrange fish over croutons with generous helping of sauce. Garnish with sprigs of parsley or water cress. Serve piping hot.

COD SAUTÉED WITH SHRIMP SAUCE
TIME: 30 MINUTES; SERVES 6

3 lbs. codfish steaks	¼ lb. butter
1 cup milk	½ tsp. salt
1 cup corn meal	¼ tsp. pepper

SHRIMP SAUCE

1 cup cooked shrimps, chopped	3 tbs. butter
	⅛ tsp. paprika
1½ cups milk	Salt and pepper, extra
3 tbs. flour	

Prepare *Shrimp Sauce* first. Melt butter in top section double boiler; add salt and pepper to taste; add paprika. Blend cold milk and flour in mixing bowl; stir until very smooth; add to melted butter.

Place top section over lower part of double boiler half filled with boiling water. Stir sauce constantly until it begins to thicken (about 6 minutes); add chopped shrimp; keep hot while codfish is being sautéed.

Wipe cod with damp cloth; dip cod in milk, then in corn meal; salt and pepper. Melt butter in skillet; sauté cod in hot butter 5 minutes on each side, or until golden brown. Arrange steaks on preheated platter. Garnish as preferred. Serve immediately with steaming hot shrimp sauce.

VARIATION: *Steam, bake,* or *boil,* serve with favorite rich sauce. Use *any lean-meated fish.*

◀§ CROAKER   A lean fish, averaging 1 pound, its comparatively small size places it in the pan-fish category and usually it is sold whole.

CROAKER AU FARINA
TIME: 20 MINUTES; SERVES 6

6 *croaker* (1 *lb. each*)	¼ *lb. butter*
Paprika	*Salt and pepper*
1 *cup farina*	1 *egg, well beaten*
	6 *sprigs water cress*

Have fish drawn only; wipe with damp cloth. Break egg into bowl; beat until foamy. Pour farina on mixing board. Dip fish in egg, then in farina; salt and pepper to taste.

Melt butter in large frying pan; heat but do not allow to smoke. Fry fish on one side 5 minutes; turn carefully with spatula; fry other side 5 minutes or until golden brown, being careful not to overcook. Serve hot on preheated plates. Sprinkle each serving with paprika. Garnish with water cress or preferred green herb.

VARIATION: Pan-fry as "Calico Bass American Indian," page 22; or plain, using ½ cup flour.

❧ EEL   Unlike the salmon, which spends most of its life at sea and comes into fresh water to spawn, the common American EEL does just the opposite. It spawns at sea and comes into fresh water to live. Eels enter the bays and sounds in enormous numbers early in the spring. Always shipped alive in tank trucks, it is kept fresh in tanks of cold water in retail markets. The sizes vary from 2 to 4 feet in length. It is a fish without pelvic fins and is almost snakelike in appearance. Its skin is smooth and has such minute scales embedded in it that they are not easily detected. The fresh fish has a rich flavor both delicious and satisfying when properly prepared and served either hot with sauces or cold in salads. Great quantities of eel are now hickory-smoked and are shipped to retail markets during the entire year. Smoked eel is considered one of the most unusual of luncheon delicacies.

EELS BROILED WITH SAGE
TIME: 25 MINUTES; SERVES 4 TO 6

2 *lbs. thick eels*	8 *sage leaves*
6 *tbs. olive oil.*	*Salt and pepper*
Pinch of paprika	*Water cress*

Have eels skinned and cleaned; cut crosswise into 4-inch pieces; wipe with damp cloth.

Blend olive oil and paprika; dip eel pieces in seasoned olive oil; salt and pepper eels lightly to taste; place on broiler rack 4 inches below flame in preheated broiling compartment; broil 10 minutes; turn; baste with olive oil; broil other side 10 minutes, or until eels are golden brown and flake when tested with fork. Serve piping hot on preheated platter. Garnish with water cress or chopped parsley.

VARIATION: Eels may be herb-broiled with *rosemary, thyme,* or *sweet basil,* blended with 1 teaspoon of olive oil.

EELS ROASTED EN CASSEROLE
TIME: 20 MINUTES; MARINATE 1 HOUR; SERVES 4 TO 6

2 *lbs. thick eels*	6 *tbs. olive oil*
Salt and pepper	1 *tbs. chopped parsley*
Juice of 1 lemon	1 *lemon, extra*

Have eels skinned and cleaned; cut crosswise into 4-inch pieces; wipe with damp cloth.

Blend olive oil, parsley, and lemon juice. Dip eel pieces in seasoned olive oil; salt and pepper lightly; place in shallow casserole or baking dish, and put in preheated broiling compartment (350° F.) 4 inches below flame; broil 10 minutes; baste with balance of seasoning; broil 5 to 10 minutes, or until eels are golden brown and flake when tested with fork. Serve piping hot on preheated individual plates. Garnish with lemon wedges.

EEL TARTARE VILLENEUVE
TIME: 45 MINUTES; SERVES 4 TO 6

2½ *lbs. thick eels*	½ *cup olive oil*
1½ *cup water*	1 *cup cracker crumbs*
1 *onion, minced*	1 *egg, well beaten*
2 *cloves*	1 *tsp. olive oil, extra*
2 *sprigs parsley*	6 *sprigs parsley, extra*
1 *stalk celery*	*Salt and pepper*
1½ *cups dry sauterne wine*	

Have eels skinned and cleaned; cut crosswise in 3-inch pieces; place in saucepan; pour in wine and water; add onion, cloves, parsley, and celery; bring to broiling point over medium flame; cover; lower flame; simmer very gently 25 minutes; remove from flame; drain.

Break egg into mixing bowl; add 1 teaspoon olive oil; beat until foamy. Dip pieces of eel, one by one, first into beaten egg, then into cracker crumbs. Preheat broiler compartment to 550° F.

Arrange eels on well-greased broiler pan placed 2 inches below flame; brown 3 minutes quickly. Garnish with parsley.

◆§ FLOUNDER   A family name that includes *gray sole*, *black backs* or *winter flounder*, *lemon sole*, *yellowtails*, and *dabs*, it is a flat, lean-meated fish with an average weight of 2 pounds; marketed whole, filleted, and fresh-frozen. The *gray sole* is regarded by many as one of the best of all flat fishes in flavor. The *black backs* or *winter flounder* are considered the best flavored of the five varieties of flounder since they are the thickest and meatiest. The *lemon sole*, taken only on Georges Bank, is very similar to the winter flounder in flavor. The *yellowtail* is a thinner-bodied fish but it has a good flavor and is marketed in large quantities.

The DAB has a thick layer of meat, free from bones, on both upper and lower sides, and is sweet, not oily, with a very distinctive flavor and texture. Our "fillet of sole" is not related to the renowned English sole, but is usually one of the species of flounders taken in American waters.

FLOUNDER FILLETS DR. HAWES'
TIME: 25 MINUTES; SERVES 4

4 flounder fillets	1 can mushroom soup
(½ lb. each)	Pinch of nutmeg
1 tbs. melted butter	Pinch of paprika
1 tbs. flour	1 tbs. grated Parmesan cheese
1 tbs. sweet cream	Salt
Juice of ½ lemon	4 sprigs parsley

Wipe fillets with damp cloth; sprinkle with few drops lemon juice and very little salt.

Melt butter in saucepan; blend in flour, nutmeg, and paprika; cook 4 minutes, stirring constantly; add mushroom soup; simmer 3 minutes, stirring gently.

Arrange fish fillets in shallow fireproof baking dish; pour sweet cream over, then pour hot mushroom sauce over. Sift grated Parmesan cheese over top. Bake in preheated moderate oven (350° F.) 15 minutes. Serve piping hot in preheated individual plates. Garnish each serving with parsley.

◄§ FLUKE   Also called SUMMER FLOUNDER, this is a flat fish, white-meated, weighing from 1 pound to 5 pounds. (*See also* Flounder, page 42.)

FLUKE BAKED IN WHITE WINE
TIME: 45 MINUTES; SERVES 4 TO 6

4 fluke fillets	½ cup dry sauterne wine
½ cup Fumet (page 21)	2 ozs. butter
Juice of 1 lemon	2 ozs. butter, extra
¼ cup cream	8 mushrooms, sautéed
2 egg yolks, beaten	Salt and pepper

Sauté whole mushrooms 20 minutes in 1 ounce melted butter; keep hot on side of stove.

Wipe fillets with damp cloth; place in shallow fireproof baking dish.

Blend wine with *fumet*; add juice of ½ lemon; pour liquid over fillets; salt and pepper to taste. Bake in preheated moderate oven (350° F.) 10 minutes; remove from oven; drain sauce carefully. With spatula, hold fillets in baking dish.

Pour sauce from baking dish into top section of double boiler placed over bottom section half filled with boiling water; heat.

In separate pan melt 1 ounce butter over low flame; blend in flour, stirring constantly; add 2 tablespoons fish sauce to dilute. When sauce in double boiler is very hot, add butter and flour mixture, stirring constantly for 5 minutes. Blend beaten egg yolks with cream; gradually add to sauce, continue stirring; when sauce thickens (about 2 minutes), remove from flame.

Pour piping hot sauce over fillets. Garnish with hot sautéed mushrooms. Sprinkle lemon juice. Place baking dish in very hot preheated broiler compartment 3 inches below flame for 1 minute; remove quickly while still very light brown. Serve immediately in oven baking dish.

VARIATION: Substitute *1 cup Fish Fumet* (page 21).

◄§ GROUPER   Belongs to the sea bass family. Full-grown

groupers weigh 50 pounds, market sizes range from 5 to 15 pounds. Larger ones are prepared as steaks or fillets. The steak flavor is best broiled; the fillets, baked in sauce.

GROUPER FILLET ROLLS WITH SPICED TOMATO SAUCE

TIME: 30 MINUTES; SERVES 6

2 lbs. grouper fillets
1 onion, sliced
½ tsp. salt

½ cup flour
2 ozs. butter or margarine
⅛ tsp. white pepper

SPICED TOMATO SAUCE

1 No. 2 can tomatoes
1 small can tomato paste
½ tsp. thyme
¼ tsp. rosemary
½ tsp. salt
2 tbs. chopped chives

½ clove garlic, minced
½ tbs. lemon juice
⅛ tsp. pepper
1 tbs. Cheddar cheese, crumbled
Pinch of red pepper seeds

Prepare sauce first. Combine all ingredients except cheese and lemon juice in saucepan; bring to boiling point; lower flame; simmer gently 20 minutes; add crumbled cheese; stir well; while sauce is simmering 5 minutes, prepare fish. Wipe fillets with damp cloth; cut into 6 serving pieces. Blend salt and pepper with flour. Dust each fillet lightly with mixture; place 1 slice onion in center of fillet; roll and tie with string or skewer with toothpicks.

Cut 2 sheets of oiled paper the size of baking dish; butter paper well on one side; place one sheet of paper on bottom of baking dish; arrange rolled fillets on bottom; cover with second sheet of buttered oiled paper. Bake in preheated hot oven (450° F.) 20 minutes. Arrange fillets on preheated platter; pour spiced sauce over fillets. Serve immediately.

VARIATION: Serve with white sauce, or garnish with green herb. Grouper steaks are best broiled.

↜§ HADDOCK   It is easy to distinguish the HADDOCK from cod, though they are closely related. The haddock is conspicuously marked by a black lateral line and a black patch on its side below the lateral line and above the pectoral fin. The size is much smaller than cod. The haddock's average weight in New England waters runs from 2 to 6 pounds. When smoked, it is called "Finnan Haddie." A very firm, white-meated fish of pleasant flavor, it is much improved by smoking. When fresh, served either as fillets or flaked, it is unusually tasty.

HADDOCK SCALLOPED AU GRATIN

TIME: 45 MINUTES; SERVES 4 TO 6

1 lb. haddock fillets	½ cup grated, or crumbled
2 ozs. butter or margarine	Cheddar cheese
½ green pepper, minced	½ cup cracker crumbs
½ onion, minced	1 cup rich milk
½ tsp. salt	2 tbs. flour
⅛ tsp. pepper	½ tsp. Worcestershire sauce

Wipe fillets with damp cloth; cut fillets into cubes.

Melt butter in saucepan; add minced pepper, onion, fillet cubes, salt, and pepper to taste; sauté gently over low flame 10 minutes, or until pepper is half done.

Meanwhile, blend cold milk and flour in mixing bowl; when very smooth, pour into top section of double boiler and cook 10 minutes, or until sauce begins to thicken; stir in Worcestershire sauce, then add sautéed haddock cubes; stir well.

Grease fireproof casserole; evenly pour fish mixture into it.

Combine crumbled or grated Cheddar cheese with cracker crumbs; spread combination over top of fish mixture; bake in preheated moderately hot oven (300° F.) 10 minutes, or until golden brown. Garnish with mint sprigs, if desired.

VARIATION: Use flaked, leftover fish.

HADDOCK FILLETS WITH MUSHROOM SAUCE

TIME: 45 MINUTES; SERVES 4

1½ lbs. haddock fillets	1 tbs. chopped parsley
¼ tsp. salt	2 ozs. butter
⅛ tsp. pepper	Mushroom Sauce (page 81)
1 tbs. flour	

Prepare sauce first.

Wipe haddock fillets with damp cloth; cut fillets into 4 serving pieces.

Combine salt, pepper, and flour; sprinkle lightly over fillets; place pats of butter in center of each piece; arrange on greased broiler pan; broil in preheated moderate oven

(350° F.) 12 minutes, or until golden brown; do not turn. When done, arrange fillets on preheated platter; pour steaming hot sauce over top. Garnish with chopped parsley. Serve immediately.

VARIATION: Haddock fillets may be *steamed*. Serve with favorite *mild* or *tangy sauce* for variety. Garnish with favorite green herb or lemon wedges. Use *any variety lean-meated sweet fish*; preparation time approximately same for broiled fillets and sauce.

◦§ HALIBUT   It belongs to the flatfish family and resembles a gigantic, overgrown flounder. The average sizes are from 50 to 100 pounds, but many weigh from 500 to 600 pounds. Halibut reaches the retail markets dressed and in steaks, fresh, frozen, and smoked. Its firm, white, flaky-textured meat is of delicious flavor and the steaks are prepared in many unusual ways all over the world.

HALIBUT STEAK EAST INDIAN
TIME: 40 MINUTES; SERVES 6

2 *lbs. halibut steak*	3 *tbs. flour*
1 *bay leaf*	1 *cup Fish Stock (page 21)*
2 *ozs. butter*	1 *cup dry sauterne wine*
1 *small onion, minced*	2 *drops tabasco sauce*
½ *green pepper, minced*	2 *tbs. chopped parsley*
1 *stalk celery, chopped*	*Salt and pepper*
¾ *tsp. curry powder*	

Wipe halibut steaks with damp cloth; place fish in shallow saucepan; cover with cold water; add bay leaf; cover; bring to boiling point; lower flame; simmer gently 10 minutes, then drain, saving stock, which is set aside to cool. Keep halibut hot over steam.

Meanwhile, melt butter in saucepan; add onion, green pepper, and celery; sauté over low flame 10 minutes.

Blend flour and curry powder with 1 cup cooled Fish Stock; pour into saucepan; cook over low flame 5 minutes, stirring constantly; add sauterne wine; stir well; add tabasco sauce, salt and pepper to taste; stir well; heat to boiling point.

Remove skin and center bone from halibut; arrange fish on preheated hot platter; pour hot sauce over. Garnish with chopped parsley. Serve immediately on preheated individual plates.

HALIBUT SERVICHE
TIME: 20 MINUTES; MARINATE 3 HOURS; SERVES 8

1½ lbs. halibut steak   Juice of 4 bitter oranges
1 tsp. salt   Tabasco to taste
1 onion, sliced very thin   8 crisp lettuce leaves

Wipe halibut steaks with damp cloth; cut into small ½-inch pieces (about size of thumbnail); place in large mixing bowl; add sliced onion; mix well. Cover fish with bitter orange juice; add salt and tabasco to taste. (South Americans like the fish very hot.) Cover mixture and let stand at room temperature 3 hours, or until fish is firm and very white. Do not allow to stand longer or the juice will destroy the texture of the fish. Place in refrigerator; chill seasoned fish 1 hour, or until ready to serve. When ready, line pre-chilled cocktail glasses with crisp lettuce leaf; fill glasses and serve immediately as first course.

◆§ KINGFISH A giant relative of the prized Spanish Mackerel, its average weight is 15 to 30 pounds, though smaller ones are often marketed whole; otherwise sold in steaks. It has excellent flavor and few bones. The small fish, ¾ to 3 pounds, are often called KING WHITING.

KINGFISH VINAIGRETTE
TIME: 20 MINUTES; SERVES 4 TO 6

2 lbs. kingfish steaks   ½ cup Fish Stock (page 21)
2 ozs. butter   ½ cup wine vinegar
Salt and pepper   ½ tsp. dill

Wipe steaks with damp cloth; arrange steaks in broiling pan.

Melt butter in small saucepan; add Fish Stock, wine vinegar, and dill; blend well; heat but do not boil; add salt and pepper to taste; pour sauce over fish steaks; place in pre-heated broiler compartment (450° F.) 3 inches below flame; baste several times as fish broils; do not turn; broil 15 minutes. Serve immediately on preheated individual plates.

VARIATION: Also prepare baked or pan-broiled; serve with favorite tangy sauce. If baked, allow approximately 30 minutes.

⋅§ LINGCOD Its long, slender body may be a mottled gray, or brown with yellow and brown spots. Some of the darker specimens are a beautiful pale green. It may weigh as much as 30 or 40 pounds and reach a length of 4 feet. The average weight for those marketed dressed is about 4 pounds.

LINGCOD WITH MUSHROOMS
TIME: 1¼ HOURS; SERVES 6

1 whole lingcod (4 lbs.)	⅛ tsp. basil
½ cup flour	4 slices bacon
1½ tsp. salt	1½ cups Fish Stock
⅛ tsp. pepper	(page 21)
Pinch of cayenne	6 small potatoes, whole
½ lb. mushrooms, sliced	6 sprigs mint

Have fish cleaned; head and backbone removed if desired; wipe with damp cloth; cut 4 two-inch gashes across one side.

Blend flour, salt, pepper, cayenne, and basil; sprinkle fish with mixture; arrange fish in shallow baking dish; lay bacon slices in gashes; pour stock around fish; bake in preheated oven (350° F.) 1 hour. When half done, arrange mushrooms and potatoes around fish; baste with Fish Stock, or Court Bouillon (page 20). When done, place fish on preheated platter; arrange mushrooms and potatoes around; pour remaining baking-pan liquid over fish. Garnish with mint sprigs. Serve immediately on preheated individual plates.

VARIATION: Use 1 cup fish stock and ½ cup dry rhine wine instead of fish stock only. Use any whole fish.

⋅§ MACKEREL There are 22 mackerels. One called BOSTON MACKEREL is native to the northeast Atlantic; another is known as SPANISH MACKEREL and is found from Maine to Brazil. A beautiful fish, deep blue with iridescent tones, the average market weight is 2 pounds. Since the texture is firm and rather oily, the fish is best when broiled or baked, or served with a tangy sauce.

MACKEREL MUSTARD BROILED
TIME: 20 MINUTES; SERVES 4 TO 6

1 whole mackerel (3 lbs.)	1 tbs. prepared mustard
2 tbs. chopped parsley	⅛ tsp. fennel

2 ozs. butter
1 lemon, sliced

2 tbs. lemon juice
Salt and pepper

Have mackerel cleaned and split for broiling; wipe with damp cloth.

Melt 1 ounce butter in shallow saucepan; add chopped parsley, salt, and pepper; stir well. Season mackerel well by brushing with butter mixture; place on broiler rack (skin side down) 2 inches below flame in preheated hot broiler compartment (450° F.); while broiling 5 minutes, melt other ounce butter; add prepared mustard, lemon juice, and fennel; mix well. Pour this mustard mixture over mackerel; broil 5 minutes longer.

Place fish on preheated hot platter. Garnish with lemon slices. Serve immediately on preheated plates.

VARIATION: To prepare "Mackerel Royal Broiled" follow recipe as for "Swordfish Royal Broiled," page 66.

◄§ MULLET OR STRIPED MULLET Not to be confused with the fresh-water mullet, it is marketed whole in sizes 2 to 3 pounds; the larger sizes are now filleted. The roe is also eaten. Small sizes from ½ pound to 2 pounds are best broiled; larger sizes are baked. It has a tender, firm-textured meat which contains a clear yellow oil with a mild nutlike flavor. (*See also* "Smoked, Salted, and Canned Fish" chapter.)

MULLET BAKED IN CHEESE
TIME: 40 MINUTES; SERVES 4 TO 6

1 dressed mullet (2 lbs.)
1 small onion, sliced
2 tbs. lemon juice
2 stalks celery, chopped
2 ozs. butter, melted
6 tbs. grated American
   cheese

1 cup water
2 tbs. flour
1 cup rich milk
⅛ tsp. Worcestershire sauce
Salt and pepper

Have mullet cut into individual portions; wipe with damp cloth; place mullet in casserole; sprinkle with salt, pepper, and lemon juice. Arrange onion and celery over top of fish; pour in water; bake in preheated moderate oven (350° F.) 10 minutes. Meanwhile, melt butter in saucepan; add flour;

blend well; when smooth, gradually add milk, stirring constantly until thickened (about 5 minutes); add salt, pepper, Worcestershire sauce, and 4 tablespoons cheese; blend well.

Pour sauce over fish; sprinkle with remaining cheese; bake 10 minutes longer, or until fish flakes easily when tested with fork. Arrange fish on preheated platter. Garnish with parsley. Serve immediately on preheated plates.

VARIATION: Use ½ *cup rhine wine and* ½ *cup water.*

MULLET SPICY FRIED
TIME: 15 MINUTES; MARINATE 1 HOUR; SERVES 4 TO 6

2 lbs. mullet fillets, skinned	⅓ cup wine vinegar
1½ tsp. salt	Pinch of cayenne
⅛ tsp. pepper	½ cup olive or vegetable oil
¼ tsp. thyme	½ cup flour
½ tsp. tarragon herb	3 tbs. vegetable oil, extra
1 bay leaf, crumbled	6 sprigs water cress
1 small onion, chopped	

Wipe fillets with damp cloth; cut fillets into serving portions.

In large bowl mix well salt, pepper, thyme, tarragon, bay leaf, onion, wine vinegar, cayenne, and olive or vegetable oil; marinate fillets 1 hour in this mixture; drain; roll in flour.

Pour vegetable oil in large skillet; heat but do not allow to smoke; fry fillets over medium flame 4 minutes on each side, or until golden brown and easily flaked when tested with fork. Serve piping hot on preheated individual plates. Garnish fish with sprig of water cress or favorite green herb.

VARIATION: Marinated, striped mullet fillets may be *broiled.* Place on broiler rack in preheated broiling compartment (400° F.) 2 inches below flame; broil 10 minutes; do not turn; garnish with melted butter and water cress.

◄§ POLLOCK   A lean fish which resembles the cod. It is darker and more lustrous. Average weight is from 4 to 12 pounds, maximum is near 50 pounds. A shapely fish of handsome green color, also known as BOSTON BLUEFISH or DEEP-SEA FILLETS. Firm-textured, white-meated fish unusually palatable when prepared with a delicate sauce or sautéed with herbs.

POLLOCK OVEN-SAUTÉED IN HERBS

TIME: 1 HOUR; SERVES 6

1 pollock (4 lbs.)
1 oz. butter
2 ozs. butter, extra
2 egg yolks, beaten slightly
2 tbs. capers
1 small onion, minced
2 sprigs parsley, chopped
2 tbs. chopped sour pickles

⅛ tsp. tarragon herb
½ tbs. tarragon vinegar
1 tbs. lemon juice
½ tsp. salt
¼ tsp. paprika
1 lemon, sliced
6 sprigs parsley

Have pollock cleaned, boned, and split for baking; wipe with damp cloth; salt lightly inside only. Butter well a sheet of wax paper the size of shallow baking dish; place paper on bottom; arrange fish carefully over paper; bake in preheated moderate oven (350° F.) 20 minutes, while softening 2 ounces butter in mixing bowl, add beaten egg yolks; when creamy, add next 9 ingredients; blend thoroughly.

Spread mixture evenly over fish; bake 25 minutes more, or until fish flakes easily when tested with fork.

Arrange pollock carefully on preheated hot platter. Garnish with parsley sprigs and thin slices lemon.

◆§ POMPANO   A fat fish, blue, silvery, or golden luster often 18 inches long; average weight is 1½ pounds.

POMPANO FLORIDA PLANKED

TIME: 1 HOUR; SERVES 6

1 pompano (4 lbs.)
1½ tsp. salt
⅛ tsp. pepper
1 lb. semi-cooked peas
4 stuffed tomatoes

3 cups seasoned mashed
   potatoes
½ semi-cooked cauliflower
6 sprigs parsley

Use hardwood plank or greased oven glass. Wood is preferable. Oil well; place plank in cold oven and heat thoroughly as oven preheats.

Have pompano drawn only; wipe with damp cloth; sprinkle fish lightly inside and out with salt and pepper. Place fish on hot plank; bake in a preheated oven (350° F.) 35 minutes, or until fish begins to flake easily when tested with fork. Quickly arrange a border of hot mashed potatoes at edge of plank. In space between fish and potatoes arrange other vegetables in attractive design. Place plank in hot oven 5 minutes, or until potatoes are slightly browned and vegetables are tender but not soft; remove from oven. Garnish with parsley sprigs. Serve immediately on plank.

VARIATION: Prepare as "Pompano Marguery," *see* page 64 "Sole Marguery."

◆§ PORGY   This brown fish, in New England often called SCUP, is tinged with pink above and paling to silvery underparts. Reaches a length of 18 inches and weighs 3 or 4 pounds; average market weight is from 1½ to 2 pounds. Usually marketed as fresh, pan-dressed fish. Tender, flaky, and of excellent flavor, it fries well when rolled in cracker crumbs or corn meal and is most unusual when baked with a tangy sauce.

PORGIES WITH TOMATOES
TIME: 40 MINUTES; SERVES 4 TO 6

4 pan-dressed porgies	4 large tomatoes
(1 lb. each)	3 tbs. olive oil
1 small onion, chopped	½ cup water
½ tsp. basil	¼ tsp. salt
1 bay leaf	½ cup cracker crumbs
¼ tsp. pepper	8 sprigs water cress

Have porgies pan-dressed; wipe with damp cloth; salt lightly inside and out. Pour oil in saucepan over medium flame; add onion; sauté 3 minutes, or until light brown; add basil, bay leaf, pepper, and salt; simmer 2 minutes.

Arrange porgies in shallow casserole or baking dish; pour hot herbs over fish; place whole tomatoes around porgies; add ½ cup water; bake in preheated moderate oven (350° F.) 30 minutes. A few minutes before taking from oven, sprinkle cracker crumbs over tomatoes. Serve immediately in casserole. Garnish with water cress or preferred green herb.

VARIATION: Use 2 *anchovy fillets* on each tomato; reduce salt to ⅛ teaspoon. *See also* "Pan-fried American Indian Style," p. 22.

◆§ RED SNAPPER   Average size is 4 pounds, though this most colorful item is a seafood market's display sometimes weighs 30 pounds and is 2½ feet long. Usual market forms include steaks, fillets, both quick-frozen and fresh. The meat is juicy, white, and of fine, delicate flavor, and is good either broiled, baked, steamed, or boiled, though most people consider a baked red snapper one of the choicest delicacies the sea provides. The GRAY SNAPPER market sizes are from ½ pound to 5 pounds. The MUTTONFISH averages about 3 pounds. The YELLOWTAIL snapper, not to be confused with the flounder, is considered one of the choicest of local food fishes; average weight is about a pound.

RED SNAPPER FLORIDA SUPRÊME
TIME: 40 MINUTES; SERVES 4

2 *lbs. red snapper steaks*	4 *fresh prawns, minced*
1 *tbs. chopped parsley*	1 *cup rhine wine*
¼ *tsp. basil*	2 *ozs. butter*
½ *carrot, minced*	*Salt and pepper*
1 *stalk celery, minced*	1 *lemon, sliced*

Wipe red snapper steaks with damp cloth; salt and pepper fish to taste. Place 1 ounce butter in baking dish; arrange steaks in dish; cover with parsley, carrot, and celery; sprinkle basil over top; pour in rhine wine; bake in preheated moderate oven (350° F.) 20 minutes while shelling and cleaning raw prawns; mince.

Melt other ounce butter in shallow saucepan; add prawns; sauté 3 minutes, or until light brown, stirring constantly; then pour over steaks; bake 10 minutes longer, or until red snapper steaks flake easily when tested with fork.

Arrange steaks on preheated platter; pour herb and prawn sauce over. Garnish with lemon slices.

VARIATION: Use 6 raw *shrimp*; preparation time same. Also prepare red snapper fillets as "Sole Marguery," p. 64.

◄§ ROCKFISH The skin varies in color from dark gray to bright orange and the meat from almost a pure white to a deep pink. Its texture is firm and when cooked it is white and flaky, resembling crab meat. Shredded cooked rockfish tastes as sweet and delicious as the best crab meat.

ROCKFISH BÉCHAMEL

TIME: 25 MINUTES; SERVES 6

½ cup shredded cooked
   rockfish
2 tbs. butter
3 tbs. flour
Pinch of cayenne
1 cup of chicken broth

1 cup rich milk
2 egg yolks, beaten
1 tbs. chopped parsley
1 pimiento, cut in strips
1 green pepper, cut in strips
6 slices buttered toast

Use freshly steamed (page 54) or leftover rockfish.

Melt butter in saucepan over medium flame; gradually blend in flour and cayenne; when smooth, slowly pour in chicken broth and milk, stirring constantly until thick (about 6 minutes). Add shredded rockfish; stir vigorously; gradually add beaten egg yolk and chopped parsley. Serve piping hot over buttered toast placed on preheated individual plates. Garnish each serving with strips of pimiento and green pepper.

VARIATION: Use *any variety leftover flaked fish.*

ROCKFISH OVEN-STEAMED

TIME: 30 MINUTES; SERVES 6

1 lb. rockfish fillets
½ tsp. salt

1 small onion, chopped
2 cups Newburg Sauce
   (page 84)

Wipe fillets with damp cloth; sprinkle fillets lightly with salt; place in ungreased covered casserole with onion between fillets; bake in preheated moderate oven (350° F.) 30 minutes; remove; shred fillets with fork.

Serve with Newburg Sauce, or prepare shredded rockfish, as preferred.

VARIATION: *Serve Rockfish Oven-Steamed and shredded with Cheese Sauce* (p. 81) *or prepared with any other mild or tangy sauce. Garnish with chives or parsley.*

ROCKFISH DEVILED PACIFIC

TIME: 15 MINUTES; SERVES 6

2 cups steamed rockfish,
   shredded
2 cups soft bread crumbs
¼ cup melted butter
⅔ cup tomato catsup
2 tbs. minced parsley
2 hard-boiled eggs, chopped

2 tbs. lemon juice
½ cup dry, buttered bread
   crumbs
¼ tsp. salt
⅛ tsp. pepper
Paprika

Use freshly steamed rockfish (page 54) or leftover cooked rockfish. Combine all ingredients except *dry*, buttered bread crumbs; mix lightly. Fill individual buttered ramekins with mixture; cover with buttered crumbs; heat in preheated moderate oven (350° F.) 15 minutes. When piping hot, sprinkle each ramekin with paprika. Garnish with favorite chopped herb, such as parsley, chives, or mint. Serve immediately.

◄§ ROE The name for eggs still enclosed in the thin membrane in which they are found in the female fish. Roe is taken from many species of fish and is now available in the retail markets in most sections of the country all year. Shad roe is perhaps the most popular and best known. However, roes from many different fish: *alewife, cod, herring, mackerel, mullet, salmon, shad,* and *whitefish* roe are marketed in three forms—fresh, frozen, and canned. The roe of *sturgeon* is widely reserved for *caviar*, as is a large part of salmon and whitefish roe. (*See* "Smoked, Salted, and Canned Fish" chapter.)

The size varies with the size of the fish. The fresh roe of shad usually measures from 5 to 6 inches long, about 3 inches wide, and an inch or more thick. The *white milt* of the *herring, shad,* and *smelt* is considered a real delicacy also.

ROE OF SHAD BROILED WITH BACON
TIME: 20 MINUTES; SERVES 4

1½ lbs. roe of shad	8 slices bacon
Pepper to taste	4 slices buttered toast
Pinch of rosemary	8 sprigs water cress

Place roe in saucepan over medium flame; cover with boiling water; simmer gently 5 minutes only. Drain; cut roe into 4 or 8 serving portions.

Arrange roe on broiler rack; place slice of bacon over each piece of roe; broil 4 inches below flame in preheated broiler compartment (350° F.) 8 minutes, or until bacon and roe are golden brown. Serve piping hot on preheated plates. Garnish each serving with water cress and generous helping of tartar sauce if desired.

VARIATION: To prepare "Fried Shad Roe with Bacon," simply wipe roe dry. Dip in beaten egg, then in cracker crumbs, fry in deep fat 6 minutes. Meanwhile, fry bacon in separate frying pan. Serve immediately, very hot, with bacon slices and parsley sprigs as garnish.

ROE OF SHAD OVEN-TOASTED
TIME: 30 MINUTES; SERVES 4

1½ lbs. shad roe	1 tbs. butter, melted
½ tbs. prepared mustard	3 tbs. dry sherry wine
1 tsp. anchovy paste	3 drops Angostura bitters
1 tbs. Worcestershire sauce	4 slices hot buttered toast
Pinch of cayenne	4 sprigs fresh mint
Pinch of rosemary	1 lemon, sliced

Place roe in saucepan over medium flame; cover with boiling water; simmer gently 15 minutes. Drain; cut roe into 1-inch pieces. While roe is simmering, blend in mixing bowl all other ingredients except last three. When roe is done, dip pieces into mixture until well coated; arrange on hot buttered toast; put in preheated hot oven (400° F.) for 5 minutes to allow mixture to permeate roe. Garnish with mint and lemon slices.

VARIATION: Use *cod, salmon,* or *any canned variety roe.*

◆§ ROSEFISH   Average weight 1 pound. It is also called REDFISH. Marketed whole; larger sizes filleted. Meat is firm and of a rich and agreeable flavor.

ROSEFISH MARSEILLAISE
TIME: 40 MINUTES; SERVES 4 TO 6

2 lbs. rosefish fillets	½ cup dry sauterne wine
1 onion, minced	3 firm tomatoes, diced
1 tbs. chopped parsley	3 tbs. olive oil
1 clove garlic, minced	Salt and pepper

Wipe fillets with damp cloth.

Pour olive oil in fireproof oven dish placed over medium flame; add onion, parsley, garlic, tomatoes, salt and pepper to taste.

Place fillets carefully over top of vegetables; cover; bring to boiling point; lower flame. Simmer gently 15 minutes. Add sauterne wine; bring to boiling point, then transfer dish to preheated moderate oven (350° F.); bake 10 minutes more, or until fish flakes easily when tested with fork.

Carefully remove fish from sauce, using large spatula; arrange fillets on preheated hot platter; keep hot over steam.

Quickly strain sauce through fine sieve; heat to boiling point. (Sauce should be reduced one half by this time.) Pour steaming hot sauce over fillets. Serve immediately on preheated plates.

VARIATION: Use *any preferred fish fillets*.

◄§ SALMON   There are two distinct groups of that king of fishes: one is the ATLANTIC SALMON, known as KENNEBEC, and the other is the PACIFIC SALMON. The Kennebec is still found in great abundance; unlike all species of Pacific salmon, the only fish that die immediately after spawning, the Atlantic or Kennebec may survive as many as three spawnings. The weight of the Atlantic salmon averages 10 to 20 pounds but it may run over 80 pounds; its deliciously flavored meat is orange-pink in color. The five distinct species of the PACIFIC SALMON are all strikingly different in size and color. The BLUEBACK of the Columbia River is called SOCKEYE; in Alaska it is known as the RED SALMON. A beautiful bright blue and silver when in the ocean, the fresh-water color changes entirely. The head turns an olive-green and the back and sides a dark blood-red. The weight of the blueback averages 5 pounds and it never weighs more than 12. The meat is a rich, deep red color, the quality very firm, and the flavor succulent and sweet.

The CHINOOK is largest of the five species of Pacific salmon. The Flathead Indians called it *chinook,* meaning spring. Average weight is about 25 pounds, but it often weighs from 40 to 60 pounds and sometimes as much as 100 pounds. The CHUM or DOG SALMON is silvery in color and sometimes has black specks to distinguish it from the other species. It rarely exceeds 10 pounds, but some weigh 20 pounds. The COHO or SILVER SALMON averages about 6 pounds and never weighs more than 30 pounds. Because of its silvery hue and the lightness of its meat, the Russians call the coho the *White Salmon* or Whitefish. The HUMPBACK or PINK SALMON, also called the *Dog Salmon,* it averages 3 pounds and is rarely over 7 pounds. After beginning their long journey to the spawning rivers all Pacific salmon take no food of any kind. They are the only fish that die immediately after spawning. Science has never been able to solve this tragic and dramatic secret.

SALMON* AMERICAN INDIAN
TIME: 40 MINUTES; SERVES 6

3 lbs. salmon steak (1 piece)	1 bay leaf
6 slices bacon	2 ozs. butter
1 clove garlic, minced	1 No. 2 can tomatoes
Salt to taste (about 1 tsp.)	2 green peppers, chopped
1 large onion, sliced	¼ tsp. crushed red pepper

Wipe steak with damp cloth. Blend salt and minced garlic; rub steak well with this mixture; place in casserole; arrange bacon slices over top. In large mixing bowl blend well next 6 ingredients. Pour this mixture around and over salmon; bake in preheated hot oven (450° F.) 30 minutes, or until fish flakes easily when tested with fork. Serve immediately from casserole.

SALMON SAUTÉED BASEL STYLE
TIME: 20 MINUTES; SERVES 4

1½ lbs. salmon steaks	1 bay leaf
3 ozs. butter or margarine	¼ tsp. dill
1 small onion, minced	Salt and pepper
1 tbs. chopped chives	4 sprigs parsley
1 cup rhine wine	

Wipe steaks with damp cloth; cut into 1-inch cubes; salt and pepper to taste. Place 1 ounce butter in skillet; add cubed steaks; pour in wine; add bay leaf; cover; simmer gently 10 minutes while melting other 2 ounces butter in frying pan; add onions, chives, and dill; sauté until golden brown. Arrange on preheated hot platter; pour hot wine sauce over, then hot butter and onion. Garnish with sprigs of parsley.

VARIATION: *Simmered in half wine and half water.*

◆§ SCROD WITH OYSTER SAUCE
TIME: 30 MINUTES; SERVES 6

2 lbs. scrod fillets	½ tsp. pickling spices
1 tbs. vinegar	4 cups water
½ tsp. salt	Paprika
1 bay leaf	Water cress

* Baked in an outdoor oven, this dish is called "Barbecued Salmon." *Whole game fish* also are unusually tasty this way.

Wipe scrod with damp cloth; tie scrod in piece of cheese-cloth; place in saucepan; add vinegar, salt, bay leaf, spices, and water; cover; bring to boiling point; lower flame; simmer gently 8 minutes; remove scrod from water. Save this stock for making sauce. While scrod is simmering prepare

OYSTER SAUCE

½ doz. oysters, in liquor	1 tbs. butter
1 tbs. flour	4 mushrooms, sliced
1 cup Fish Stock (page 21)	Pinch of nutmeg
½ cup cream	1 tsp. lemon juice
1 hard-boiled egg	

Chop egg white; press yolk through sieve; set aside.

Drain oysters; cut into quarters. Slice mushrooms; sauté gently, 3 minutes in butter; gradually add flour, stirring constantly.

When fish stock is ready, mix egg yolk in 1 cupful; add to sauce in pan; stir; add chopped egg white and lemon juice; stir over low flame until creamy; add cream and nutmeg, stirring constantly.

Arrange fish on preheated hot platter; pour hot sauce over. Garnish with water cress. Serve immediately on preheated individual plates. VARIATION: See also "Cod" pages 38 to 39. Prepare scrod fillets in same manner.

◆§ SEA HERRING Some species called BRANCH HERRING, ALEWIFE, GRAY HERRING, and GOLDEN SHAD are taken in fresh water when they spawn. Their weight is less than a pound and they seldom exceed 15 inches in length. Young herring, canned as SARDINES, are about 3 inches long.

The meat of the herring is rich and oily. Its flavor is sweetest at spawning time (unlike the other fishes).

SEA HERRING AU RAGOUT UTTWIL
TIME: 30 MINUTES; SERVES 4 TO 6

2 lbs. fresh sea herring	2 slices bacon, chopped
1 tsp. butter	1 tbs. capers, washed
1 tbs. flour	¼ tsp. dill
1 small onion, minced	Juice of 1 lemon
1 carrot, chopped	Pinch of paprika
1 cup water	Salt and pepper
1 tbs. chopped parsley	

Have herring cleaned and boned; wipe with damp cloth; cut herring into 2-inch pieces; set aside.

Melt butter in saucepan over medium flame; add chopped bacon; brown slightly; add onion; sauté 3 minutes, or until golden brown; gradually stir in flour; brown lightly; add dill; gradually stir in water and cook until sauce thickens slightly (about 5 minutes); add carrot, parsley, capers, and fish; salt and pepper to taste; cover; cook over low flame 10 minutes, or until fish flakes easily when tested with fork. Remove to side; allow to stand 15 minutes, then serve piping hot by reheating quickly.

VARIATION: Use ½ *cup dry sauterne wine and ½ cup water* instead of all water.

ᐁ§ SEA TROUT OR WEAKFISH   Is related to the drums, croakers, and spots, but is not to be confused with the well-known fresh-water trout. The GRAY SEA TROUT, average weight is 1 to 6 pounds, is usually marketed in the small sizes only: whole, drawn, pan-dressed, and filleted. The SPOTTED SEA TROUT, average weight is 1 pound to 2 pounds; its meat is white, tender, and of a very delicate flavor. Marketed whole. The WHITE SEA TROUT is the smallest species.

SEA TROUT BAKED SOUTH AMERICAN
TIME: 1 HOUR; SERVES 4

1 *sea trout, whole (2 lbs.)*	*Juice of 1 lime*
6 *small carrots*	½ *cup olive oil*
1 *large onion, sliced*	¼ *tsp. dill*
2 *egg yolks, beaten*	*Salt and pepper*

If one large trout is not obtainable, select two smaller ones. Have trout cleaned, split, and backbone removed; wipe with damp cloth; cut fish into 4 or 6 serving portions; place pieces in baking dish; arrange 1 slice onion and 1 carrot on each piece; sprinkle lime juice over fish; salt and pepper to taste. Pour olive oil over top; dust lightly with dill; bake in preheated moderate oven (350° F.) 40 minutes, or until fish flakes easily when tested with fork. When done, pour liquid from around fish into saucepan; place saucepan over low flame; gradually stir in lightly beaten egg yolks; continue stirring 3 minutes, or until sauce thickens.

Arrange fish pieces on preheated platter. Pour piping hot sauce over fish. Serve immediately.

VARIATION: *See also* suggestions for *broiling*, pages 9-10; *steaming*, page 12. Serve fish with mild or tangy sauce.

◄§ SHAD   The "shad runs" begin in North Carolina in February or March; also in the Chesapeake Bay in March; usually in April, along the New Jersey coast and in the Hudson River. Like the salmon, the shad spends most of its time in the ocean but runs the coastal rivers to spawn above tidewater. Usually marketed fresh in sizes from 1½ to 8 pounds, it is considered one of the finest of sea-food dishes when stuffed and baked. Shad roe is regarded a "gourmet's choice."

SHAD FILLETS IN HERB SAUCE
TIME: 1 HOUR; SERVES 6

3 lbs. shad fillets, boned	⅛ tsp. marjoram
Salt	⅛ tsp. rosemary
2 ozs. butter	Pinch of nutmeg
½ tsp. prepared mustard	Pinch of cayenne
½ cup rhine wine	

Use boned shad fillets or steaks; wipe with damp cloth.

HERB SAUCE WITH RHINE WINE

Melt butter in saucepan over very low flame; add mustard, marjoram, rosemary, nutmeg, and cayenne; blend well; add rhine wine; heat slightly; when warm, baste fillets thoroughly with this mixture.

Place fillets or boned shad steaks on well-greased rack in baking dish; brush well with mixture again; place some of mixture between fillets; bake in preheated moderate oven (350° F.) 45 minutes, or until fish flakes easily when tested with fork; baste from time to time with Herb Sauce. Serve immediately.

VARIATION: Boned shad steaks may be *broiled*. If so, brush generously with Herb Sauce. Lay steaks on preheated broiler rack 2 inches below flame; *broil* 10 minutes; turn; pour balance of mixture over steaks; broil 10 minutes more. Garnish with parsley. Serve piping hot. (2 pounds steaks ½ inch thick serves 4 generously.)

SHAD GOLDEN BROILED
TIME: 30 MINUTES; SERVES 4

2 lbs. shad steaks
1 tbs. grated onion
2 tbs. lemon juice
¼ lb. butter

1 tsp. salt
¼ tsp. pepper
¼ tsp. marjoram
2 tbs. minced parsley

Have shad steaks cut approximately ¾ inches thick; wipe with damp cloth.

In mixing bowl combine all seasonings except minced parsley.

Arrange shad steaks on greased broiler rack; pour half mixture over steaks; place in preheated broiling compartment 2 inches below flame; broil 10 minutes; turn steaks; pour balance of mixture over them; broil 8 minutes more or until golden brown. Serve piping hot on preheated platter. Garnish with parsley or preferred green herb.

VARIATION: Use *any fish marketed in steak form.* Watch broiling time carefully; do not overcook.

SHAD ROYAL PLANKED
TIME: 1 HOUR; SERVES 6

1 shad, drawn (4 lbs.)
½ tsp. salt
⅛ tsp. pepper
Pinch of tarragon herb
1 lb. semi-cooked peas
4 whole baked tomatoes

3 cups seasoned mashed potatoes
½ head semi-cooked cauliflower
1 lemon, sliced
6 sprigs parsley

Use hardwood plank if possible (otherwise a greased oven glass); oil well; place in cold oven and heat thoroughly, as oven preheats to 400° F.

Clean fish well and wipe with damp cloth; sprinkle fish inside and out with salt and pepper to taste; place on hot plank; bake in preheated moderate oven 35 minutes, or until fish flakes easily when tested with fork.

Meanwhile, prepare vegetables.

Remove shad from oven. Quickly arrange border of hot potatoes at edge of plank. In space between fish and potatoes arrange other vegetables in an attractive manner. Replace in oven for about 10 minutes, or until potatoes are slightly browned and cauliflower is tender but not soft. Remove. Garnish with lemon slices and parsley. Serve immediately on plank.

◄§ SHARKS   Becoming increasingly popular as the markets are able to secure steadier supplies, many different species are taken, among them the *Leopard, Dusky, Brown, Hammerhead,* and *Soupfin.* The latter is one of the most important to consumers because of the Vitamin A content of its liver oil as well as the food value of its meat. The soupfin shark ranges up to 6 feet in length and from 25 to 40 pounds in weight. It is excellent when kippered and compares very favorably with kippered salmon. When cooked, the broad dark band under the skin turns white and the firm shark meat suggests that of the swordfish in texture and flavor.

SHARK OVEN-FRIED PACIFIC
TIME: 30 MINUTES; SERVES 4 TO 6

2 lbs. Soupfin shark fillets	⅓ cup oil or melted butter
½ cup rich milk	1½ tsp. salt
1 cup dry bread crumbs	⅛ tsp. pepper
⅛ tsp. basil	2 tbs. chopped parsley

Wipe shark fillets with damp cloth.

Pour milk into small mixing bowl; add salt, pepper, and basil; stir well.

Dip each fillet first in seasoned milk, then in bread crumbs; arrange in buttered shallow baking dish; pour oil or melted butter over fish; bake in preheated moderate oven (350°-375° F.) 25 minutes. Serve piping hot on preheated plates. Garnish each serving with parsley or preferred green herb, such as mint, tarragon, or dill.

VARIATION: Fillets are unusually tasty when *baked with Spiced Tomato Sauce* (page 44).

◄§ SOLE   *See also* Flounder

SOLE MARGUERY
TIME: 30 MINUTES; SERVES 4

8 fillets lemon sole	1 cup Fish Stock (page 21)
4 fresh mushrooms, minced	1 egg yolk, beaten
1 cup dry sauterne wine	Paprika
4 ozs. butter	Salt and pepper
6 green shrimp	

Purchase fillets of lemon sole, allowing ½ pound for each

person; wipe fillets with damp cloth; season lightly with salt and pepper to taste.

Shell green (raw) shrimp; cut in half lengthwise. Wash and peel mushrooms, using caps only; mince fine.

Melt 2 ounces butter in saucepan over low flame; add fillets, shrimp, mushrooms, sauterne wine, and Fish Stock; cover; bring to boiling point; simmer gently 8 minutes.

Carefully lift out fillets; arrange in shallow baking dish. With perforated spoon lift shrimp and mushrooms from saucepan; spread evenly over fillets.

Reduce wine and fish stock liquid to half by boiling over high flame for 10 minutes. Remove from heat; gradually add other 2 ounces butter to reduced liquid; stirring constantly, add egg yolk slowly; blend well.

Pour sauce over fillets; place in preheated broiling compartment 3 inches below flame; broil 3 minutes, or until golden brown. Serve immediately on preheated individual plates.

VARIATION: Use *any delicately flavored fillets.*

SOLE AU COGNAC
TIME: 45 MINUTES; SERVES 4 TO 6

8 fillets lemon sole	½ wineglass cognac
1 cup water	1 cup rhine wine
1 small onion, minced	¼ lb. mushrooms, chopped
1 bay leaf	5 ozs. butter
½ tsp. thyme	1 cup rich cream
1 clove garlic	1 tsp. lemon juice
Paprika	Salt and pepper

Purchase 4 whole lemon sole; have them filleted; save head, skin, and bones; wipe fillets with damp cloth; sprinkle lightly with paprika and set aside.

Pour water and rhine wine into saucepan over medium flame; add onion, bay leaf, thyme, garlic, salt and pepper to taste; add fish heads, skin, and bones; simmer gently 20 minutes. Strain liquid through fine sieve and set aside.

While liquid is simmering, melt 1 ounce butter in small saucepan over medium flame; add mushrooms; sauté gently 15 minutes, or until tender.

When liquid is strained, add sautéed mushrooms to it. Keep hot over low flame.

Meanwhile, melt 4 ounces butter in frying pan over medium flame; when hot but not smoking, fry fillets quickly 3 minutes on each side. Remove from heat; pour cognac over fillets. Quickly set ablaze with lighted match. Blaze only ½ minute. Remove fillets from pan and arrange them on preheated hot platter. Keep hot over steam.

Blend butter and cognac from frying pan with the mushroom mixture in saucepan; gradually stir in 1 cup rich cream; blend well; add 1 teaspoon lemon juice. Heat thoroughly. Pour steaming hot sauce over fillets. Serve piping hot.

VARIATION: Use *fillets of any firm, sweet-meated fish.*

◄§ SQUID   A distant relative of the octopus, it is shaped almost like a pen, and is usually about 12 inches long. Called the *cuttlefish* by Europeans, it is eaten more frequently abroad than here in America. Squid is sweet and rather rich. It is delicious when simply broiled with butter and a dash of rosemary, though the flavor becomes more intriguing when served with a tart or wine sauce.

SQUIDS SAUTÉED BOURGEOISE
TIME: 20 MINUTES; SERVES 4 TO 6

2 lbs. squids	1 tbs. chopped parsley
¼ lb. butter	¼ tsp. salt
1 clove garlic, minced	⅛ tsp. pepper
Pinch of cayenne	Buttered toast
¼ cup rhine wine	

Have squids thoroughly cleaned; cut into 2-inch cubes; wipe with damp cloth.

Melt butter in saucepan over medium flame; add garlic, cayenne, parsley, salt, and pepper; sauté gently 3 minutes, or until garlic is golden brown; add fish cubes; brown lightly 3 minutes; add rhine wine; simmer gently 8 minutes, or until squids are done but not overcooked. Serve piping hot over buttered toast placed on preheated plate.

◄§ SWORDFISH   Derives its name from the long swordlike beak. When the fish is harpooned and its anger aroused, it has been known to pierce the side of a fishing dory. A lean fish, weighing from 200 to 600 pounds in the North Atlantic waters, the meat is much firmer and more oily than halibut, but it has an indescribable rich flavor when properly prepared and not overcooked. It is best when broiled or planked.

SWORDFISH ROYAL BROILED

TIME: 15 MINUTES; SERVES 4 TO 6

2 lbs. swordfish steak	8 green olives, chopped
1 tsp. salt	⅛ tsp. paprika
¼ tsp. pepper	8 sprigs water cress
3 ozs. butter or margarine	

Have swordfish steak cut at least 1 inch thick; wipe with damp cloth.

Blend salt, pepper, and paprika; rub swordfish lightly on both sides with this mixture; spread 1 ounce butter over top of fish.

Preheat broiler compartment 10 minutes; place swordfish on preheated broiler pan 2 inches below flame; broil 3 minutes on one side; turn; dot with 1 ounce butter; broil 4 minutes, or until light brown. Meanwhile, melt other ounce butter (do not heat); add chopped olives; stir well.

Arrange swordfish on preheated platter; spread olive mixture over top; garnish with water cress. Serve immediately.

VARIATION: *Olives may be omitted;* use lemon slices as garnish with water cress. All fish marketed in steak form are unusually delicious when royal broiled; especially *salmon steaks* and *fresh tuna.*

◆§ TUNA   Light meated, it often weighs as much as 1,-600 pounds, but the average commercial sizes run from 8 to 65 pounds. Because of its rich, oily texture, the tuna is well suited for canning. The small tuna, called ALBACORE, is the only true white-meated tuna and is marketed in fresh steak form as well as canned.

TUNA STEAK BORDEAUX

TIME: 25 MINUTES; MARINATE 24 HOURS; SERVES 4 TO 6

2 lbs. tuna steak	2 firm tomatoes, quartered
3 tbs. olive oil	Salt and pepper
2 small onions, minced	4 slices buttered toast
1 cup white wine vinegar	

Have tuna steak cut 1½ inches thick; wipe with damp cloth; place steak in shallow dish with cover; pour in wine vinegar sufficient to cover steak well; replace cover on dish; set aside to marinate 24 hours at room temperature.

When ready to prepare, pour olive oil in skillet; heat but do not allow to smoke; brown fish quickly 2 minutes on each side; remove from skillet; arrange in fireproof casserole; set aside a few minutes.

Place onions in oil in skillet; add salt and pepper to taste; cover; sauté gently over low flame 3 minutes; add tomatoes; sauté 3 minutes more.

Now place casserole (with fish) over low flame; pour sauce over fish; cover; simmer gently 15 minutes. Just before serving add 1 tablespoon vinegar and stir carefully. Serve portions piping hot fish over buttered toast placed on preheated plates.

VARIATION: *Tuna may be marinated in dry sauterne.*

❦ WHALE The *Humpback*, *Sei*, and *Finback* WHALES are considered the very best for eating. The flavor resembles that of venison, while its color and texture are much like young beef. The boneless, gristleless meat is dressed, cut in chunks or steak form, and marketed fresh, frozen, corned, and canned. The steaks are sliced ready for broiling, then chilled, and packed in boxes for shipment to the markets. The chunks are excellent for soup stocks, stews, and pot roast, while the broiled, sizzling steaks are as palatable as T-bones when served with plenty of melted butter and a baked potato at the side.

WHALE POT ROAST SEATTLE
TIME: 2 TO 3 HOURS; SERVES 6 TO 8

3 *lbs. whalemeat*	½ *cup burgundy wine*
1 *large onion, sliced*	3 *tbs. vegetable oil*
1 *large carrot, sliced*	2 *tbs. flour*
1 *bay leaf*	*Pinch of fennel*
½ *cup water*	*Salt and pepper*

Wash whalemeat thoroughly in cold salted water; wipe well with damp cloth.

Blend salt, pepper, and fennel; rub whalemeat with this mixture, then sprinkle with 1 tablespoon flour, patting it into meat.

Heat oil in frying pan; brown whalemeat on all sides quickly to seal in flavor; transfer to heavy pot or casserole; add onion and carrot.

Blend water and burgundy wine; pour about ¼ cup over

whalemeat; cover; cook over medium high flame for ½ hour; add ¼ cup water and wine; lower flame slightly; add balance of water and wine. Cook from 2 to 3 hours, or until meat is tender. Watch carefully to avoid sticking; if necessary add little water or wine.

When tender, remove; thicken gravy in pot with the other tablespoon flour; season with salt and pepper to taste. Serve piping hot with mashed potatoes.

VARIATION: Put *cold leftover roast whale* through food chopper, put in a buttered baking dish with fresh peas, covered with mashed potatoes, and bake 40 minutes.

WHALEMEAT FILLET WITH MUSHROOMS
TIME: 1½ HOURS; SERVES 6

2 lbs. whalemeat fillets	2 tbs. lemon juice
¼ lb. butter	1 tbs. flour
1 cup water	Salt and pepper
1 lb. mushrooms, sliced	

Have whalemeat cut into small steaks or fillets; wipe with damp cloth; sprinkle whalemeat with salt and pepper to taste. Melt 2 ounces butter in frying pan; arrange fillets carefully; fry over low flame ½ hour on each side, turning only once. Meanwhile, melt other 2 ounces butter in saucepan; add sliced mushrooms; sauté 3 minutes over low flame; salt to taste; add 1 cup water; sauté 15 minutes, or until mushrooms are tender.

After whalemeat has been in frying pan 1 hour, pour off butter into small pan; blend in 1 tablespoon flour; when very smooth, stir flour mixture nto mushrooms; blend well, add lemon juice, and keep gravy hot over low flame.

Finish preparing whalemeat fillets by turning the flame high under the frying pan and browning quickly on both sides. Arrange on a preheated platter. Serve mushroom gravy in separate dish. Serve immediately on individual preheated plates, arranging mushrooms around each portion.

VARIATION: *Broiled whalemeat steak.* Have steaks cut across the grain of meat and pounded with back of cleaver, then broil like any beefsteak. Time approximately same.

◄§ WHITING   Sometimes called the SILVER HAKE, it is closely related to *cod* and *hake*. A slender, dark-gray fish with silvery underparts, its average length is about a foot, and the average market weight from 1 pound to 4 pounds. The larger ones are prepared as fillets. Unusually tasty when pan-fried or baked with a delicate sauce.

WHITING BAKED WITH CUCUMBERS
TIME: 25 MINUTES; SERVES 4 TO 6

2 lbs. whiting fillets
1 small onion, minced
½ cup chicken broth
2 cucumbers, cubed

⅛ tsp. dill
Salt and pepper
6 stuffed olives, chopped

Wipe fillets with damp cloth. Peel and mince onion; cube cucumbers; chop olives.

Place fillets in shallow fireproof baking dish; sprinkle lightly with salt and pepper to taste; cover with onion and cucumber; sprinkle with dill; pour chicken broth over top; bake in preheated moderate oven (350° F.) 20 minutes. Serve piping hot in oven dish. Garnish with chopped olives.

VARIATION: Use *any lean-meated fillets* or *flaked leftovers with ½ cup dry sauterne* instead of broth.

6. FISH PATTIES AND PUFFS

~~~~~~

Patties and Puffs

BAKED PATTIES HAWAIIAN
TIME: 30 MINUTES; SERVES 6

2 cups steamed fish, flaked	2 pimientos, diced
1 cup cooked rice	1 tbs. lemon juice
¼ onion, grated	½ tsp. salt
¼ tsp. dry mustard	1 cup cracker crumbs
1 tsp. Worcestershire sauce	Chutney
4 tbs. shredded coconut	

Use any sweet-meated flaky fish, such as *hake, pike,* or *halibut;* or utilize leftovers which have been simply baked without sauces or boiled.

Place all ingredients, except cracker crumbs, in large mixing bowl; mix gently and thoroughly; add enough crumbs to hold mixture together; mold into patties; roll in cracker crumbs; arrange in greased baking dish; bake in preheated moderate oven (350° F.) 10 minutes, or until golden brown. Serve on preheated platter with chutney or favorite sweet relish.

VARIATION: *Crushed corn flakes* may be substituted.

HALIBUT PATTIES WITH RELISH
TIME: 30 MINUTES; SERVES 4

1 lb. halibut steak	2 tbs. pickle relish
1 egg	1 cup dry bread crumbs
½ cup milk	2 ozs. butter or margarine
½ tsp. salt	Pinch of sage

Wipe halibut with damp cloth; place halibut in wire steaming basket. Pour 2 cups water in saucepan; boil. Place wire basket in pan. Do not allow fish to touch water; cover; steam 15 minutes, or until fish flakes easily when tested with fork. Remove fish; flake with fork; set aside. Meanwhile prepare patty mixture: break egg into mixing bowl; beat lightly with fork; add milk, salt, relish, sage, and ¾ cup bread crumbs; blend well; add flaked fish; mix well; shape into patties (about 8); roll in balance of bread crumbs.

Melt butter or margarine in frying pan; heat but do not allow to smoke; fry patties 3 minutes, or until golden brown.

VARIATION: Use *haddock, salmon,* or *cod,* and serve with tangy or shellfish sauce.

NORWEGIAN FISH PUFFS NORBY
TIME: 1 HOUR; SERVES 6

1 *lb. haddock fillets*	½ *cup rich milk*
1 *lb. haddock tails*	¼ *tsp. baking powder*
1 *cup potato flour*	½ *tsp. salt*
1 *egg, well beaten*	⅛ *tsp. white pepper*
½ *tsp. salt, extra*	1 *qt. cold water*
Parsley sprigs	1 *bay leaf*

Wipe fish fillets and tails with damp cloth. Set fillets aside. Prepare fish stock by pouring 1 quart cold water into saucepan; add ½ teaspoon salt and bay leaf; add haddock tails; bring to boil; cover; simmer 20 minutes. Strain fish stock through fine sieve; set stock aside. While fish stock is simmering, prepare mixture.

Grind raw fillets through food chopper. Sift flour and baking powder into mixing bowl; add ½ teaspoon salt and ⅛ teaspoon white pepper; add beaten egg; blend well; add ground raw fish; mix well; add enough milk to make soft, light mixture.

Reheat fish stock to boiling point; dip dessert spoon into hot broth to prevent fish mixture sticking to spoon. Drop fish mixture by spoonfuls into boiling fish stock; boil 10 minutes. Remove puffs from stock; keep hot over steaming water until all mixture is used. Serve piping hot with favorite "White Sauce" (p. 81). Garnish with parsley sprigs or chopped green herb.

VARIATION: Prepare puffs as usual. Remove from broth; cool 1 hour at room temperature. *Fry puffs in deep butter 3 minutes,* or until golden brown.

Puddings

NORWEGIAN FISH PUDDING NORBY
TIME: 1 HOUR; SERVES 6

2 lbs. cod fillets	4 egg whites, well beaten
1 tsp. salt	⅛ tsp. nutmeg
⅛ tsp. pepper	⅛ tsp. cayenne
3 cups rich cream	

Wipe fillets with damp cloth; grind *raw* fish through food chopper; place fish in large mixing bowl; add salt, pepper, cayenne, nutmeg, and egg whites; mix well.

Force this mixture through fine sieve into another mixing bowl; use a pestle for the work. Place bowl in large dish filled with cracked ice. Gradually stir rich cream into fish mixture; place in buttered pudding mold. Place mold in boiling water in baking pan; bake very slowly in preheated moderate oven (300° F.) 12 minutes.

Unmold steaming hot pudding on preheated platter. Garnish with water cress, or serve with preferred cream sauce, such as cheese or mushroom. Steaming hot pudding may be served directly from mold if preferred.

Soufflé

ROCK BASS SOUFFLÉ SWEDISH STYLE
TIME: 1 HOUR; SERVES 6

2 rock bass (1½ lbs. each)	4 eggs
2 cups milk	¼ tsp. nutmeg
½ cup flour	Dash of cayenne
2 ozs. butter or margarine	Dash of paprika
½ tbs. butter, extra	Salt and pepper

Clean and dress rock bass; wipe with damp cloth; place in wire steaming basket. Pour 2 cups water in saucepan; bring to boiling point. Place wire basket in pan. Do not allow fish to touch water; cover; steam 10 minutes, or until fish flakes easily when tested with fork. Remove fish; take out all bones; remove skin; flake with fork; chop into fine pieces.

While fish is steaming, prepare soufflé mixture: pour milk in deep saucepan; heat but do not boil; add 2 ounces butter or margarine.

Blend flour with enough cold water to make very smooth mixture; carefully add to hot milk, stirring constantly, until mixture thickens (about 5 minutes). Add fish, nutmeg, cayenne, salt and pepper to taste; stir well; remove from flame; cool 5 minutes. Separate egg yolks from whites; beat each separately; add yolks to fish mixture; stir well, then fold in stiffly beaten whites.

Grease casserole with ½ tablespoon butter; pour fish mixture into casserole; sprinkle with paprika; place casserole in shallow pan of boiling water; bake in preheated moderate oven (350° F.) 30 minutes or more, until soufflé rises and is delicately brown. (Leftover soufflé, when cold, can be sliced and fried in butter.)

7. Fish Salads

~~~~~~

Salad Bowls

PACIFIC ROCKFISH SALAD BOWL SUPRÊME

TIME: COOKED FISH 30 MINUTES; RAW FISH 1 HOUR; SERVES 6

2 cups shredded cooked
   rockfish, or
1 lb. rockfish fillets
3 hard-boiled eggs, chopped
6 radishes, sliced
¼ green pepper, chopped
¾ green pepper, in strips
½ cup mayonnaise
12 crisp lettuce leaves

3 stalks celery, chopped
½ cucumber, diced
2 small sweet pickles, minced
1 tbs. lemon juice
½ tsp. salt
⅛ tsp. pepper
12 sprigs water cress
Paprika

Purchase rockfish fillets from which skin has been removed. Oven-steam rockfish * as follows: Sprinkle fillets with salt (about 1 teaspoon to each pound). Slice 1 small onion. Place rockfish in ungreased covered casserole with slices of onion over and between fillets; bake in preheated moderate oven (350° F.) 30 minutes. Cool quickly at room temperature; shred fibers with fork; set rockfish aside.

Blend mayonnaise with lemon juice in large mixing bowl. Add all salad ingredients except green pepper strips, water cress, and lettuce leaves; toss well.

Arrange lettuce leaves in prechilled salad bowl; fill with fish mixture; garnish with water cress and green pepper strips. Serve on prechilled individual salad plates.

ROE SALAD RHODE ISLAND

TIME: FRESH, 45 MINUTES; CANNED, 30 MINUTES; SERVES 4

½ lb. fresh shad roe
2 stalks celery, chopped

1 tbs. prepared horse-radish
¾ cup mayonnaise

---

* Pacific rockfish cooked "oven-steamed" as in this recipe cannot be distinguished from fresh crab-meat flakes.

8 *stuffed green olives,*
   chopped
½ *cucumber, diced*
¼ *tsp. salt*
⅛ *tsp. pepper*

⅛ *tsp. thyme*
1 *small head chicory*
Water cress
Crisp lettuce leaves

Simmer fresh roe as shown on page 56; cool at room temperature; carefully cut into cubes, using sharp knife; set aside.

In large bowl mix celery, olives, cucumber, salt, and pepper. Blend horse-radish, mayonnaise, and thyme; pour over vegetables in bowl; mix well; add roe cubes, being careful not to break; mix gently with vegetables.

Line prechilled salad bowl with crisp lettuce leaves and chicory; arrange roe mixture over greens; garnish edge of salad bowl with water cress. Serve very cold with extra helping of mayonnaise at side.

VARIATION: *Canned or fresh roe of alewife, cod, herring, mackerel, mullet, salmon,* and *whitefish may be used. Tangy garnishes, such as green olives, capers, dill pickles, or sour gherkins, are best with roe.*

ROSEFISH DEVILED SALAD

TIME: 30 MINUTES; SERVES 4

½ *cup flaked rosefish*
1 *stalk celery, minced*
1 *tbs. green pepper, minced*
1 *tbs. mayonnaise*
1 *tsp. lemon juice*
¼ *tsp. dry mustard*

4 *hard-boiled eggs*
⅛ *tsp. salt*
Pinch of cayenne
2 *large tomatoes, quartered*
1 *green pepper, cut in rings*
Crisp lettuce leaves

Use freshly steamed or leftover rosefish; flake into very small pieces with fork; set aside.

Mix lemon juice and dry mustard in bowl; add mayonnaise; blend well. Cut eggs in half lengthwise; remove yolks; mash and mix with seasoned mayonnaise; add salt and cayenne to taste; add rosefish flakes.

Fill whites of eggs with fish mixture. Arrange crisp lettuce leaves on prechilled oval platter; place filled eggs in center; border platter with tomato quarters and green pepper rings. Serve very cold with extra mayonnaise if desired.

VARIATION: Use *any preferred variety freshly steamed, or leftover fish which can be very finely flaked. Smoked fish* is delicious when prepared in this manner.

SALMON SUMMER SALAD
TIME: 30 MINUTES; SERVES 4

1 lb. steamed salmon
2 stalks celery, chopped
1 small Bermuda onion, sliced
8 ripe olives
1 green pepper, cut in rings
Crisp lettuce leaves

2 hard-boiled eggs
¼ tsp. salt
⅛ tsp. pepper
¼ tsp. celery seed
¼ tsp. dill
Mayonnaise

Use freshly steamed or leftover salmon steak; break up into large chunks; mix carefully with desired amount mayonnaise in large bowl; set aside.

Prepare all vegetables; chop celery; slice onion and hard-boiled eggs; cut green pepper into rings. Blend celery with mayonnaise, salt, pepper, and celery seed. Mix seasoned celery with salmon, being careful not to break up fish.

Line prechilled salad bowl with crisp lettuce leaves; place salmon salad carefully in bowl. Arrange alternate slices hard-boiled egg, onion, and green pepper rings around border; sprinkle lightly with dill. Garnish top with ripe olives.

VARIATION: Any variety firm-meated freshly steamed or leftover fish may be used.

Salad Molds

JELLIED WHITEFISH RING
TIME: 40 MINUTES; CHILL 1 HOUR; SERVES 6

1 cup cooked whitefish flakes
¼ oz. gelatine (1 envelope)
1 tbs. prepared horse-radish
½ cup diced raw celery
½ tsp. salt
3 hard-boiled eggs, quartered
1½ cups tomato juice

3 tbs. wine vinegar
1 tsp. onion juice
¼ cup minced green pepper
⅛ tsp. white pepper
¼ cup hot water
6 tsp. mayonnaise

Use steamed or boiled whitefish; flake with fork.

Dissolve gelatine in hot water. Add tomato juice, horse-radish, salt, vinegar, and onion juice; place in refrigerator to chill for 1 hour, or until slightly thickened. Fold in celery, green peppers, and fish. Turn into salad-mold ring which has been rinsed in cold water; chill in refrigerator until firm.

Unmold on crisp lettuce leaves. Garnish with quartered hard-boiled eggs and mayonnaise.

VARIATION: Minced green peppers may be omitted; use 8 *stuffed green olives* instead. Plain water may be substituted for tomato juice. *1 cup freshly flaked hake or halibut,* may be substituted for whitefish.

SHREDDED ROCKFISH SALAD MOLD

TIME: 30 MINUTES; CHILL 3 HOURS; SERVES 4 TO 6

1½ cups shredded rockfish	1 tbs. gelatine
2 stalks celery, chopped	½ cup cold water
1 pimiento, chopped	1 bay leaf
½ tsp. Worcestershire sauce	¼ tsp. cayenne
½ tsp. salt	1 cucumber, sliced
⅛ tsp. pepper	Crisp lettuce leaves
1½ cups tomato juice, heated	Mayonnaise

Use freshly oven-steamed rockfish (page 54) or leftover rockfish. In mixing bowl blend fish, celery, pimiento, salt, and pepper. Set rockfish mixture in refrigerator.

Pour tomato juice in small saucepan over medium flame; add bay leaf, Worcestershire sauce, and cayenne; heat but do not boil; remove from heat; take out bay leaf.

Meanwhile, soften gelatine in ½ cup cold water; dissolve in hot tomato juice. Cool 1 hour, or until slightly thickened; then add rockfish mixture; stir well.

Pour salad mixture into mold which has been chilled in cold water; place in refrigerator; chill 2 hours, or until firm. Unmold on prechilled platter garnished with crisp lettuce leaves and cucumber slices. Serve very cold with generous helping mayonnaise.

VARIATION: Use *any freshly cooked or leftover fish.*

TUNA JELLIED CRESCENT

TIME: 30 MINUTES; CHILL 3 HOURS; SERVES 4 TO 6

1 cup tuna flakes	1 tbs. unflavored gelatine
1 tbs. capers, drained	½ cup cold water
½ cup chopped celery	1½ cups hot water
½ tsp. celery seed	½ tsp. salt
½ cup shredded cabbage	⅛ tsp. pepper
4 sour gherkins	⅛ tsp. paprika
Russian Dressing	Crisp romaine lettuce leaves

Use freshly cooked leftover tuna or canned flakes; place in mixing bowl; add capers, celery, celery seed, and shredded cabbage; mix gently but well. Set in refrigerator until needed.

Soften gelatine in cold water; dissolve in hot water; season with salt, pepper, and paprika. Set aside to cool 1 hour, or until slightly thick. When ready, add fish mixture to gelatine; blend well by stirring gently. Pour mixture into crescent-shaped mold which has been rinsed in cold water; place in refrigerator; chill 2 hours, or until firm.

Unmold on crisp romaine lettuce leaves arranged on prechilled round plate. Garnish with sour gherkins. Serve very cold with generous helping of Russian dressing.

VARIATION: *Use any fresh or canned flaked fish.*

8. Fish Sauces and Stuffings

~~~~~~

Cold Sauces

COCKTAIL SAUCE SUPRÊME

TIME: 10 MINUTES; CHILL 30 MINUTES; SERVES 6 TO 8

1 cup catsup	1 tbs. minced onion
2 tbs. tarragon vinegar	½ tsp. salt
1 tbs. horse-radish	1 tsp. Worcestershire sauce
1 tbs. minced celery	3 drops tobasco sauce

Pour catsup in large mixing bowl; add all other ingredients; blend well. Place in refrigerator; chill well 30 minutes. Use as needed, with cold flaked fish.

VARIATION: Omit minced onion; add *4 stuffed olives, chopped;* use only ⅛ teaspoon salt with olives. Or omit celery and onions; add *4 teaspoons sweet-pickle relish.*

COOKED CHILLED CUCUMBER SAUCE

TIME: 15 MINUTES; CHILL 30 MINUTES; SERVES 6

1 cup diced cucumbers	½ cup mayonnaise
1 tbs. butter	½ cup milk
2 tsp. lemon juice	⅛ tsp. pepper
Pinch of oregano	⅛ tsp. paprika
1 tbs. flour	½ tsp. salt

Melt butter in top section double boiler placed over lower section half filled with boiling water; blend in flour, stirring constantly. When smooth, gradually stir in milk; blend well; add oregano, salt, pepper, paprika, and mayonnaise; stir well; add lemon juice and cucumbers; cook 3 minutes. Remove from heat; chill in refrigerator.

HORSE-RADISH CREAM SAUCE

TIME: 20 MINUTES; SERVES 6 TO 8

4 tbs. freshly grated horse-radish	1 pt. cream, whipped
	Juice of 1 lemon
2 egg yolks, well beaten	½ tsp. salt
2 egg whites, well beaten	

79

Separate egg yolks from whites; place each in bowls. Beat egg yolks until light yellow; add grated horse-radish; beat 2 minutes; add salt.

Beat egg whites until stiff. Beat cream until stiff; blend the two well. Gradually add horse-radish mixture; add lemon juice. Blend well; chill in refrigerator 30 minutes. Serve with hot or cold fish, as desired.

SOUR GHERKIN SAUCE
TIME: 30 MINUTES; YIELD: APPROXIMATELY 1 CUP

4 *sour gherkins, minced*
½ *cup olive oil*
¼ *tsp. dry mustard*
¼ *cup red wine vinegar*
1 *tsp. sugar*
½ *tsp. dill*
Salt and pepper

Blend dry mustard and sugar. Combine minced gherkins, olive oil, mustard, sugar, and dill in mixing bowl; blend well; add wine vinegar; mix well; add salt and pepper to taste; chill in refrigerator 15 minutes.

VARIATION: Sauce may be *heated* and *served hot.*

TARTAR SAUCE: *See page* 143, "Frogs' Legs Deep-Fried."

VINAIGRETTE* SAUCE
TIME: 20 MINUTES; SERVES 4 TO 6

1 *cup olive oil*
⅛ *cup vinegar*
1 *clove garlic*
½ *tsp. celery seed*
Pinch of cayenne
1 *tsp. sugar*
½ *tsp. salt*
½ *tsp. Worcestershire sauce*
1 *tsp. lemon juice*
¼ *tsp. thyme*

Blend celery seed, cayenne, sugar, salt, and thyme in mixing bowl; gradually stir in olive oil, vinegar, Worcestershire sauce, and lemon juice; blend well; add clove garlic.

Pour sauce into covered jar. Place in refrigerator for 1 hour. When ready to serve, remove clove of garlic.

VARIATION: *Serve sauce* piping hot over boiled or baked fish.

* See also "Kingfish Vinaigrette," page 47.

Hot Sauces

BASIC WHITE SAUCE
TIME: 15 MINUTES; SERVES 4 TO 6

2 ozs. butter	1 cup rich milk
2 tbs. flour	Pinch of nutmeg
¼ tsp. salt	⅛ tsp. pepper

Melt butter in top section double boiler placed in lower section half filled with boiling water; gradually add flour, stirring constantly; add salt, pepper, and nutmeg. Slowly pour in cold milk. Stir sauce continually until it is very smooth and thickens (about 6 min.); cook 5 minutes longer.

Basic White Sauce may be used to prepare creamed fish or shellfish and as a basis for preparing a variety of seasoned sauces. Always serve piping hot.

VARIATION: *Celery Sauce.* Follow recipe; add ½ cup minced celery. *Cheese Sauce.* Follow recipe; add ½ cup mild or sharp cheese. *Curry Sauce.* Follow recipe; add ½ to 1 teaspoon curry powder. *Egg Sauce.* Follow recipe; add 2 hard-boiled eggs, chopped fine. *Golden Sauce.* Remove Basic White Sauce from heat just before serving; fold in 1 well-beaten egg; stir briskly until hot sauce absorbs and cooks egg. Garnish with *fresh mint, fresh dill sprays,* or *sprigs of fresh fennel. Herb Sauces; Caper Sauce.* Follow recipe; add 1 tablespoon drained capers. For other herb sauces, omit nutmeg, add 1 tablespoon chopped *fresh herbs,* such as *chives, dill, minced onion, parsley, pimiento, peppers,* or *mint.* When using dried herbs for flavoring, use ½ to 1 teaspoon only. *Mushroom Sauce.* Follow recipe; add ½ to 1 cup cooked minced mushrooms. Prepared sauces may be poured over *boiled, baked,* or *steamed fillets* and *steaks.* If sauce if prepared ahead of time and becomes thicker than desired, dilute with small quantity milk just before serving, then reheat to boiling point but do not boil.

BÉCHAMEL SAUCE
TIME: 30 MINUTES; SERVES 4

2 cups milk	2 tbs. flour
3 sprigs parsley	⅛ tsp. mace
1 small onion	½ tsp. salt
1 whole clove	¼ tsp. pepper
4 peppercorns	Pinch of nutmeg
2 tbs. butter	

Pour 1 cup milk in small saucepan over medium flame; add parsley, onion, clove, and peppercorns; cover; simmer 15 minutes. Strain sauce through fine sieve.

Melt butter in saucepan over medium flame; gradually blend in flour, mace, salt, and pepper. When smooth, gradually add all milk, stirring constantly until thick (about 5 minutes); add pinch of nutmeg; blend well. If sauce is thicker than desired, add small amount milk. Sauce may be prepared ahead of time, ready for use as required.

BEER SAUCE BASEL STYLE
TIME: 30 MINUTES; SERVES 6

1 *bottle light beer or ale*	1 *bay leaf*
(12 ozs.)	½ *stick cinnamon*
1 *tsp. vinegar*	⅛ *tsp. salt*
½ *tsp. sugar*	*Pinch of pepper*
1 *onion, minced*	2 *ozs. butter*
1 *clove*	2 *tbs. potato flour*

Pour beer or ale into saucepan; add all seasonings (8 ingredients); bring to boiling point; add 1 ounce butter; cover; simmer gently 15 minutes; remove from fire; strain sauce through fine sieve.

Blend potato flour well in small amount cold water; when very smooth, gradually add to strained sauce. Place saucepan over low flame; stir constantly and bring to boiling point (about 3 minutes). (If thinner sauce is preferred, add small amount beer.) Serve piping hot, with boiled, broiled, pan-fried, or steamed fish.

CREOLE SAUCE
TIME: 20 MINUTES; SERVES 4 TO 6

2 *cups canned tomatoes*	1 *clove garlic, minced*
1 *large onion, minced*	⅛ *tsp. rosemary*
4 *tbs. melted butter*	⅜ *tsp. pepper*
1 *tsp. salt*	⅛ *tsp. paprika*
1 *cup minced green pepper*	

Melt butter in saucepan over medium flame; add onion, green pepper, and garlic; sauté 10 minutes, or until tender; add salt, pepper, paprika, and tomatoes; bring to boiling point; cover; turn down flame; simmer 15 minutes or longer.

(The longer tomatoes simmer, the better the flavor of sauce.) Serve piping hot over baked fish.

VARIATION: *Fillets and steaks of fish cut into serving pieces* may be simmered in Creole Sauce 10 to 12 minutes and then served.

DILL SAUCE LAUTERBRUNNEN
TIME: 30 MINUTES; SERVES 4

½ tbs. chopped dill	1 cup Fish Stock (page 21)
2 ozs. butter	¼ tsp. salt
2 tbs. potato flour	⅛ tsp. pepper

Melt butter in top section of double boiler placed in lower section half filled with boiling water; gradually add flour, stirring constantly; add Fish Stock, stirring constantly until sauce begins to thicken. (If thinner sauce is preferred, use more fish stock.) Add salt, pepper, and dill; blend well; simmer gently 20 minutes. Serve piping hot over baked, pan-fried, steamed, or boiled fish.

If fresh dill is not obtainable, use 1 tablespoon dried dill, well crushed.

HERB SAUCE WITH RHINE WINE: See page 61, "Shad Fillets in Herb Sauce."

HOLLANDAISE SAUCE: See page 141, "Crayfish Cardinal."

LEMON BUTTER SAUCE
TIME: 10 MINUTES; SERVES 4 TO 6

2 ozs. butter	⅛ tsp. pepper
2 tsp. lemon juice	

Melt butter in small saucepan over low flame.

Blend lemon juice and pepper; add to melted butter; mix well.

Serve hot with steamed, boiled, baked, or planked fish.

VARIATION: *Lemon Butter with Mustard.* Add ½ cup prepared French mustard; stir well; serve piping hot. Excellent with cod and haddock.

MAÎTRE D'HÔTEL BUTTER SAUCE: See pages 142-43, "Frogs' Legs Broiled Maître d'Hôtel."

MUSHROOM SAUCE: *See* page 81.

NEWBURG SAUCE
TIME: 10 MINUTES; SERVES 6

3 tbs. butter
3 tbs. flour
¼ tsp. dry mustard
¼ tsp. salt
⅛ tsp. pepper

4 tbs. sherry wine
1½ cups light cream
2 egg yolks, beaten
2 drops tabasco sauce
Pinch of cayenne

Melt butter in top section double boiler placed in lower section half filled with boiling water; gradually add flour; blend well; add seasonings; cook over medium flame 2 minutes; gradually pour in cream, stirring constantly. When well blended, remove from flame; cool 5 minutes.

Pour egg yolks into large mixing bowl; beat until foamy; slowly pour sauce over egg yolks, stirring constantly. Return mixture to top section double boiler; add sherry wine; heat 1 minute. Serve piping hot over steamed fish.

OYSTER SAUCE. *See* pages 58-59, "Scrod with Oyster Sauce."

SAUCE RAVIGOTE: *See* pages 36-37, "Blowfish with Sauce Ravigote."

SHRIMP SAUCE: *See* page 39, "Cod Sautéed with Shrimp Sauce."

SPICED TOMATO SAUCE: *See* page 44, "Grouper Fillet Rolls with Spiced Tomato Sauce."

Wine Sauces

BURGUNDY SAUCE
TIME: 20 MINUTES; YIELD: APPROXIMATELY 2 CUPS

2 tbs. butter
2 tbs. flour
⅛ tsp. mace

1 cup burgundy wine
½ cup Fish Stock (page 21)
Salt and pepper

Melt butter in saucepan over medium flame; gradually blend in flour; when very smooth, add burgundy wine and Fish Stock; blend well; add mace; salt and pepper to taste; stir constantly until thick (about 6 minutes); cook over low flame 5 more minutes, continue stirring. Serve piping hot over fish. Sauce may also be prepared in top section of double boiler.

VARIATION: Use *claret, chianti* or *any tart red wine.*

CHAMPAGNE SAUCE
TIME: 20 MINUTES; SERVES 4 TO 6

1 cup champagne	1 cup White Sauce (page 81)
2 cloves	
4 peppercorns	½ tsp. sugar
Pinch of mace	

Pour champagne into top section of double boiler placed in lower section half filled with boiling water; add cloves, peppercorns, sugar, and mace; bring to boiling point; cover; simmer 5 minutes.

Stir in 1 cup Basic White Sauce; heat. Serve piping hot over steamed or boiled fish fillets.

VARIATION: Use *sweet* or *dry sauterne,* or *rhine wine.*

MADEIRA SAUCE PIQUANTE
TIME: 1¾ HOURS; SERVES 6

½ cup madeira wine	1½ cups consommé
1 small onion, minced	1 lemon rind, grated
2 sprigs thyme, minced	1 tbs. butter
1 sprig parsley, minced	1 tbs. flour
1 stalk celery, minced	½ bay leaf
Salt and pepper	Pinch of cayenne

Melt butter in top section of double boiler placed over lower section half filled with boiling water; gradually blend in flour; when smooth, lift out top section and place over low flame; brown flour, stirring constantly; replace top section. Pour in consommé; bring to boiling point; add all other ingredients except cayenne and madeira wine; simmer gently 1½ hours; remove from flame; strain through fine sieve; return to flame; add cayenne and madeira wine; bring to boiling point; simmer 2 minutes. Serve immediately with fish fillets or steaks.

VARIATION: Use *dry* or *sweet sherry wine.*

SAUTERNE WINE SAUCE: *See* page 32, "Whitefish with Sauterne Wine Sauce."

SHERRY-ALMOND SAUCE: *See* pages 31-32, "Rainbow Trout Rocky Mountain."

SHERRY WINE SAUCE
TIME: 15 MINUTES; SERVES 4

½ cup dry sherry wine	2 tbs. flour
2 anchovy fillets, minced	⅛ tsp. pepper
2 cups milk	Pinch of salt
2 tbs. butter	

Mince anchovy fillets until almost a paste.

Melt butter in top section of double boiler placed over lower section half filled with boiling water; gradually blend in flour with melted butter; add anchovies, pepper, and very little salt; when well mixed, slowly add milk, stirring constantly until the sauce thickens; simmer gently 5 minutes.

Just before serving stir in sherry wine; heat 1 minute. Serve piping hot on steamed or boiled fillets. Excellent with crab and lobster.

VARIATION: Use *tawny port* or *sweet sherry wine*.

Stuffings

BREAD STUFFING
TIME: 15 MINUTES; FILLS 4-LB. FISH

3 cups soft bread crumbs	¼ cup rich milk
2 ozs. butter	½ tsp. salt
1 small onion, minced	⅛ tsp. pepper
¼ tsp. rosemary	½ tsp. thyme

Melt butter in saucepan; add onion; sauté over low flame 5 minutes, or until light brown; remove from heat; add salt, pepper, rosemary, and thyme; blend well.

Place bread crumbs in large mixing bowl; add blended seasonings; mix well. Add only enough milk to moisten stuffing slightly. For smaller fish, use half amounts given here.

VARIATION: *Celery Stuffing*. Follow recipe; omit milk; add 1 cup chopped raw celery.
Cheese Stuffing. Follow recipe; add 1 cup grated mild cheese.
Chestnut Stuffing. Follow recipe; add 1 cup minced raw chestnuts.

Green Pepper Stuffing. Follow recipe but omit milk; add ½ cup minced raw green pepper.

Mushroom Stuffing. Follow recipe; add ¼ pound minced raw mushrooms.

Rockfish Stuffing. Follow recipe; add 1 cup minced cooked rockfish. Small fish: *bass, butterfish, crappies, croaker, porgies,* and *trout,* are unusually good when stuffed and baked.

HERB STUFFING

TIME: 20 MINUTES; FILLS 2- TO 3-LB. FISH

½ cup cracker crumbs	1 tsp. chopped parsley
½ cup dry bread crumbs	¼ tsp. dill
2 ozs. butter	¼ tsp. salt
½ tsp. basil	⅛ tsp. pepper
1 tsp. capers, minced	¼ onion, minced

Melt butter in saucepan; add onion; sauté over low flame 5 minutes, or until light brown; remove from heat.

Place cracker and bread crumbs in large mixing bowl; add all seasonings; blend well. This makes a *dry* stuffing. If moist stuffing is preferred, use soft bread crumbs and moisten with ¼ cup milk or fish stock.

VARIATION: The savor of Herb Stuffing may be varied by using different combinations of herbs; always use sparingly. For example, substitute *sage, celery leaves,* and *marjoram* for basil, parsley, and dill; or use *marjoram, thyme,* and *rosemary;* or *sage* and *basil* without the dill.

CAPER DRESSING: See page 37, "Bluefish with Caper Dressing."

9. SMOKED, SALTED, AND CANNED FISH

The large variety of *smoked, salted,* and *canned* fish available in our stores and markets all year is increasing rapidly. Limited space does not allow a specific recipe for each kind of fish; for example: in the recipe for "Canned Bonito Mousse with Golden Sauce," it is possible to use that recipe in preparing canned *albacore, mackerel, salmon,* or *tuna.* The same idea is carried out in the other three divisions of this section of the book. The recipes given for *salted dried, salted in brine,* and *smoked fish* can be easily and appetizingly interchanged with the specific one named in the recipe. Also in many of the recipes in which fresh flaked fish is used canned fish may be substituted; for example: in patties, puffs, puddings, pies, and soufflés. Also in preparing salads a great deal of time is saved when canned fish is used in place of fresh. Naturally the flavor is not the same, but often the dish has a particularly distinctive flavor.

Smoked Fish

◆§ BLOATER   *See* "Sardines or Sea Herring," page 99.

BLOATER PAN-FRIED WITH CHEESE
TIME: 20 MINUTES; SERVES 4

4 bloaters	2 ozs. grated Cheddar cheese
2 eggs, beaten	½ cup flour
2 ozs. butter	Water cress

Purchase soft-smoked bloaters for pan-frying. Select fish of medium size. Split; remove bones, skin, head, and tail.

Break eggs into oblong dish; beat until foamy; add 1 ounce grated cheese. Dip bloaters in seasoned eggs, then in flour.

Melt butter in skillet; heat but do not allow to smoke. Fry bloaters quickly 2 minutes on each side, or until thoroughly heated. Arrange on preheated individual plates; sprinkle with cheese. Garnish with water cress. Serve immediately.

BOWFIN Considered by gourmets to be one of the best of all smoked fishes, its flavor is tangy and full of rich hickory smoke. The bowfin may be eaten cold with a favorite garnish, or steamed in the same way as finnan haddie.

EEL *See* Eel, page 40.

SMOKED EEL HOLIDAY PLANKED

TIME: 45 MINUTES; SERVES 6 TO 8

1½ lbs. smoked eel
1 small head lettuce
12 radishes
1 large tomato, sliced
12 sprigs water cress
1 small bunch celery,
  with tops

12 ripe olives
12 green stuffed olives
1 large pimiento, cut in strips
½ cucumber, sliced
2 hard-boiled eggs, sliced
½ tsp. basil

Purchase smoked eel in one piece. Prepare all vegetable garnishes and chill in ice water 1 hour. Arrange bed of lettuce leaves on long, prechilled platter; place eel in center. Garnish by beginning at center of platter and working toward the edge; alternate red and green garnishes, saving cucumber slices and water cress for outside rim. Place pimiento strips over egg slices and sprinkle tomato slices very lightly with basil just before serving. Serve on chilled salad plates with generous helping of mayonnaise and 1 hot buttered roll.

VARIATION: Use *any variety smoked fish.*

FINNAN HADDIE *See* Haddock, page 44.

FINNAN HADDIE BROILED FILLETS
TIME: 15 MINUTES; SERVES 4

1 *finnan haddie fillet*	8 *tbs. olive oil*
(1½ lbs.)	4 *tsp. chopped parsley*

Select smoked fillet or split finnan haddie; brush lightly with olive oil; place in preheated broiling compartment on rack 4 inches below flame; broil slowly 10 minutes, or until fish is thoroughly heated.

Place on preheated platter. If split finnan haddie is used, lift out bone carefully. Pour olive oil over hot fish. Garnish with chopped parsley. Serve piping hot with boiled or baked potatoes.

VARIATION: Substitute ¼ *pound melted butter* in place of olive oil, if preferred; garnish with chopped fresh mint.

FINNAN HADDIE NEWBURG
TIME: 30 MINUTES; SERVES 6

1 *finnan haddie fillet (¾ lb.)*	4 *egg yolks, beaten*
2 *ozs. butter*	¾ *cup cream*
1½ *cups milk*	*Pinch of cayenne*
1½ *tbs. flour*	¼ *tsp. nutmeg*
⅛ *tsp. salt*	2 *tbs. chopped parsley*
⅛ *tsp. paprika*	6 *slices toast*
¼ *cup sherry wine*	

Purchase smoked fillet or split finnan haddie. If latter is used, remove bones and skin; flake fish; set aside.

Melt butter in saucepan; add milk; heat over low flame but do not boil. Meanwhile, blend flour with little cold water into smooth paste; add to hot milk, stirring constantly until sauce thickens (about 5 minutes). Season with salt, paprika, cayenne, and nutmeg; stir well; add flaked finnan haddie; stir gently 5 minutes to heat fish thoroughly. Remove from flame; allow to cool 2 minutes.

Meanwhile beat egg yolks lightly with cream and sherry in mixing bowl; when well blended, add to warm fish mixture. Reheat carefully 3 minutes; stir well. When piping hot, but *not* boiling, serve over toast placed on preheated plates. Garnish with chopped parsley or chopped ripe olives.

VARIATION: Use *any preferred variety smoked fish.*

◆§ HERRING   *See* "Sardines—Sea Herring," page 99.

KIPPERED HERRING PLAIN BROILED

TIME: 20 MINUTES; SERVES 6

6 soft-smoked kippers
Juice of 1 lemon
4 ozs. butter, melted

Paprika
3 tsp. chopped chives

Split kippers without breaking the back skin; place skin side down in oiled shallow baking dish; brush with melted butter and lemon juice; season with paprika to taste; bake in preheated moderate oven (350° F.) 10 minutes, or until kippers are thoroughly heated. Serve piping hot on preheated individual plates. If kippers are small, each person should be served 2. Garnish with chopped chives or preferred green herbs or pickles.

◦§ MULLET

SMOKED MULLET WITH SPICED BUTTER

TIME: 30 MINUTES; SERVES 4

1 large smoked mullet (1½ lbs.)
1 bunch water cress
1 tsp. chopped chives
1 lemon, sliced

¼ lb. butter
⅛ tsp. pepper
⅛ tsp. dill
⅛ tsp. paprika

Arrange smoked mullet in shallow baking dish; place in preheated moderate oven (350° F.); bake 10 minutes, or until mullet is thoroughly heated. Meanwhile, melt butter in small saucepan over medium flame; brown carefully but do not allow to smoke; add pepper, paprika, and dill to taste.

Place hot mullet on preheated platter; quickly split fish open; pour spiced butter over fish; sprinkle lightly with chopped chives; garnish with water cress and lemon slices. To serve, cut through backbone and skin with sharp knife.

VARIATION: Use *any soft-smoked, whole fish.*

◦§ SALMON

SMOKED SALMON WITH BROWNED RICE

TIME: 30 MINUTES; SERVES 4

4 ozs. smoked salmon
4 ozs. butter
⅛ tsp. paprika
⅛ tsp. nutmeg
⅛ tsp. rosemary

2 cups cooked rice
3 hard-boiled eggs
12 ripe olives
1 dill pickle, sliced
Water cress

Purchase soft-smoked (kippered) salmon; have it cut very thin. Dice half amount with sharp knife; cut other half into strips ¼ inch wide; set aside.

Chop egg whites; press egg yolks through coarse sieve; set both aside. Place hot cooked rice in large mixing bowl; add diced salmon only; blend well; add chopped egg whites.

Melt butter in frying pan over medium flame; add paprika, nutmeg, and rosemary; blend well; add rice mixture, stirring constantly; brown carefully by stirring. When light brown (about 6 minutes), pile in mound on preheated dish. Quickly garnish with salmon strips, ripe olives, dill pickles, and water cress. Serve immediately.

VARIATION: Use *any variety soft-smoked fish.*

SMOKED SALMON WITH FRESH HALIBUT
TIME: 30 MINUTES; SERVES 4

⅛ lb. smoked salmon	4 ozs. butter
Juice of ½ lemon	2 tbs. chopped walnuts
4 tbs. sherry wine	Pepper
2 lbs. halibut steak	

Purchase soft-smoked (kippered) salmon; cut into strips ¼ inch wide; set aside.

Have halibut steak sliced 1 inch thick; wipe with damp cloth.

Melt butter in skillet over medium flame; when very hot but not smoking, brown steaks quickly 2 minutes on each side; add lemon juice and sherry wine; season with pepper to taste; heat 1 minute only; remove from flame.

Place halibut in preheated shallow glass dish; pour hot liquid over fish; sprinkle with chopped walnuts; decorate with strips of smoked salmon; bake in preheated moderate oven (350° F.) 10 minutes, or until fish flakes easily. Serve immediately in glass baking dish at table.

VARIATION: Use *any white-meated steaks* or *fillets.*

◄§ LAKE STURGEON   The largest fish of the Great Lakes, species measuring 7 feet have been caught in Lake Huron. It has become very scarce in spite of all efforts in artificial methods of fish culture.

SMOKED STURGEON SHERRY RAMEKINS

TIME: 30 MINUTES; SERVES 6

½ lb. smoked sturgeon	4 tbs. sherry wine
4 ozs. butter	2 cups rich milk
4 tbs. flour	⅛ tsp. nutmeg
¼ tsp. salt	2 tsp. minced parsley
½ tsp. celery seed	2 hard-boiled eggs, chopped
½ cup dry bread crumbs	2 ozs. buter, extra

Cut sturgeon into 1-inch cubes; set aside.

Melt butter in saucepan over low flame; gradually blend in flour, salt, celery seed, nutmeg, and minced parsley. When smooth, gradually add milk, stirring constantly. Cook 5 minutes, or until sauce thickens; add sherry wine, eggs, and sturgeon; stir gently; remove from flame.

Place mixture in individual buttered ramekins; sprinkle each lightly with bread crumbs; dot with butter; bake in preheated hot oven (400° F.) 5 minutes, or until crumbs are golden brown. Serve piping hot with favorite tossed salad.

VARIATION: Use *any variety soft-smoked fish, such as butterfish, carp, mullet,* or *salmon.* Garnish with chopped fresh mint just before serving.

SMOKED WHITEFISH EAST INDIAN

TIME: 30 MINUTES; SERVES 4 TO 6

1 smoked whitefish (½ lb.)	2 cups fluffy cooked rice
2 ozs. butter	¼ tsp. curry powder
½ cup rich milk	⅛ tsp. pepper
4 hard-boiled eggs, diced	12 sprigs water cress

Select lightly smoked whitefish; split open; remove bones and skin; flake fish with fork.

Melt butter in top section double boiler placed over lower section half filled with boiling water; add curry powder and pepper; blend well; add milk, eggs, and rice; stir gently; add flaked fish; stir gently again. Heat 5 minutes, or until mixture is almost steaming. Serve piping hot on preheated plates. Garnish each serving with water cress or preferred chopped green herb, such as chives or parsley.

VARIATION: Use *any variety soft-smoked fish.*

Salt Fish—Dried

SALT COD SPANISH STYLE

TIME: 2 HOURS; SOAKING TIME 10 HOURS; SERVES 6

1 lb. salt cod (whole)	4 tbs. olive oil
1 No. 2 can tomatoes	2 cloves garlic, minced
2 large onions, chopped	4 sprigs parsley, chopped
1 large sweet red pepper, minced	2 bay leaves
	1/4 tsp. thyme
2 tbs. flour	Salt and pepper

Soak the cod overnight. When ready to prepare, place fish in saucepan with enough cold water to cover; place saucepan over medium flame; boil 45 minutes; remove; take out any bones; *set fish aside until sauce is finished,* then arrange fish on oven platter; border with mashed potatoes or croutons; cover with sauce; place in preheated hot oven (400° F.); brown 10 minutes. Serve piping hot on preheated plates.

While fish is boiling, sauce may be prepared. Melt 1 table-spoon olive oil in deep skillet over medium flame; add 1 onion and 1 clove minced garlic; sauté 3 minutes, or until onion is golden brown; add tomatoes, bay leaves, parsley, thyme, and another tablespoon oil; season with salt and pepper to taste; cover; simmer slowly 1½ hours. Strain sauce through coarse sieve; keep sauce warm over low flame.

Blend thoroughly 1 tablespoon olive oil with flour until very smooth. Place in small saucepan over low flame; brown lightly 3 minutes, stirring constantly to prevent burning; add browned flour to strained sauce, stirring slowly for 5 minutes.

Place the fourth tablespoon olive oil in small skillet; melt over medium flame; add other onion and minced garlic; sauté 3 minutes, or until golden brown; stir in minced sweet pepper; blend well. Add this mixture to the sauce; blend well; heat; pour over codfish and brown as directed.

VARIATION: *Salted herring (dry)* may be prepared in same manner; soak 10 hours; then drain, take out bones, and cut herring into serving pieces. It requires *no* boiling. Prepare sauce and follow recipe.

◄§ CAVIAR The salted roe or fish eggs, is considered an epicurean extravagance. The eggs for caviar are removed from the fish before the female is ready to spawn, while the roe is still hard. In making caviar, the membrane surrounding the eggs is gently rubbed away over a fine screen. This process separates each tiny globule. The eggs are then placed in large wooden tubs and salted. The salt draws all water from the eggs and forms a brine. Later the eggs are poured into a large draining sieve where they stay until they are thoroughly dried. Then they are vacuum sealed in jars or cans. Caviar is served chiefly as an appetizer, prepared as a canapé, and occasionally as a toasted sandwich.

SALT MACKEREL BAKED IN CREAM
TIME: 30 MINUTES; SOAKING TIME 10 HOURS; SERVES 6

1 salt mackerel (1½ lbs.)	¾ cup cream
½ cup flour	½ cup milk
⅛ tsp. pepper	Paprika
1 oz. butter	2 tbs. chopped fresh mint

Soak mackerel in cold water 10 hours; change water twice, if convenient; drain fish when ready to use.

Season flour with pepper and pinch of paprika; roll mackerel in flour; place in buttered casserole; pour milk over; bake in preheated moderate oven (375° F.) 10 minutes; add cream; bake 10 minutes more. Serve piping hot from casserole. Garnish each serving with chopped fresh mint.

VARIATION: Substitute *Finnan Haddie. Do not soak.*

SALT MACKEREL BUTTER BROILED
TIME: 40 MINUTES; SOAKING TIME 2 HOURS; SERVES 6

1½ lbs. salt mackerel fillets	4 ozs. butter, melted
6 slices toast	1 tbs. chopped parsley
1 cup Curry Sauce (p. 81)	Juice of ½ lemon

Soak the fillets in cold water 2 hours; drain; place in saucepan; cover with fresh water; simmer over low flame 30 minutes. Drain; wipe dry with cloth.

Blend butter, parsley, and lemon juice; brush fillets generously with this mixture. Place fish, skin down, on buttered broiler rack; broil in preheated broiler compartment (350° F.) 10 minutes; baste once with butter.

Arrange mackerel fillets on preheated platter; pour hot Curry Sauce over.

VARIATION: Served with *highly seasoned sauce* is best.

Salt Fish—Brine

◄§ ALEWIFE   The American Indian name for a fish also called BRANCH HERRING, the southern species is called the BLUEBACK.

Alewives attain a length of 8 or 10 inches and are marketed chiefly salted in barrels for home consumption and export. Compared with flounders, the alewife is small (average weight is half a pound) and rather bony, but the meat is very agreeably flavored and is somewhat less oily than shad. Lesser quantities of alewives are smoked and some alewives are alewife roe are canned.

ALEWIFE LEMON BAKED
TIME: 20 MINUTES; SOAK 12 HOURS; SERVES 4

4 alewives, salted	Juice of 2 lemons
4 tbs. melted butter	2 tbs. minced parsley

Purchase 4 alewives *salted in brine;* soak in cold water 12 hours. Drain; wipe dry. Split fish open without breaking back skin; place skin side down in well-greased shallow baking dish.

Blend melted butter and lemon juice. Baste fish generously with this mixture. Heat fish thoroughly in preheated moderate oven (350° F.) 10 minutes. Baste with balance of lemon juice mixture; heat 1 minute. Serve piping hot on preheated plates with plain, *unsalted,* boiled potato. Garnish potato and fish with minced parsley.

VARIATION: *Mackerel, salted in brine,* may be prepared in same manner. Freshen mackerel by soaking in cold water 12 hours. Follow recipe.

ANCHOVY SOUR CREAM DIAMONDS
TIME: 30 MINUTES; SERVES 6

3 cans anchovy fillets (1½ ozs. each) or	12 ripe olives, diced
	4 cups diced cooked potatoes
18 dried anchovy fillets	2 cups sour cream
1 large onion, minced	1 tsp. chopped parsley
2 ozs. butter	1 tsp. chopped fresh dill
⅛ tsp. pepper	6 slices toast

Purchase fillets salted in brine (canned) or dry fillets. If latter are used, sprinkle with lemon juice and allow to stand

2 hours. Melt butter in large saucepan over medium flame; add onion; sauté 5 minutes, or until tender; add potatoes; stir 3 minutes, or until golden brown; lower flame; stir in sour cream; add pepper; blend well; add anchovies, olives, and parsley; heat carefully 3 minutes.

Cut toast in large diamond shapes. Arrange on preheated individual plates. Pour piping hot anchovy mixture over toast. Garnish with fresh dill. Serve immediately.

VARIATION: Use *small herring, salted in brine;* soak 10 hours; drain; remove bones and skin; cut into small serving pieces.

HERRING LOAF
TIME: 50 MINUTES; SOAK HERRING OVERNIGHT; SERVES 6

1 salted herring	2 ozs. shelled almonds
1 tart apple	½ tsp. sugar
2 hard-boiled eggs	6 potatoes
Pinch of pepper	1 tbs. chopped parsley

Select large herring salted in brine; place.in oblong dish; cover with cold water; soak overnight; remove bones and skin; set herring aside.

Peel and quarter apple; boil eggs; slice them. Grind herring, apple, eggs, and almonds through food chopper; blend thoroughly in large mixing bowl; add lemon juice, pinch of pepper, and sugar. Arrange mixture in mold; set in pan of hot water; bake in preheated oven (350° F.) 30 minutes.

Meanwhile, boil potatoes in salted water 25 minutes, or until tender. Unmold hot salad on preheated plate; arrange potatoes around salad. Garnish potatoes with chopped parsley. Serve piping hot.

VARIATION: *Herring Loaf also may be served cold.*

Canned Fishes

◆§ BONITO   A member of the mackerel family, it is also related to the *albacore*, the *kingfishes*, and the *tuna*. It sometimes weighs as much as 15 pounds, but the average weight is nearer 6 pounds. When marketed fresh, the bonito is usually cut in thick steaks. However, most of the commercial catch on both coasts is *canned*.

CANNED BONITO BAKED WITH VEGETABLES
TIME: 1 HOUR; SERVES 4 TO 6

1 can bonito (1 lb.)	6 medium potatoes, baked
3 ozs. butter	1 small can peas
1 small onion, minced	1 cup rich milk
3 tbs. flour	1 tbs. lemon juice
1 tsp. salt	¼ tsp. nutmeg
⅛ tsp. pepper	2 ozs. grated Cheddar cheese
Pinch of paprika	4 tbs. chopped parsley

Select potatoes of same size; scrub well; brush with melted butter; place in preheated hot oven (450° F.); bake 45 minutes, or until tender.

Meanwhile, melt butter in top section double boiler directly over medium flame; add onion; sauté 3 minutes, or until golden brown; gradually add flour, salt, pepper, and paprika; blend well. Then place top section double boiler in lower section half filled with boiling water. Add milk to mixture in double boiler, stirring constantly until thick (about 5 minutes). Add bonito with ¼ cup of its own liquid from can; stir gently into milk mixture. Pour ¾ of bonito-blended mixture into buttered casserole; cover with drained peas; top with balance of bonito; sprinkle with nutmeg, then with grated cheese. Place casserole in oven 10 minutes before potatoes are done; when cheese is melted and golden brown, remove casserole; garnish with chopped parsley.

VARIATION: Use *Canned salmon, mackerel* or *tuna.*

CANNED BONITO MOUSSE WITH GOLDEN SAUCE
TIME: 45 MINUTES; SERVES 6

1 can bonito (1 lb.)	⅛ tsp. mace
4 egg whites, beaten	2 cups Golden Sauce (page
1 cup sour cream	81)
¾ tsp. salt	2 tbs. chopped chives
⅛ tsp. pepper	

Drain bonito; flake fine with fork, then rub through coarse sieve. Beat egg whites only until bubbly but not stiff. Place bonito in chilled mixing bowl standing in pan of ice water. Gradually add egg whites, stirring gently; gradually add sour cream; continue stirring until texture is delicate; add salt, pepper, and mace.

Pour mixture into buttered mold; place in pan of hot

water; bake in preheated moderate oven (350° F.) 15 minutes, or until set.

Unmold on preheated plate. Serve with generous helping
Golden Sauce. Garnish with chopped chives.

VARIATION: Use *canned mackerel, salmon,* or *tuna.*

SARDINES OR SEA HERRING There are young SEA
HERRING which are marketed canned, salted, smoked,
spiced, and fresh. Some are processed and marketed as
"smoked boneless herring." The larger fish, 6 to 8 inches,
are utilized for smoking. Either soft- or hard-smoked in the
round, they are called BLOATERS and KIPPERS.

CANNED HERRING OR SARDINES DEVILED WITH HERBS

TIME: 20 MINUTES; SERVES 4

2 cans herring or sardines	¼ tsp. dry mustard
(4 ozs. each)	¼ tsp. basil
2 ozs. butter	½ tsp. celery seed
½ cup dry bread crumbs	½ tsp. Worcestershire sauce
Lemon wedges	24 scallop or clam shells

If herring are used, remove skin and center bones. If sardines, purchase skinless and boneless to save time. Drain
canned fish; mash gently with fork.

In mixing bowl cream butter; add mustard, basil, celery
seed, and Worcestershire sauce; blend well; add bread
crumbs and fish.

Fill scallop or clam shells with mixture; arrange in shallow
baking dish; place in preheated hot broiling compartment
(400° F.) 3 inches below flame; broil 4 minutes, or until
golden brown.

Serve piping hot with lemon wedges or chopped green
herb. VARIATION: Use 8 ounces *any variety canned fish.*

CANNED HERRING OR SARDINE SOUFFLÉ

TIME: 1 HOUR; SERVES 6

2 cans herring or sardines	4 ozs. grated American
(4 ozs. each)	cheese
4 ozs. butter	½ lb. mushrooms, diced
½ cup flour	4 eggs, separated
1½ cups milk	2 cups soft bread crumbs
Pinch of cayenne	1 tbs. chopped fresh dill

If herring are used, remove skin and center bones. If sardines, purchase boneless and skinless to save time. Drain canned fish; break into small pieces with fork.

Melt 2 ounces butter in saucepan; add mushrooms; sauté 5 minutes only; set aside.

Melt other 2 ounces butter in separate saucepan over medium flame; gradually stir in flour and pinch of cayenne; when smooth, slowly stir in milk; cook 5 minutes over low flame, stirring constantly; when thick, set aside to cool.

In mixing bowl beat egg yolks until foamy; gradually add to cooled sauce. Return sauce to flame; cook 2 minutes; gradually stir in cheese; remove from flame; add mushrooms, bread crumbs, and fish; stir well; cool 5 minutes.

Meanwhile, beat egg whites until stiff; carefully fold into cooled fish mixture; pour into 6 large ramekins; bake in preheated moderate oven (350° F.) 40 minutes, or until firm. Serve piping hot. Garnish ramekins with chopped fresh dill.

VARIATION: Use *any variety canned* or *cooked flaked fish*.

10. How to Purchase Shellfish

〰〰〰〰〰〰〰〰〰〰〰〰〰〰〰〰〰〰〰〰〰〰〰

The term "Shellfish" includes both mollusks and crustacea. The *bivalve mollusk* is any species with two valves which open and shut, such as *oysters, clams, mussels,* and *scallops.* The crustacea are *all* the shellfish covered with a crust which can be peeled off, such as *prawns, shrimps, crayfish, crabs, lobsters,* and *turtles.*

Purchasing any fresh shellfish is far easier than selecting fish, because nature has provided such obvious aids to assist us in identifying a live shellfish. *Clams, mussels,* and *oysters* are alive *only when the shell is tightly closed.* Gaping shells which do not close when the shellfish is handled indicate that it is dead and should not be used.

Live *crabs, lobsters,* and *turtles* are easily identified by the lively movements of claws or head. Crustacea must be alive up to the moment of cooking.

Fresh *prawns* and *shrimp,* generally marketed headless, are greenish in color and firm to the touch. Both the *bay* and *deep-sea scallops* are marketed shucked and should have a white, firm appearance when absolutely fresh.

◆§ HOW TO IDENTIFY THE USUAL MARKET FORMS OF SHELLFISH

1. ALIVE. Marketed *in shells,* such as clams, crabs, lobsters, mussels, oysters, and snails.

2. CANNED. Practically all shellfish are available in cans. Usually packed in brine, they are shucked, peeled, and cooked, ready to be eaten and used in recipe combinations.

3. COOKED IN THE SHELL. Hard-shell crabs and lobsters may be bought this way. Select only those which have been kept under refrigeration from time of cooking.

4. COOKED MEAT. The edible portion cooked and ready to eat. The meat is picked from the shells, handled chilled, and packed in 1-pound containers. Prawns, shrimp, lobster, and crabs are marketed in this form. The BLUE CRAB of the East and Gulf coasts may be had as

  a. LUMP MEAT. Meat from the large muscles, sometimes known as *special* or *back-fin lump*. The meat is all white.
  b. FLAKE MEAT. The remaining portion; all white.
  c. FLAKE AND LUMP MEAT.
  d. CLAW MEAT. Meat from the claws; outside coloring has brownish tinge. The ROCK CRAB of New England is also a brownish color and only one grade is marketed. PACIFIC COAST or DUNGENESS CRAB. Meat from the body and claws is packed together; the color is reddish.

5. QUICK-FROZEN. Fresh, *shucked oysters,* should not be thawed until ready to use and never refrozen. *Crayfish, shrimp,* and *spiny lobster* are also marketed fresh-frozen.

6. SHUCKED. Shellfish removed from their shells. *Oysters, clams,* and *scallops* are marketed in this form.

7. SMOKED. Smoked oysters and oyster slices in cans.

11. How to Clean Shellfish

~~~~~~

§ HOW TO SHUCK HARD-SHELL CLAMS   The shell
of the hard-shell clam is not too difficult to open when these
simple steps are taken. If clams purchased alive in shells
have not been shucked at the market then

1. Scrub shells thoroughly under cold running water; discard any clams in broken or open shells.

2. Hold clam in left hand with shell hinge against palm.

3. Insert thin, strong, sharp knife between shells.

4. Cut around entire clam; twist knife to pry open.

5. Cut muscle free from shell; remove clam.

6. Wash clams in salted water to remove all sand.

7. Remove small dark mass; snip off end of siphon.

8. Wash clams again in salted water.

If cherrystone or little-neck clams are to be served on the
half shell, *do not remove from shell after opening*, but carefully remove all shell particles. Clams may also be opened
by placing them in a small quantity of boiling water for
5 minutes; drain and remove from shells. Wash meat carefully in salted water and they are ready to be cooked.

§ HOW TO CLEAN HARD-SHELL CRABS   Always
boil alive. Plunge into 2 quarts rapidly boiling water seasoned with ½ cup vinegar, 2 tablespoons of salt, and 1
teaspoon of cayenne pepper. Boil rapidly 5 minutes; then

simmer 15 minutes. When cool enough to handle, remove flakes from shell:

1. Break off claws and legs; crack; remove meat.

2. Break off segment that folds under body from rear.

3. Force shell apart by wedging strong knife into opening made by removing segment or apron.

4. Insert thumbs in opening between shell halves and pull upper shell away from lower shell; or hold crab in left hand, with back toward you, and slip fingers under top shell and pull downward to release the top shell.

5. Remove spongy digestive tract under running water.

6. If East Coast hard-shell, split shell along central crease

7. In left hand hold half the crab body and with sharp knife cut hard covering around outer edge.

8. Remove meat with nut pick.

9. If Pacific Coast variety (Dungeness), simply tap each half crab firmly against the inside of dish in which meat is being placed. Most of meat will fall out easily.

◄§ HOW TO CLEAN SOFT-SHELL CRABS   Most of the retail markets prepare and clean the soft-shells at the time they are purchased. If you have caught them yourself, here is the way to clean them:

1. With a sharp knife cut off segment or apron that folds under body from rear.

2. Turn crab; cut off face at point back of eyes.

3. Lift each point at sides with fingers.

4. Clean out gills.

5. Wash crabs in cold salted water.

6. Dry on absorbent paper.

7. When cooked, entire body is eaten.

HOW TO CLEAN AND BOIL LOBSTER Always handle a live lobster with care to avoid any possible injury from its sharp claws. Pick up the lobster from behind the head and plunge it head first into a large kettle of rapidly boiling salted water (1 tablespoon to each quart of water). Or insert sharp knife between body and tail of lobster to sever spinal cord before putting it into boiling water.

If lobster weighs 2 pounds, boil approximately 10 minutes, being careful not to overcook; otherwise meat becomes tough and stringy. If the lobster is less than 2 pounds, boil only 7 minutes, counting from the time the boiling water begins to boil again *after* lobster has been plunged into it. When done, cool lobster and remove meat as follows:

1. Place lobster on its back.

2. With sharp knife split open from end to end, starting at mouth.

3. Remove back vein running from head to tail.

4. Remove small sac back of head.

5. Green and coral parts are edible; do not remove.

6. Pry body meat loose with fork; extract meat.

7. Crack claws with mallet; extract meat.

8. Lobster meat is ready to use.

HOW TO CLEAN AND BROIL LOBSTER Always sever spinal cord *before preparing for boiling*. To do so:

1. Place lobster on back.

2. Insert sharp knife between body shell and tail segment.

3. Cut down quickly to break spinal cord.

4. Split lobster open from head to tail.

5. Remove black vein running from head to tail.

6. Remove small sac back of head.

7. Do not remove edible green and coral parts.

8. Crack claws with mallet.

9. Brush lobster meat with melted butter; season with salt and pepper to taste.

10. Spread on broiler pan, meat side up; broil 10 minutes for a 2-pound lobster; larger sizes 2 or 3 minutes more; smaller sizes, 3 minutes less.

◄§ HOW TO CLEAN AND STEAM MUSSELS The same rule for freshness applies to mussels as to other bivalve mollusks, such as clams and oysters. Use only those mussels with tightly closed shells. Before steaming mussels

1. Scrub shells well under cold running water.

2. Place mussels in large deep pot; cover with water.

3. Allow mussels to stand 2 hours.

4. Discard all mussels that float.

To steam: *

1. Pour 1 inch of water into large kettle.

2. Add 1 teaspoon salt; add mussels; cover.

3. Steam 3 minutes only, or until shells begin to open.

---

* *Clams may be steamed in same manner:* After scrubbing thoroughly, place them in large kettle with small quantity water and the juice of 1 lemon. Steam only 6 minutes, or until shells begin to open. *See also pages 134-35.*

To prepare mussels for use:
1. Remove from kettle.

2. Take meat from shells.

3. Remove dark, hairy beard; set mussel meats aside to be used as desired.

HOW TO SHUCK OYSTERS

When oysters are purchased alive in shells and have not been shucked for you at the market, it is not too difficult to shuck them at home. These simple steps will help:

1. Scrub shells thoroughly under cold running water.

2. Break off the "bill" at thin end with a hammer.

3. Hold oyster flat on table with left hand and with the oyster hinge toward that hand.

4. With right hand force a shucking knife between shells at thin end.

5. Cut large abductor muscle attached to shell and remove shell with twisting motion.

6. Cut the other end of same muscle attached to opposite shell.

7. For oysters on the half shell, leave oyster in shell; otherwise drop oyster into container.

8. Remove bits of shell; use oyster as desired.

HOW TO CLEAN AND BOIL SHRIMP AND PRAWNS

Fresh green shrimp are usually marketed either chilled or frozen. The head and the thorax have been removed and the shrimps need only a thorough washing, peeling, and the one small vein taken out before they are used. Prawns are also marketed headless. Both these crustacea may be peeled either *before* or *after* boiling. When they are used in cooked dishes, it is better to peel and use them *raw*, since the flavor will be sweeter and the meat much juicier.

To prepare plain boiled shrimp or prawns:

1. Wash in the shells under cold running water.

2. Drop into rapidly boiling salted water (1 tablespoon salt to each quart water).

3. After water reaches boiling point, lower heat; simmer 5 minutes; drain.

4. Peel shells from cooked shrimp or prawns.

5. Make a cut along outside curvature; remove black vein; crustacea are ready to use.

To peel *raw* shrimp or prawns:

1. Wash thoroughly under cold running water.

2. Peel off shells with sharp knife.

3. Take out black vein; crustacea are ready to use.

◦§ HOW TO DRESS A TURTLE

1. The head must be removed. If a *snapping turtle*, cause it to grasp a stick; pull the head forward and cut it off. If *other species*, force the head to portrude by pressing down on the upper shell.

2. Run a sharp knife along the edges of skin where it joins the shell.

3. Pull the skin back over the legs to the feet.

4. Disjoint feet with sharp knife.

5. Cut through bridges which join upper and lower shell. (In both the *snapper* and the *soft-shell*, the bridges are soft; if a *terrapin*, the bridge is hard and must be sawed or chopped in two.)

6. Insert sharp knife under lower shell and lift it up and off.

7. Take out entrails.

8. Remove meat from 4 quarters of upper shell.

9. If desired, the "tenderloin" in the "ceiling" of upper shell may be extracted by cutting into this ceiling with a hatchet.

10. Prepare turtle meat as desired.

Bisques

CLAM BISQUE WITH WINE

TIME: 30 MINUTES; SERVES 4

2 doz. fresh clams, in liquor	3 egg yolks
1 cup water	Thyme
½ cup dry sauterne wine	Paprika
½ cup cream	Salt and Pepper
2 tbs. butter	

Drain clams, saving liquor, and chop fine.

Pour clam liquor, water, sauterne wine, and minced clams in top section of double boiler; salt and pepper to taste; stir well; simmer over low flame 10 minutes.

While clams simmer, beat egg yolks until foamy; fill lower section of double boiler half full of boiling water.

When clams have finished simmering, place top section in lower section of double boiler over high flame; add egg yolks; stir; add cream, stirring constantly. Heat for 10 minutes, or until mixture begins to thicken, then remove immediately. Never let mixture boil, otherwise it will curdle. Serve immediately in preheated cups. Sprinkle with dash of thyme and paprika to add flavor and color.

VARIATION: Use ½ pound fresh lobster meat, mince fine; use 2 dozen shucked oysters; simmer oysters 3 minutes only; or use 1 pound fresh cooked shrimp; no simmering required.

LOBSTER BISQUE À LA MINUTE

TIME: CANNED LOBSTER, 15 MINUTES; FRESH, 40 MINUTES; SERVES 4

1 can lobster (8 ozs.)	½ cup cracker crumbs
or	1 small onion, minced
1 small lobster (1½ lbs.)	Paprika

2 tbs. butter   *Salt and Pepper*
1 qt. milk

Remove lobster from can; chop into fine pieces.

If fresh lobster is used, put head first into 2 quarts rapidly boiling salted water; cover; boil 10 minutes. Remove; cool enough to handle; break off claws; crack. Turn lobster on back and cut open from head to tail; take out sac back of head; remove all meat from shell including the edible green and coral; mince into fine pieces.

Melt butter in deep saucepan over low flame; stirring constantly, gradually add milk, cracker crumbs, onion, salt and pepper to taste; blend thoroughly. When smooth, add lobster. Simmer over low flame about 5 minutes, or until lobster is thoroughly heated. Serve immediately in preheated bouillon cups. Sprinkle with paprika.

VARIATION: Use *canned crab flakes* or *canned shrimp.*

MUSSEL BISQUE WITH TOMATO
TIME: 30 MINUTES; SERVES 6

2 qts. mussels, *in shells*	4 tbs. butter
1 tbs. flour	1 qt. milk
1 slice onion	1 tsp. salt
1 No. 2 can tomatoes	¼ tsp. pepper

Scrub mussels thoroughly; place in large wide pot; pour ½ cup water over mussels; cover pot; steam slowly 10 minutes, or until shells open; remove from shells and chop fine.

Pour milk in deep saucepan; add onion; scald milk about 2 minutes over low flame but do not boil; set aside; remove onion slice. Melt butter in top of double boiler over low flame, then place over lower section of double boiler half filled with boiling water; gradually blend in flour; add milk, stirring constantly; cook about 10 minutes, or until thick.

Meanwhile, strain tomatoes, then gradually add to the milk mixture, tomatoes, mussels, salt, and pepper, stirring constantly. Heat to boiling point but *do not* boil. Serve immediately with croutons.

VARIATION: Use 1 *quart soft-shell clams.*

OYSTER BISQUE AMERICAN
TIME: 40 MINUTES; SERVES 6

1 pt. oysters, in liquor	1 qt. milk
1 slice lemon	⅓ cup butter
2 stalks celery, chopped	⅓ cup flour
1 sprig parsley	1 tsp. salt
1 bay leaf	¼ tsp. pepper

Drain oysters, saving liquor, and chop fine.

Pour milk into deep saucepan; add onion, bay leaf, and parsley; scald about 2 minutes but do not boil; set aside.

Place celery in small pan; cover with water; cook 15 minutes, or until celery is tender; add to milk; strain mixture through very fine sieve. While celery is cooking, fill lower section of double boiler half full with boiling water. Melt butter in top section of double boiler; gradually blend in flour; add milk slowly, stirring constantly. Now place top section in lower section of double boiler over high flame; cook mixture 10 minutes, or until thick; add oysters, liquor, salt, and pepper; heat thoroughly about 5 minutes, but do not allow to boil. Serve immediately. Season with dash of paprika.

SHRIMP BISQUE AMERICAN
TIME: 30 MINUTES; SERVES 4 TO 6

1 lb. fresh shrimp	⅓ cup butter
4 cups milk	⅓ cup flour
2 slices onion	¾ tsp. salt
1 bay leaf	⅛ tsp. pepper
1 cup celery, diced	3 tbs. chopped parsley

Wash shrimp thoroughly in cold running water; put into rapidly boiling salted water; cover; boil 15 minutes; drain. When cool enough to handle, remove from shells; take out black vein which runs down center back. Save 6 whole shrimp; chop balance into tiny pieces.

Pour milk into saucepan; add bay leaf, onion slices, celery, and parsley; scald milk about 2 minutes; do not boil.

Melt butter in deep saucepan over low flame; stir in flour, salt, and pepper. When very smooth, gradually add scalded milk, stirring constantly until mixture boils; add

:hopped shrimp; cook 5 more minutes, stirring constantly.
Garnish with a whole shrimp floating in each bowl on top of
bisque.

Chowders

ABALONE CHOWDER CATALINA ISLAND
TIME: 1½ HOURS; SERVES 4 TO 6

1 lb. abalone meat, trimmed	⅛ tsp. dill
4 cups water	⅛ tsp. thyme
1 tsp. salt	2 cups milk
¼ lb. bacon, diced	2 tbs. butter
1 large onion, chopped	¼ cup cracker crumbs
1 tbs. chopped parsley	Paprika
4 potatoes, cubed	

Remove abalone from shell; pound with wooden mallet
until soft. (Trimmed abalone meat, purchased from market,
is already pounded.) Pour water into deep pot; add salt, dill,
and thyme; add abalone; cover; simmer over medium flame
1 hour, or until abalone is tender. Remove abalone from
broth; force through food chopper to mince; return to broth.
   Meanwhile, place bacon in skillet; brown lightly over low
flame; add onion; sauté 5 minutes, or until golden brown.
   When minced abalone has been returned to broth, add
bacon, sautéed onion, and cubed potatoes to broth; cook 15
minutes, or until potatoes are tender. When ready to serve,
add butter; gradually stir in milk and cracker crumbs; bring
to boiling point. Garnish with chopped parsley. Sprinkle
with paprika. Serve piping hot in preheated soup plates.

NEW ENGLAND CLAM CHOWDER NO. 1
TIME: 45 MINUTES; SERVES 6 TO 8

1 qt. shucked clams, in liquor	1 pt. milk
4 slices bacon, diced	1 tbs. chopped parsley
1 large onion, chopped	⅛ tsp. pepper
1 cup water	⅛ tsp. thyme
1 cup clam liquor	½ tsp. salt
2 large potatoes, diced	

Drain clams from liquor; strain liquor through fine sieve;
reserve. Split clams; remove dark parts; rinse in cold water;
chop fine.

Place bacon in deep kettle over low flame; fry slowly 5 minutes, or until golden brown; remove from fat. Cook onion in bacon fat 5 minutes, or until golden brown; add water, clam liquor, crisp bacon, and potatoes; cover; simmer slowly 15 minutes, or until potatoes are tender; add clams, thyme, salt, and pepper to taste; cook 2 minutes; add milk; bring to boiling point but do *not* boil. Serve piping hot in preheated chowder bowls. Sprinkle each serving with chopped parsley.

VARIATION: Use *cream* instead of milk.

NEW ENGLAND CLAM CHOWDER NO. 2
TIME: 50 MINUTES; SERVES 6 TO 8

2 *doz. chowder clams, in*	½ *tsp. salt*
shells	1 *pt. rich milk or cream*
¼ *lb. salt pork, diced*	¼ *tsp. thyme*
2 *cups clam broth*	1 *large onion, chopped*
2 *large potatoes, diced*	1 *cup boiling water*
⅛ *tsp. pepper*	1 *tbs. chopped parsley*

Scrub clams thoroughly under cold running water; place in deep kettle; pour 1 quart water over them; cover; steam 8 minutes, or until shells begin to open. Remove clams from shells; save all juice; cut out small dark parts; chop fine. Strain clam broth; keep in separate bowl.

Place pork in deep pot; cook slowly over low flame 5 minutes, or until golden brown. Remove pork from fat; put chopped onion in fat; cook 5 minutes, or until golden brown; add water, clam broth, pork, potatoes, thyme, salt, and pepper; cover; simmer 10 minutes, or until potatoes are tender but not soft; add chopped clams and milk slowly; bring to boiling point but do not boil. Serve piping hot in preheated chowder bowls. Sprinkle each serving with chopped parsley.

MANHATTAN CLAM CHOWDER
TIME: 1¾ HOURS; SERVES 6 TO 8

1 *qt. shucked clams, in liquor*	2 *cups water*
¼ *lb. salt pork, diced*	2 *carrots, diced*
1 *large onion, diced*	2 *medium potatoes, cubed*
1 *green pepper, diced*	3 *stalks celery, diced*
½ *cup bread crumbs*	¼ *tsp. pepper*
2 *tsp. salt*	1 *cup clam liquor*
3 *cups canned tomatoes*	

Drain clams from liquor; split; remove small dark mass;

rinse clams in cold water; chop fine; set aside. Strain liquor through fine sieve.

Place diced pork in large, deep kettle over medium flame; cook 15 minutes, or until golden brown; add onion; sauté 5 minutes, or until golden brown; add all other vegetables, water, and seasonings; cover; simmer gently 1 hour; add chopped clams and 1 cup clam liquor; cook 5 minutes. Add bread crumbs; stir well. Serve piping hot in preheated chowder bowls.

OYSTER CHOWDER
TIME 30 MINUTES; SERVES 6

1 pt. oysters, in liquor	2 medium potatoes, diced
1 large onion, minced	1 qt. rich milk
3 tbs. butter	1½ tsp. salt
2 stalks celery, diced	½ tsp. pepper
1 cup water	Paprika

Melt butter in deep pot; add onion; fry 3 minutes, or until light brown; add water, celery, potatoes, salt, and pepper; cover; cook 15 minutes, or until vegetables are tender; add milk and bring to boiling point.

In separate pot simmer oysters in their liquor 3 minutes, or until edges curl. Drain; add to milk and vegetables. Serve piping hot in preheated chowder bowls with dash of paprika sprinkled over top.

SHRIMP CHOWDER
TIME: 45 MINUTES; SERVES 4 TO 6

1 lb. fresh shrimp	1 cup cream, heated
2 slices bacon, diced	Pinch of mace
2 tbs. butter	Pinch of cayenne pepper
2 tbs. flour	⅛ tsp. salt
1 qt. rich milk, heated	

Wash shrimp thoroughly in cold running water; remove from shells; chop into small pieces, not fine. Place bacon in skillet; fry over low flame 5 minutes, or until light brown.

Melt butter in separate deep saucepan. Blend flour with mace, cayenne, and salt; add to melted butter, stirring constantly until very smooth.

Heat milk; gradually add to flour, stirring constantly until slightly thickened. Place in top of double boiler over hot water; add shrimp to milk mixture; cook over low flame 15 minutes. Meanwhile, heat cream, then add bacon and hot cream to chowder; heat to boiling. Serve piping hot in pre-heated chowder bowls.

VARIATION: Use 1 *pound minced lobster meat, crab flakes, shredded crayfish,* or ¾ *pound minced scallops.*

Soups

CREAMY CRAB MEAT SOUP
TIME: 45 MINUTES; SERVES 4 TO 6

½ lb. fresh crab flakes	½ cup sherry wine
2 hard-boiled eggs	1 tbs. flour
Grated rind of 1 lemon	½ cup cream
1 tbs. butter	1 qt. rich milk

Remove any possible shell fragments from crab flakes; place in deep mixing bowl.

Remove yolks from hard-boiled eggs and rub through a fine sieve; chop egg whites fine; add to crab flakes; blend well, then add grated lemon rind, butter, and flour; blend well; add 1 quart milk; pour into top part of double boiler placed over boiling water; heat thoroughly. When heated, remove and add ½ cup cream, stirring gently. Heat thoroughly again; season with sherry. Serve piping hot in pre-heated soup bowls.

CREAM OF MUSSEL SOUP
TIME: 25 MINUTES; SERVES 6 TO 8

2 lbs. fresh mussels	1 egg yolk, beaten
3 cups mussel broth	1 pimiento, minced
3 small onions, minced	Dash of cayenne
2 ozs. butter	Salt
2 tbs. flour	Pinch of nutmeg
1 pt. rich milk	

Select fresh mussels with tightly closed shells; wash under cold running water; place in deep kettle; pour 1 pint water over mussels; cover, steam 3 minutes, or until shells begin to open. Meanwhile, beat egg yolk lightly; mince pimiento; set aside. Remove mussels from shells; take off dark, hairy beard. Save all liquor and juice. Strain through fine sieve. Set broth and mussel meats aside. Melt butter in hot skillet; sauté onions 3 minutes, or until golden brown. Meanwhile, pour 1½ cups cold milk into deep saucepan. Blend flour well with other half cup milk in small mixing bowl; when smooth, stir into milk in saucepan; cook over low flame 5 minutes, stirring constantly, then add mussel meats, broth, sautéed onions, salt to taste, and dash of cayenne. Gradually add egg yolk and pimiento, stirring constantly. Bring to boiling point but do not boil. Sprinkle each serving with nutmeg.

LOBSTER SOUP WITH ALMONDS
TIME: 1 HOUR; SERVES 6 TO 8

1 lb. frozen lobster meat
2 cups boiling water
3 tbs. butter
1 bay leaf
½ tsp. basil
2 carrots, minced
½ cup mushrooms, minced
1 large onion, minced
1 tbs. chopped parsley

1 doz. almonds, chopped
½ lb. cooked ham, minced
1 clove garlic, minced
2 tbs. flour
1 cup canned tomatoes
½ tsp. allspice
2 hard-boiled eggs, minced
Salt and pepper
½ cup sherry wine

Place lobster meat in wooden mixing bowl; chop fine; add chopped almonds; blend well; set aside. Mince carrots, ham, mushrooms, onion, and eggs; set aside.

Melt 1 tablespoon butter in deep kettle over medium flame; add bay leaf, basil, and parsley; heat; add carrots, mushrooms, onion, and garlic; cover; simmer 5 minutes, then add ham; simmer 5 minutes more.

Blend flour with other 2 tablespoons butter in mixing bowl; add to mixture in kettle, stirring constantly; add tomatoes and allspice; cover; simmer 15 minutes.

Pour in 2 cups boiling water; add lobster meat and chopped almond mixture; cover; simmer 5 minutes; add chopped eggs and sherry wine. Heat well but do not boil.

VARIATION: Use *crab flakes, cooked shrimp, crayfish.*

TURTLE SOUP NEW ORLEANS
TIME: 4 HOURS; SERVES 4 TO 6

3 lbs. turtle meat	2 medium onions, minced
3 qts. water	2 bay leaves
4 tbs. bacon drippings	2 sprigs parsley
4 tbs. flour	6 cloves
1 tbs. bacon drippings, extra	½ tsp. mace
1 cup canned tomatoes	1 tsp. sugar
½ clove garlic, minced	2 tbs. lemon juice
Turtle stock and water	½ cup sherry wine
½ lemon, minced	2 hard-boiled eggs, minced

Have turtle meat cut into 1-inch cubes. Pour 3 quarts water into deep kettle; add turtle meat; bring to boiling point over high flame; parboil 10 minutes. Strain; reserve stock; set turtle pieces aside. Melt 4 tablespoons bacon drippings in skillet over medium flame; add turtle pieces; brown carefully on all sides for 10 minutes; remove; set aside. Mince 1 cup turtle meat; reserve as garnish.

In separate skillet melt 1 tablespoon bacon drippings; add onions; sauté 5 minutes, or until golden brown; gradually stir in flour; brown well by stirring constantly over medium flame, then add 1 cup tomatoes, garlic, bay leaves, parsley, cloves, mace, sugar, and lemon juice; blend all thoroughly. Transfer to large deep kettle. Blend turtle stock and enough water to make 4 quarts; add to vegetable-herb mixture; stir well; bring to boiling point over high flame; add turtle meat; cover; simmer gently 3 hours. Strain; add sherry wine; reheat. Garnish each serving with minced hard-boiled eggs or minced turtle meat and minced lemon.

VARIATION: Serve soup *unstrained* if preferred.

Stews

CLAM STEW À LA MINUTE
TIME: 10 MINUTES; SERVES 4

2 doz. small shucked clams	4 ozs. butter
6 cups milk	⅛ tsp. mace
Salt and pepper	1 tbs. chopped parsley

Pour clams into frying pan over low flame; cover with their own juice; add 2 ounces butter, salt and pepper to taste; add mace; cover; simmer 3 minutes.

Heat milk in top section double boiler placed over lower

section half filled with boiling water. Bring milk to boiling point but do not boil.

Pour 6 clams in individual preheated bowls; add small piece of butter; pour in hot milk. Sprinkle each serving with chopped parsley. Serve piping hot.

VARIATION: Use *2 dozen shucked oysters.*

CRAB STEW AU LAIT

TIME: 15 MINUTES; SERVES 6 TO 8

1 lb. fresh crab flakes	1 qt. milk
2 tbs. butter	½ cup cream
¾ cup cracker crumbs	½ cup water
Paprika	Salt and pepper

Melt butter in top section double boiler placed over lower section half filled with boiling water; add cracker crumbs and crab flakes to melted butter; stir in ½ cup water; boil 1 minute only; stir in milk; heat to boiling point but do *not* boil; season with salt and pepper to taste; add cream; stir well; let this come to boiling point but do *not* boil. Serve piping hot in preheated bowls. Sprinkle each serving with dash of paprika.

VARIATION: Use *½ pound minced lobster meat.*

LOBSTER STEW WITH CORAL

TIME: 1 HOUR; PREPARE DAY IN ADVANCE; SERVES 4

1 medium lobster (1½ lbs.)	1 qt. rich milk
¼ lb. butter	Paprika or nutmeg

Insert sharp knife between body and tail of lobster to sever spinal cord. To boil lobster, pour 2 quarts water into large pot; add 1 teaspoon salt. Put lobster in rapidly boiling water; boil 10 minutes. Remove; when cool enough to handle, break off claws; crack. Place lobster on back and split open; remove all meat; cut into cubes; save the green tomalley, coral, and the thick, white substance close to shell.

Melt butter in deep, heavy kettle; add tomalley, coral, and white substance; simmer 8 minutes; add lobster pieces; simmer 8 more minutes over low heat. Remove from flame; cool slightly. When cooled, very gradually stir in milk, being careful the milk does not curdle; the stew takes on a rich pink color. Allow to stand overnight.

When ready to serve, heat gradually in top section of double boiler. Sprinkle with dash of paprika or nutmeg.

LOBSTER STEW QUICKIE
TIME: 15 MINUTES; SERVES 4

½ lb. fresh lobster meat	1 cup heavy cream
4 cups milk	½ lb. butter
Nutmeg	Salt and pepper

Cut lobster meat into cubes. Melt butter in deep, heavy saucepan. Sauté lobster in butter 3 minutes; add pinch of nutmeg; blend well.

Pour milk and cream into separate saucepan; heat well but not to boiling point, then gradually pour heated milk over lobster, stirring constantly; add salt and pepper to taste; heat to boiling point but do *not* boil. Serve piping hot in preheated bowls.

VARIATION: For thicker stew, use *1 lb. lobster meat.*

OYSTER STEW À LA MINUTE
TIME: 10 MINUTES; SERVES 6

1 qt. oysters, in liquor	⅛ tsp. pepper
1 qt. milk	Paprika
4 tbs. butter	2 tbs. chopped parsley
½ tsp. salt	

Drain oysters. Melt butter in saucepan over medium flame; add oysters; cook 3 minutes, or until edges begin to curl; add milk, salt, and pepper. Bring almost to boiling point but do *not* boil. Serve at once in preheated bowls. Sprinkle each serving with dash of paprika and chopped parsley.

VARIATION: Substitute *1 pint cream with 1 pint milk.*

SCALLOP STEW WITH PIMIENTO
TIME: 25 MINUTES; SERVES 4 TO 6

1 lb. scallops	1 qt. milk
1 large pimiento, chopped	⅛ tsp. rosemary
4 tbs. butter	2 sprigs parsley, chopped

Remove any particles of shell and wipe scallops with damp cloth; cut into small ½-inch pieces.

Heat butter in skillet; add rosemary; sauté scallops gently 10 minutes.

Pour milk into top section of double boiler; when slightly warm, add pimiento and scallops; season with salt and pep-

per to taste; bring to boiling point but do not boil. Sprinkle
each serving with chopped parsley.

SELECTED SHELLFISH STEW WITH SAUTERNE

TIME: 15 MINUTES; SERVES 4

¾ lb. fresh cooked shellfish   ¼ cup dry sauterne wine
  meat (lobster, shrimp, or   1 qt. rich milk
  crab)   1 tbs. chopped parsley
2 ozs. butter   Salt and pepper
Paprika

Cut shellfish meat into fairly large cubes 1 inch square;
set aside. Pour milk into top section double boiler placed
over lower section half filled with boiling water; add butter,
salt and pepper to taste. Heat milk but do not bring to boiling point. Add shellfish meat to hot milk; bring to boiling
point but do not boil; add sauterne wine; heat 1 minute.
Serve piping hot in preheated bowls. Sprinkle each serving
with chopped parsley and dash of paprika.

VARIATION: Substitute *dry sherry wine*.

SNAPPING TURTLE STEW MADEIRA

TIME: 1¼ HOURS; SERVES 6 TO 8

3 lbs. snapping turtle meat   1 clove garlic, minced
3 medium onions, minced   1 bay leaf
¼ cup olive oil   ½ tsp. thyme
2 tbs. flour   1 wineglass madeira wine
3 cups water   Salt

Cut turtle meat into cubes 1 inch square; sprinkle with
flour. Pour oil into deep saucepan over medium flame; add
minced onion and garlic; sauté 3 minutes, or until golden
brown; add turtle meat; brown quickly; gradually add water.
When boiling, pour in madeira wine; add bay leaf, thyme,
and salt to taste; cover tightly; simmer 1 hour. Serve piping
hot in preheated bowls.

SHELLFISH STEW HAWAIIAN
TIME: 1 HOUR; SERVES 6 TO 8

½ lb. fresh cooked crab flakes
½ lb. fresh cooked lobster
   meat
1 doz. small clams, in juice
¼ lb. butter
¼ cup flour
2 medium onions, sliced
⅛ tsp. paprika

1 qt. milk
6 stalks celery, chopped
3 slices bacon, diced
1 pt. clam juice
2 bay leaves
⅛ tsp. cayenne
Salt and pepper
2 tbs. chopped parsley

Drain clams, reserving juice. Cut lobster meat into large pieces. Peel and slice onions; chop celery; dice bacon.

Pour milk into deep saucepan; add onions, bay leaves, and celery; simmer 10 minutes; remove celery and onions.

In separate deep saucepan melt butter; gradually add flour and blend well; add clam juice slowly, stirring constantly, then gradually add milk. When very smooth, add clams, crab, and lobster meat. Season with cayenne, paprika, and salt and pepper to taste, being careful to *use too little* rather than too much. Bring stew to boiling point, stirring gently. Garnish each serving with chopped parsley.

13. SHELLFISH BOUILLABAISSE AND GUMBOS

Bouillabaisse

There are as many different versions of *bouillabaisse* as
there are little villages along the southern coast of France.
But the basic ingredients of bouillabaisse never change.
Olive oil, garlic, and saffron must always be included; butter never should be substituted for olive oil. It is best to
use the firm-meated fish, though fish of soft texture may be
included if they are added *after* the bouillabaisse is at least
half cooked. The proportion is usually two to one: that is,
twice as many pounds of fish as shellfish; 8 pounds of fish
to 4 pounds of shellfish, is sufficient to serve 12 generous
portions.

BOUILLABAISSE AQUITAINE
TIME: 1 HOUR; SERVES 6 TO 8

1 lb. mackerel	1 tbs. chopped parsley
1 lb. black sea bass	2 ozs. butter
1 lb. cod (tail)	8 slices French bread, toasted
1 medium lobster (1½ to	2 cloves garlic, chopped
2 lbs.)	2 large tomatoes, quartered
1 doz. soft-shell clams	¼ tsp. saffron
2 doz. mussels, in shells	¼ tsp. black pepper
1 medium leek, chopped	1 bay leaf
1 medium onion, chopped	Pinch of thyme
1 carrot, chopped	½ cup olive oil
2 tsp. salt	½ cup dry sauterne wine

Have fish cleaned but do not bone; cut crosswise into
slices 2 inches thick. Insert sharp knife between body and
tail of live lobster to sever spinal cord; cut crosswise
(through shell and all) into fairly large serving pieces. Scrub
clams and mussels under cold running water to remove all
sand; set aside. Place next 11 ingredients in large deep ket-

tle; place lobster pieces on top of vegetables; add mackerel and sea bass; pour olive oil over all; add enough boiling water to cover mixture well; cover; boil hard for 8 minutes. Pour in wine; add cod; cook 5 minutes more; add clams and mussels; continue cooking 5 to 8 minutes, or until shells open.

Carefully remove fish and shellfish; serve separately some of each kind of fish and shellfish on individual preheated side plates. Serve boiling hot soup in bowls in which slice of buttered toast has been placed. Serve immediately.

VARIATION: Use *½ pound fresh crab flakes* instead of mussels; add crab flakes at same time as clams. *Any firm-meated white fish* may be used with sea bass instead of mackerel and cod. *Eel* can also be included.

BOUILLABAISSE POMPANO
TIME: 1 HOUR; SERVES 6 TO 8

2 *lbs. pompano*	2 *medium lobsters (1½ lbs. each)*
2 *lbs. black sea bass*	
½ *cup olive oil*	1 *doz. soft-shell clams*
1 *leek, chopped*	2 *large tomatoes, cubed*
1 *bay leaf*	1 *large onion, sliced*
2 *tsp. salt*	2 *cloves garlic, chopped*
¼ *tsp. black pepper*	¼ *tsp. saffron*
1 *tbs. chopped parsley*	1 *qt. boiling water*
8 *slices French bread, toasted*	½ *cup dry sauterne wine*

Have fish well cleaned but do not bone; cut into small slices 2 inches thick. Insert sharp knife between body and tail of lobster to sever spinal cord. Cut through shell and all into fairly large serving pieces.

Scrub clams thoroughly under cold running water; set aside. Pour oil into deep kettle; when hot, sauté onion, leek, and garlic over low heat for 10 minutes; add bay leaf, tomatoes, salt, saffron, and pepper; stir gently.

Place lobster pieces over vegetables, then add fish. Pour enough boiling water over all to cover well; bring to boiling point quickly; cover; continue boiling 8 minutes. Pour in wine; add clams; cook 5 to 10 minutes, or until shells open.

Arrange selection of fish in individual preheated soup bowls; add 1 slice buttered toast. Pour boiling hot, unstrained soup over all. Sprinkle with chopped parsley. Otherwise, serve fish and soup separately as for "Bouillabaisse Aquitaine."

Gumbos

SEA FOOD GUMBO
TIME: 1½ HOURS; SERVES 6 TO 8

6 *hard-shell crabs*	2 *onions, sliced*
1 *lb. green shrimp, peeled*	2 *cloves garlic, minced*
2 *doz. shucked oysters*	½ *tsp. thyme*
1 *green pepper, minced*	1 *bay leaf*
2 *stalks celery, chopped*	2 *sprigs parsley*
16 *okra, sliced*	1 *tbs. flour*
2 *tbs. butter*	Pinch of cayenne
3 *pts. water*	Salt

Scrub crabs clean in cold running water. Place into rapidly boiling salted water head first; cover; cook 20 minutes. Remove; cool in cold water enough to handle; drain; break off claws; break shells open beginning at tail end; remove spongy fingers and stomach found under head as well as all substance between sides of shell and body; pick out meat; set aside. Wash, peel, and clean fresh shrimp; slice in half lengthwise; set aside.

Melt butter in deep kettle; add onions and garlic; brown 3 minutes; gradually blend in flour, stirring constantly until light brown and very smooth; add 1 pint water, stirring constantly, and bring to boiling point; lower flame; simmer 15 minutes. Stir occasionally to prevent sticking. Add balance of water, okra, all seasonings, and peeled shrimp. *Do not add crab meat or oysters.* Bring to a boil; cover; simmer gently 1 hour. Twenty minutes before serving, cooked rice should be prepared so that it is steaming and fresh. Boil ½ cup rice in 2 quarts rapidly boiling salted water; drain; keep hot in colander placed over steaming water.

Fifteen minutes before serving add crab meat, shrimp, and oysters, with their liquor, to the mixture.

When ready to serve, place 1 or 2 tablespoons hot rice in individual bowls. Arrange steaming gumbo over rice.

VARIATION: Substitute 12 hard-shell crabs only.

CRAB GUMBO SUPRÊME
TIME: 1 HOUR; SERVES 4 TO 6

12 *hard-shell crabs*	2 *cups cooked rice*
1 *cup canned tomatoes*	1 *qt. boiling water*
1 *large onion, sliced*	2 *tbs. butter*
1 *lb. okra, chopped*	Salt and pepper
½ *tsp. rosemary*	½ *clove garlic*

Scrub crabs well; scald, boil, and prepare as shown on pages 103-4.

Melt butter in deep kettle over medium flame; sauté onion and garlic 5 minutes; add okra, tomatoes, and seasonings; stir well; gradually add boiling water; cover; simmer gently 40 minutes. Add crab meat; stir well; simmer 10 minutes more.

Place 2 tablespoons hot steaming rice in deep plate; arrange steaming gumbo over rice. Serve immediately.

VARIATION: Use *2 pounds fresh cooked crab meat.*

LOBSTER GUMBO
TIME: 1 HOUR; SERVES 6

1 lb. fresh lobster meat	*3 tbs. butter*
(lumps)	*½ cup chopped celery*
½ lb. okra, sliced	*1 bay leaf*
1 No. 2 can tomatoes	*½ tsp. thyme*
1 onion, sliced	*1 qt. boiling water*
1 clove garlic	*2 cups cooked rice*
Pinch of cayenne	*Salt and pepper*

Melt butter in deep kettle. Sauté onion, garlic, and celery 10 minutes; add tomatoes, okra, bay leaf, thyme, salt, and pepper to taste, and a pinch of cayenne; stir well; gradually add boiling water; cover; simmer 40 minutes. Add lobster meat; simmer 10 minutes.

Place 2 tablespoons hot, freshly boiled rice in preheated deep plate; arrange steaming gumbo over it. Serve immediately.

VARIATION: Use *1 pound fresh crab meat,* or *1 pound cooked shrimp,* or *half crab meat* and *half shrimp.*

~~~~~~

CALIFORNIA COCKTAIL

TIME: 15 MINUTES; SERVES 4

½ cup crab meat, flaked
½ cup lobster meat, cubed
3 tbs. orange juice
1 grapefruit

4 tbs. catsup
½ tsp. Worcestershire sauce
Lettuce leaves

Purchase freshly cooked crab and lobster meat; cut into cubes; blend well. Peel and cut grapefruit sections into small pieces. Blend orange juice, catsup, and Worcestershire sauce. Mix well with shellfish; place in refrigerator to chill.

Line well-chilled cocktail glasses or sherbet cups with lettuce leaves; fill with generous portion of mixture. Serve with saltines or Melba toast.

CRAB FLAKE COCKTAIL FISHERMAN'S STYLE

TIME: 15 MINUTES; SERVES 4

1 lb. cooked fresh crab meat
8 lettuce leaves
Paprika

4 tbs. mayonnaise
1 lemon, quartered
8 sprigs water cress

Purchase cooked fresh crab meat; separate flakes. Place 2 lettuce leaves on each well-chilled luncheon plate. Arrange ¼ pound crab meat in center of each plate. Place 1 tablespoon mayonnaise near edge of plate; garnish rim with sprigs of water cress and lemon wedge. Sprinkle paprika very lightly over crab meat. Serve well chilled. To eat, dip forkful of crab meat lightly into mayonnaise at side.

VARIATION: Use cooked *lobster meat, crayfish, shrimp,* or *prawns.*

LOBSTER COMBINATION COCKTAIL

TIME: 15 MINUTES; SERVES 4

½ lb. cooked lobster meat
4 lettuce leaves
1 doz. oysters in shell

4 tbs. Cocktail Sauce
Rind of 1 lemon, grated

Purchase oysters in shell or in liquor. If in shell, have them shucked at the market. Cut fresh lobster meat into pieces of preferred size; chill each shellfish separately in refrigerator. Grate the rind of 1 lemon; set aside. Prepare cocktail sauce (page 187). Line prechilled cocktail glasses with lettuce leaf; add serving of lobster meat, then 3 oysters; sprinkle with grated lemon rind; cover with cocktail sauce. Serve well chilled.

VARIATION: Use *any combination of cooked shellfish* preparing this recipe. For example use ¼ pound crab flakes with ¼ pound lobster meat; or ¼ pound cooked shrimp with ¼ pound crab flakes. *Always arrange cooked shellfish at bottom of cocktail glass.* Garnish with preferred green herb, pickles, or chopped olives.

PICKLED SHRIMP COCKTAIL
TIME: 20 MINUTES; CHILL 2 HOURS; SERVES 4

1 *lb. green shrimp*	½ *onion, sliced*
1 *pt. water*	1 *clove garlic*
1 *tsp. salt*	2 *bay leaves*
½ *cup olive oil*	½ *tsp. salt*
¼ *cup lemon juice*	⅛ *tsp. pepper*

Pour water into saucepan; when boiling, add 1 teaspoon salt; add shrimp; boil 12 minutes; drain. When cool enough to handle, remove from shells; take out black vein which runs down center back. While shrimp are cooking, blend well olive oil, lemon juice, ½ teaspoon salt, and pepper; when smooth, add onion, garlic, and bay leaves. Place shrimp in bowl with cover; pour sauce over shrimp; cover; chill in refrigerator 2 hours.

To serve, arrange shrimp on prechilled small individual plates. Garnish each with parsley, chives, or water cress.

VARIATION: For tangier flavor, add ⅛ teaspoon cayenne and 1 small onion to water in which shrimp simmers. Substitute 2 dozen little-neck clams. Wash and scrub shells thoroughly; pry shells open; remove dark "stomach" mass. Place raw clams in deep bowl; follow recipe; chill in refrigerator 4 hours.

~~~~~~

•§ ABALONE With a large, strong, oval-shaped single shell like a huge ear 6 or 7 inches long, its spiral form is like a roof and covers a large muscular foot by which the mollusk clings tenaciously to the rocks or moves itself about. This edible muscle is practically the whole contents of the shell, which is lined with mother-of-pearl. When pounded before it is baked, broiled, or made into chowder, abalone literally melts in your mouth. The richness of its flavor is indescribable, and eating a broiled or baked abalone steak, prepared as soon as the fish is taken from the ocean, is an experience never to be forgotten.

ABALONE HOLLYWOOD

TIME: 1½ HOURS; SERVES 6

2 lbs. abalone meat, sliced	1 tsp. prepared mustard
2 eggs, beaten	Juice of 1 lemon
1 cup cracker crumbs	1 tbs. minced parsley
½ cup peanut oil	1 clove garlic, crushed
1 cup hot water	Salt and pepper
1 small onion, minced	6 sprigs parsley
1 firm tomato	

Have abalone removed from shell; trim off dark parts; cut into slices; place on board; pound with wooden mallet until meat is soft but not mushy. (Trimmed abalone meat purchased from market is already pounded.) Dip slices into beaten egg, then in cracker crumbs. Heat oil in skillet; fry abalone quickly 5 minutes, or until golden brown; remove from skillet; place in casserole.

Pour hot water into skillet in which abalone was fried; add onion, tomato, mustard, lemon juice, parsley, garlic, salt and pepper to taste. Stirring constantly, cook well 5 minutes. Pour hot sauce over abalone.

Place casserole in preheated slow oven (300° F.); bake
hour. Serve piping hot from casserole. Garnish each servin
with parsley sprig.

ABALONE STEAKS BROILED SANTA MONICA
TIME: 30 MINUTES; SERVES 4

1½ lbs. abalone steaks	2 tbs. mayonnaise
½ tsp. salt	1 tbs. minced parsley
½ tsp. paprika	Juice of 1 lemon
2 ozs. butter, melted	

Have abalone steaks cut ½ inch thick and pounded we
with wooden mallet until soft but not mushy.

Blend salt, paprika, and lemon juice in shallow dish; plac
abalone in seasoned lemon juice; allow to stand 15 minute;
arrange steaks on greased broiler rack 2 inches below flam
in preheated hot broiling compartment (400° F.); broil
minutes, or until golden brown; turn; spread with mayor
naise; broil 10 minutes, or until tender and golden brow
Garnish each serving with minced parsley or lemon wedge;

⋙ CLAMS The hard-shell clam is often called by thei
Indian name *quahaug*, also spelled "quahog." Small qua
haugs, eaten raw on the half shell, are known as CHERRY
STONES. The LITTLENECK CLAM is the smallest, and CHOW
DER clam is the largest of the hard-shells. The quahaug ha
a rounded shell, rather smooth, and is usually taken wit
huge rakes since it doesn't burrow in the sand as the soft
shell does. The southern hard-shell is the same species as the
New England quahaug, and in the South is also called the
"round clam" or the "little neck." Off the Gulf of Florida thi
clam grows much larger and may weigh more than a poun
and measure 5 or 6 inches across. The large chowder clams
which burrow in the sand, have a very strong flavor, and si;
of these are sufficient to make a wonderfully pungent clam
chowder.

The soft-shells found north of Cape Cod all the way t
the Arctic Ocean are somewhat longer than the hard-shell
and more oval-shaped. They burrow into the mud and are
taken by digging at low tide.

The COCKLE is the common European species. Its shell i
convex, radially ribbed, and somewhat heart-shaped.

CLAMBAKE NEW ENGLAND FISHERMAN'S STYLE°

TIME: 1 HOUR; SERVES 6

2 doz. hard-shell clams	Seaweed
6 live lobsters (2 lbs. each)	1 tarpaulin

Usually 1 large lobster and 1 or 2 dozen clams are served to clambake enthusiasts. Dig a large hole in the sand, then line it with rocks. Place a few large rocks at the bottom; build the base fire, then heap the hole with coals and several large rocks. When the coals are fiery red and the rocks are heated through, cover with a light layer of seaweed, then a layer of lobsters; next a layer of seaweed, and then a layer of clams. Alternate seaweed and clams until enough have been placed in the "bake" for all to be served. The top covering of seaweed should be thick. Cover with a large canvas tarpaulin securely held down by rocks. Bake 20 minutes, or until clam shells begin to open. Serve with potato chips and beer.

VARIATION: The "Western Clambake" consists of clams only.

CLAMS DEVILED IN SCALLOP SHELLS

TIME: 45 MINUTES; SERVES 4

1 doz. large clams, in liquor	2 stalks celery, minced
1/4 cup clam liquor	1 pimiento, minced
1/4 cup rhine wine	1/2 tsp. Worcestershire sauce
2 tbs. chopped chives	3/4 cup cracker crumbs
1/2 green pepper, minced	Salt and pepper
4 ozs. butter	

Drain clams; save liquor; remove small dark mass from clams; mince clams; place in saucepan; cover with clam liquor; simmer 2 minutes; remove from heat. Melt butter in saucepan. Add green pepper and celery; sauté 5 minutes, or until celery is tender. Blend well-sautéed vegetables with chives, pimiento, Worcestershire sauce, cracker crumbs, salt and pepper to taste; add clams and rhine wine; mix well; if too dry, add small quantity clam liquor.

Fill buttered scallop shells or small ramekins with mixture; bake in preheated moderate oven (350° F.) 20 minutes.

° As prepared by Charles P. Palmer of The New York *Times* staff.

CLAM FRY LONG ISLAND

TIME: 30 MINUTES; SERVES 4

4 doz. small clams	1 egg, well beaten
½ cup flour	½ cup cracker crumbs
4 ozs. butter	4 tbs. chopped chives

Purchase small clams in shells; scrub shells thoroughly under cold running water. Remove clams from shells by inserting blade of thin knife between edges and cutting around clam muscles. (See page 103.)

Salt clams lightly; dip in flour, then in well-beaten egg; roll in cracker crumbs.

Melt butter in frying pan over medium flame; heat but do not allow to smoke. Drop clams into hot butter; fry quickly only 3 minutes, until golden brown; turn; fry 2 minutes more. Drain on absorbent paper. Serve piping hot on preheated plates. Garnish each serving with chopped chives.

VARIATION: Fry *oysters*, *scallops*, and *mussels*. Allow 5 minutes on each side for scallops. Serve with Tartar Sauce (page 143).

CLAM PIE FISHERMAN'S STYLE

TIME: 1 HOUR; SERVES 4 TO 6

2 doz. small clams, in liquor	4 small potatoes, sliced thin
2 tbs. butter	1 bay leaf
1 large onion, sliced	⅛ tsp. sage
½ tsp. salt	Pinch of cayenne
Pinch of pepper	1 flaky pastry crust
½ cup rich milk	

FLAKY PASTRY CRUST

1½ cups flour	½ tsp. salt
½ cup butter	3 tbs. cold water

Prepare pastry crust first. Sift flour and salt on pastry board; gently blend in butter; gradually add only enough water to hold ingredients together; form into small ball. Roll out to desired thinness on lightly floured board; shape crust to cover casserole. Drain clams; remove small dark mass; split clams in half crosswise. Arrange alternate layers of clams, onion slices, and potatoes in casserole until all ingredients are used. Place bay leaf in center. Sprinkle salt, pepper, sage, and cayenne lightly over top; add milk; add blespoons clam liquor for additional flavor if desired.

Cover clam mixture with flaky pastry crust, press edges to im of dish; cut 2 gashes in pastry, allowing steam to escape. ake in preheated hot oven (450° F.) 15 minutes, or until op is golden brown. Serve piping hot from casserole at ble. Garnish with chopped parsley.

VARIATION: Substitute *oysters* or *scallops*; cut scallops a half crosswise; bake in oven (350° F.) 25 minutes.

LAM RAREBIT
IME: 20 MINUTES; SERVES 4

pt. clams, in liquor	2 tsp. lemon juice
2 cup clam liquor	½ tsp. salt
tbs. butter	⅛ tsp. pepper
tbs. minced onion	¼ tsp. Worcestershire sauce
2 cup rich cream	1 tbs. flour
⅛ tsp. nutmeg	2 eggs, well beaten
4 tsp. grated lemon rind	4 slices buttered toast
4 lb. Cheddar cheese	

Melt butter in top section of double boiler placed in lower ection half filled with boiling water. Sauté onion in hot utter 3 minutes, or until light brown. While onion is cook-ng, place clams and liquor, except ½ cup, in separate sauce-an; heat for 2 minutes but do not cook. Gradually add ream, nutmeg, lemon rind and juice, cheese, salt, pepper, nd Worcestershire sauce to sautéed onion; stir constantly ntil cheese is melted.

Blend flour, eggs, and clam liquor; when very smooth, stir nto cheese mixture; continue stirring until mixture thickens about 5 minutes); add heated clams; stir gently; heat 2 ninutes. Serve over buttered toast. Garnish with parsley.

VARIATION: Use *raw oysters* or *cooked crab flakes, lob-ter, crayfish, or shrimps*.

LAM SCALLOP WITH SHERRY
IME: 40 MINUTES; SERVES 4

doz. large clams, shucked	½ cup sherry wine
¼ cup cracker crumbs	1 tbs. chopped parsley
tbs. butter	⅛ tsp. paprika
cup light cream	⅛ tsp. oregano
stalks celery, chopped	½ tsp. salt

Drain clams; remove small dark mass. Use ½ tablespoon

butter to grease casserole; place layer of clams in casserole. Blend cracker crumbs with balance of butter; add paprika, oregano, and salt; mix thoroughly. Spread layer of mixture over layer of clams, then layer of celery and parsley; alternate until all ingredients are used but save enough crumbs for top. Pour cream over clams, then sherry wine; top with buttered crumbs; bake in preheated moderate oven (350° F.) 20 minutes. Serve piping hot from casserole.

VARIATION: Use *raw oysters* or *cooked crab flakes, crayfish, mussels, lobsters, prawns,* or *shrimp;* bake cooked shellfish 15 minutes only.

CLAMS TANGY STEAMED
TIME: 15 MINUTES; SERVES 4

8 doz. soft-shell clams	Juice of 1 lemon
½ lb. butter, melted	1 clove garlic
1 bay leaf	Paprika
½ cup hot water	

Scrub clams; rinse in cold running water to remove all sand. Place garlic and bay leaf in bottom of large pot; pour in hot water; add clams; cover tightly; steam 6 to 8 minutes, or until shells open, being careful not to overcook. Remove from flame; strain broth through cheesecloth; reheat.

Melt butter in saucepan; flavor with lemon juice. Serve piping hot clams in soup plates with ramekin of melted butter at side. Serve clam broth in preheated bouillon cups. Sprinkle each serving lightly with paprika.

VARIATION: Use *mussels;* allow 2 to 3 dozen for each person; steaming time approximately same.

CLAMS WITH THIN NOODLES
TIME: 45 minutes; SERVES 4

1 doz. large, hard-shell clams	2 tbs. minced parsley
4 tbs. olive oil	⅛ tsp. pepper
2 cloves garlic, minced	¾ lb. thin noodles
½ tsp. thyme	2 tsp. salt, extra
2 large tomatoes	2 qts. boiling water
½ cup clam juice	Salt

Scrub clam shells well; rinse under running water; place in large pot with ½ inch cold water; cover tightly; steam over medium flame 6 to 8 minutes, or until shells open, being careful not to overcook. Remove from flame; strain broth through fine sieve; set aside. Remove clams from shells; take off small dark mass; chop clams fine; set aside.

Pour oil into small saucepan; heat over low flame; add garlic; brown 2 minutes; add tomatoes, clam juice, thyme, parsley, pepper, and very little salt to taste; cover; simmer over low flame 20 minutes, or until sauce is fairly thick; add clams; bring to boiling point; remove from flame.

Serve piping hot over thin noodles which have been cooked while sauce is simmering. To cook noodles, pour 2 quarts boiling water into large, deep pot; add salt; add ¾ pound noodles; boil rapidly 10 minutes, or until noodles are tender but not soft; drain. Serve in preheated soup plates; pour generous portion piping hot sauce over each serving. Serve immediately.

VARIATION: Use *rice, spaghetti,* or any type *macaroni.* Also use 2 dozen small whole clams or 3 dozen large mussels.

◆§ CRABS The edible BLUE CRAB is found along the Atlantic coast from Massachusetts south to the northern part of South America. When found in fresh water, it is called SWEET-WATER CRAB. SOFT-SHELL CRAB is the term applied to any crab that has shed its old shell and whose new shell has not hardened. The peak of the season for soft-shells is July and August.

Marketed alive in the shell and as canned crab flakes, the hard-shells are also steamed where they are taken, picked out of the shell, and shipped in iced containers to the retail markets. Fresh crab flakes have a sweet, succulent flavor and may be eaten as purchased by merely adding a cocktail sauce. They are also unusually delicate when prepared with cream sauces and used in omelets. Most of the canned crab flakes in the retail markets are from the Pacific coast fisheries, where a different species, called the DUNGENESS CRAB, is taken.

CRAB FLAKE OMELET PORTUGUESE
TIME: 45 MINUTES; SERVES 4 TO 6

½ lb. fresh crab flakes
2 slices bacon, diced
1 firm tomato, diced
1 small onion, minced
½ green pepper, minced

6 mushrooms, peeled and chopped
Salt and pepper
¼ lb. butter
4 eggs

◄§ Cut crab flakes into fairly small pieces; set aside. Place diced bacon in frying pan; brown over low flame 3 minutes, or until golden brown. Add next 5 ingredients; cover; simmer 10 minutes. Just before removing from flame, stir in crab flakes. Meanwhile, break eggs; separate yolks and whites; beat each lightly with fork; blend together.

Melt butter in smooth omelet pan; when hot, but not smoking, pour in beaten eggs; cook over low flame 5 minutes, or until omelet is fluffy and lightly browned on underside. When nearly done, carefully add crab flakes mixture and fold gently together. Continue slow frying 15 minutes, or until firm. (Unless the flame is very low, it is better to place omelet pan gently in a preheated moderate [350° F.] oven, so that omelet does not burn before it is done through. If placed in oven, bake about 30 minutes.)

Place on preheated platter. Garnish with parsley. Serve immediately.

VARIATION: Use *cooked diced shellfish* or *flaked fish.*

CRAB DEVILED MADEIRA
TIME: 30 MINUTES; SERVES 4

1½ cups crab meat	1 egg yolk, beaten
¾ cup milk	¼ tsp. salt
4 ozs. butter	¼ tsp. dry mustard
½ tsp. chopped chives	⅛ tsp. mace
2 tbs. flour	⅛ tsp. nutmeg
½ cup bread crumbs	4 sprigs fresh mint
3 tbs. madeira wine	

Remove all shell particles from crab meat; break into small pieces. Melt 2 ounces butter in top section of double boiler placed over lower section half filled with boiling water; add chives. Blend milk and flour; add to melted butter; turn up flame; cook mixture 5 minutes, or until it thickens. Beat egg yolk in bowl; slowly pour milk mixture over; blend well; return to top section double boiler; place over boiling water in lower section. Add crab meat, salt, mustard, mace, and nutmeg; stir until hot.

Pour crab meat mixture into small casserole; top with bread crumbs; dot with other 2 ounces butter; bake in preheated hot oven (400° F.) 5 minutes, or until top is golden brown. Serve piping hot. Garnish with fresh mint or preferred green herb.

VARIATION: Use *sherry wine* instead of madeira.

CRAB FLAKES IN PALE ALE   TIME: 30 MINUTES; SERVES 4

1 lb. fresh crab meat, flaked
3 shallots, minced
2 tsp. caraway seed
3 tbs. chopped parsley
1 bay leaf
4 slices buttered toast
1 qt. pale ale

2 tbs. flour
2 ozs. butter
¼ tsp. salt
Paprika
Water cress
⅛ tsp. pepper

To prepare in 30 minutes, use fresh crab meat purchased at market, otherwise allow 30 minutes extra for boiling crab and removing meat from shells (see page 104). Remove any shell particles from crab meat; break up into flakes; set aside.

Pour ale into saucepan; add shallots (or 1 large onion, minced), caraway seed, parsley, bay leaf, salt, and pepper; cover; cook over medium flame 15 minutes; strain through fine sieve. Set ½ cup liquid aside to cool; pour balance in top section of double boiler placed over lower section half filled with boiling water.

Cream butter with wooden spoon; blend flour in ½ cup cooled, pale ale liquid; when very smooth, add butter; blend again; add to liquid in double boiler; place over high flame, stirring constantly; cook until thick (about 15 minutes); add crab flakes; stir well; heat through for 5 minutes. Serve piping hot over buttered toast. Sprinkle with paprika. Garnish with water cress or favorite green herb.

CRAB MEAT ROLLS CANTONESE
TIME: 45 MINUTES; SERVES 6

CRAB MEAT MIXTURE

1 cup cooked crab meat
1 stalk celery, minced
1 small onion
½ cup water chestnuts, chopped

2 tbs. chopped Chinese greens or
1 tbs. chopped parsley
1 egg yolk, beaten
Salt and pepper

BATTER MIXTURE

½ cup rice flour
½ cup flour
1 tbs. butter
1 cup water

1 egg, beaten
¼ tsp. salt
1 pt. peanut oil, for frying

Sift rice flour, flour, and salt together in mixing bowl; add egg and sufficient water to make a thin pancake batter; beat well to make mixture light. Melt butter in small frying pan (about 5 inches diameter). Pour in only enough batter to cover bottom of pan with very thin film; brown lightly on one side; turn and brown lightly on other side (about 2 minutes). Remove from pan; cool on mixing board.

Combine crab meat with all ingredients except beaten egg yolk; salt and pepper to taste. Brush top side of each pancake with beaten egg yolk; spread spoonful of mixture in center; roll lightly; brush top surface of roll with egg yolk. Place rolls in frying basket; lower into deep, hot peanut oil (375° F.); fry 4 minutes, or until crisp and golden. Drain on absorbent paper. Serve with hot French mustard or ginger chutney.

VARIATION: Use ½ cup crab meat and ½ cup shrimp or lobster meat, in place of crab meat only.

CRAB MEAT FRITTERS
TIME: 20 MINUTES; SERVES 6

1 cup fresh crab meat	2 cups flour
1 cup rich milk	1 tbs. baking powder
2 eggs	½ tsp. salt
1 tbs. butter, melted	4 tbs. butter or shortening

Remove all shell particles from crab meat; break up into small pieces. Sift flour, baking powder, and salt into mixing bowl. Break eggs into small bowl; beat until foamy; add to flour mixture; blend well; gradually add milk; when very smooth, add melted butter; stir well. (Batter should be thin for best results.) Add crab meat to mixture; stir well.

Melt other butter or shortening in shallow frying pan; heat to 375° F., hot but not smoking. Drop batter by spoonfuls into hot fat; fry 3 minutes, or until golden brown. Drain on absorbent paper. Serve plain or with favorite cream or tangy sauce on individual preheated plates.

VARIATION: Prepare cooked shellfish, flaked, such as lobster, crayfish, and shrimp. Oysters, mussels, and clams should not be cooked, but used raw and minced.

CRAB MEAT SOUR CREAM CASSEROLE
TIME: 30 MINUTES; SERVES 4 TO 6

½ lb. fresh crab meat	1 cup sour cream
½ lb. fresh cooked shrimp	4 sprigs tarragon, chopped
⅛ tsp. salt	Dash of cayenne

To prepare casserole in 20 minutes, purchase fresh crab meat and cooked shrimp at market, otherwise allow 15 minutes more to boil shrimp. (*See* pages 107-8.) Remove any shell particles from crab meat; take out black vein from shrimp. Mix crab meat and shrimp; divide into 4 equal portions; place in ovenproof ramekins.

Mix sour cream, salt, chopped tarragon, and dash of cayenne; pour mixture over shellfish; bake in preheated moderate oven (350° F.) 15 minutes, or until thoroughly heated and mixture begins to bubble. Serve immediately.

VARIATION: Use *lobster* instead of shrimp.

CRAB PATTIES DE LUXE
TIME: 30 MINUTES; SERVES 4 TO 6

1 lb. crab flakes	⅛ tsp. pepper
2 eggs	8 stuffed green olives,
4 tbs. melted butter	chopped
¼ lb. mushrooms, cooked	Pinch of cayenne pepper
and chopped	2 cups vegetable oil
½ tsp. salt	1 cup cracker crumbs

Chop crab flakes into small pieces.

Break eggs into small bowl; beat well with fork.

Put crab flakes, melted butter, chopped mushrooms, and olives into large mixing bowl; season with salt, pepper, and pinch of cayenne; add enough egg to mold into small flat patties.

Beat 2 teaspoons water into remaining egg.

Moisten patties with egg, then roll in cracker crumbs.

Heat vegetable oil to 400° F. in deep kettle. Arrange patties in well-oiled frying basket; fry quickly 3 minutes, or until rich brown. Serve piping hot on preheated plates with favorite relish.

VARIATION: Use *freshly cooked lobster* meat, *shrimp, prawns,* or *crayfish.*

SOFT-SHELL CRABS ROYAL FRIED
TIME: 20 MINUTES; SERVES 6

12 soft-shell crabs	½ cup corn meal
1 tsp. salt	1 pt. peanut oil
2 eggs, well beaten	Tartar Sauce
3 tbs. water	Water cress
1 cup bread crumbs	

Purchase crabs cleaned and dressed. (If necessary to clean remove pointed section under body, then lift up soft points of shell and discard substance which adheres. With sharp knife cut off ½ inch front portion of body to remove entrails. All that is left, including shell, is to be eaten.)

Wipe crabs with damp cloth; salt each crab on both sides. Blend bread crumbs and corn meal; blend beaten eggs and water; dip crabs in egg, then in bread crumbs.

Pour oil in deep pot; heat to sizzling (360° F.). Fry 2 or 4 crabs at a time for 3 minutes only, or until golden brown. Be careful not to overfry. While frying, crabs should always float in oil or shortening. Serve piping hot with Tartar Sauce (page 143). Garnish each serving with water cress.

◄§ CRAYFISH OR CRAWFISH Also known as the SPINY LOBSTER, the SEA CRAWFISH, and the ROCK LOBSTER. A handsome specimen mottled with blue, yellow, and brown, often confused with the true New England lobster.

The smaller AMERICAN CRAWFISH is found in fresh waters. Average length is 6 inches.

CRAYFISH HAWAIIAN
TIME: 45 MINUTES; SERVES 6 TO 8

2 crayfish	5 tbs. sherry wine
¼ lb. mushrooms, sliced	1 tsp. Worcestershire sauce
2 hard-boiled eggs, chopped	½ tsp. lemon juice
1½ cups rich cream	½ tsp. dry mustard
3 tbs. flour	½ tsp. salt
3 ozs. butter	⅛ tsp. pepper
Paprika	Water cress

Purchase sea crayfish, or spiny lobster of Florida; scrub well; rinse under running water. Boil approximately 2 cups water rapidly in large pot; add crayfish; boil 15 minutes. Remove from fire; cool enough to handle; cut in half length-

ise; remove meat; save shells; cut meat into cubes.
Melt 1 ounce butter in saucepan; add mushrooms; sauté
5 minutes over low flame. Melt other 2 ounces butter in
parate saucepan over low flame; gradually stir in flour and
y mustard; when smooth, add cream, stirring constantly
til sauce thickens (about 5 minutes); add chopped eggs,
erry wine, Worcestershire sauce, salt, and pepper; stir well;
ld crayfish cubes and lemon juice; stir gently. Fill shells or
uttered ramekins with mixture; bake in preheated mod-
ate oven (350° F.) 15 minutes. Remove from oven. Gar-
sh with paprika and water cress. Serve piping hot.
    VARIATION: Use *lobster, shrimp,* or *hard-shell crab.*

RAYFISH CARDINAL
ME: 45 MINUTES; SERVES 4 TO 6

crayfish	2 tsp. chopped fresh dill
ozs. butter	Hollandaise Sauce
ozs. cognac	

Purchase sea crayfish; scrub thoroughly; rinse under run-
ng water. Boil approximately 2 cups water rapidly in large
ot; add crayfish; water should just cover crayfish; boil 15
inutes. Remove; cool enough to handle; cut in half length-
ise; remove meat; cut into cubes. Melt butter in saucepan
ver low flame; add crayfish, dill, and cognac; mix gently.
our steaming hot Hollandaise Sauce over crayfish; stir
ently. Serve piping hot in preheated ramekins or shells.

OLLANDAISE SAUCE

⅓ cup butter	2 egg yolks
⅓ cup boiling water	¼ tsp. salt
tsp. lemon juice	Pinch of cayenne

Break egg yolks into top section of double boiler; beat
ghtly; add lemon juice; beat again. In separate bowl cream
utter with wooden spoon; add to egg mixture; blend well.
nsert top section double boiler into lower section half filled
ith boiling water; place over flame; cook sauce until butter
elts and mixture begins to thicken, stirring constantly; add
alt and cayenne; stir gently; add boiling water *very slowly;*
tir until very smooth. Serve immediately.
    VARIATION: Use *lobster, shrimp,* and *prawns;* boiling
ime for prawns and shrimp 5 minutes only.

CRAYFISH SOUTH AMERICAN
TIME: 45 MINUTES; SERVES 6

2 crayfish
3 tbs. butter
2 small onions, minced
2 fresh chili peppers, halved

1 clove garlic, minced
2 ozs. mild cheese, crumbled
6 sprigs parsley

Purchase crayfish or spiny lobster of Florida or Pacif
coast; scrub well; rinse under running water. Boil approx
mately 2 cups water rapidly in large pot; add crayfish; bo
15 minutes. Remove from flame; cool enough to handle; cu
in half; remove meat; cut into cubes; set aside.

Melt butter in large frying pan; add onions and garlic
sauté 5 minutes, or until golden brown; add chili peppers
sauté 3 minutes more; add crayfish cubes; brown evenly b
stirring 3 minutes over medium flame; add cheese; st
gently; when well blended, serve piping hot on individua
preheated plates. Garnish each serving with parsley, wate
cress, or favorite green herb garnish.

VARIATION: *Lobster, prawns, shrimp,* and *hard-shel
crab.* Boil prawns and shrimp 5 minutes only.

◄§ FROGS' LEGS   The hind legs only are eaten, and when
broiled or sautéed are a snowy white and more delicately
flavored than the tenderest young chicken. The BULLFROG
is about 8 inches long and is found all over North America
The LEOPARD FROG is the bright green one with large, ir
regular, black, white-margined blotches on its back; its leg
are barred and its belly very pale. The PICKEREL FROG i
the brown frog of eastern North America with square dark
spots over its back. Always marketed skinned, the particula
species is not too significant; it is the final epicurean effect
that is important.

FROGS' LEGS BROILED MAÎTRE D'HOTEL
TIME: 20 MINUTES; SERVES 4

16 frogs' legs
½ cup butter

Maître d'Hôtel Butter
Salt and pepper

Wipe frogs' legs with damp cloth. Join every 2 legs by
passing joint of 1 leg through muscle of other. Melt butter
in small saucepan; brush frogs' legs with melted butter; sea
son lightly with salt and pepper to taste. Arrange on broiler

k; broil 5 minutes in preheated moderate broiling com-
tment (350° F.) 3 inches below flame; turn frogs' legs;
ush with melted butter; broil 5 minutes more, or until
den brown and tender. Meanwhile, prepare

ÎTRE D'HÔTEL BUTTER

ozs. butter	2 tsp. lemon juice
tsp. pepper	1 sprig tarragon, chopped
tsp. chopped parsley	1 sprig chervil, chopped

Melt butter in small saucepan over low flame; add pepper,
rsley, lemon juice, tarragon, and chervil; mix thoroughly.
range frogs' legs on preheated platter; pour Maître
Hôtel Butter over them. Serve immediately, while hot.

ROGS' LEGS DEEP-FRIED   TIME: 20 MINUTES; SERVES 4
frogs' legs	1½ cups peanut oil
egg, well beaten	Tartar Sauce
cup cracker crumbs	Salt and pepper

Wipe frogs' legs with damp cloth. Join 2 legs by passing
nt of 1 leg through muscle of the other; dip in egg, then
cracker crumbs. Pour oil in large skillet; heat over medium
me but do not allow to smoke. Fry frogs' legs in hot oil
minutes, or until golden brown and tender. Serve piping
t with tartar or preferred sauce.

RTAR SAUCE
tbs. mayonnaise	1 tbs. cream
tbs. chopped sweet pickle	1 tbs. chopped stuffed olives

Place mayonnaise in mixing bowl; add pickle and olives;
end well; add enough cream to obtain desired consistency.
hill in refrigerator 15 minutes before serving.
    VARIATION: Serve with Mayonnaise Caper Sauce, blend
tablespoon washed capers with 3 tablespoons mayonnaise.

ROGS' LEGS GARONNE   TIME: 30 MINUTES; SERVES 4
frogs' legs	½ cup farina
ozs. butter	2 hard-boiled egg yolks
small onion, minced	Juice of 1 lemon
lt and pepper	Water cress
cup dry sauterne wine	

Wipe frogs' legs with damp cloth; sprinkle lightly w
farina, salt and pepper to taste; set aside. Melt 3 oun
butter in large skillet over medium flame; add onion; saut
minutes; add frogs' legs; sauté gently 10 minutes; add ½ c
sauterne wine; cover; sauté 5 minutes more, or until fro
legs are tender; add balance sauterne; heat.

Meanwhile, melt balance butter in small saucepan; a
lemon juice. Chop egg yolks; add to lemon and butter
pan. Arrange frogs' legs on preheated platter; pour wi
sauce (in which they were sautéed) over them; cover wi
hot egg-yolk-butter. Garnish with water cress.

◆§ LOBSTER

It takes more than six years for the lobst
to reach the permitted marketable weight of 1 pound, a
though once in a while a huge one may be taken, t
average weights reaching the retail markets run about 1
to 2½ pounds. It has a pair of stalked compound eyes,
pairs of antennae, and 5 pairs of legs. The first pair a
enormous pincers, often called "claws." One is heavier th
the other, with blunt teeth with which the lobster crush
shells of clams and other mollusks for food. The larg
pieces of the sweet white succulent meat are found in t
huge claws and tail. When the lobster is boiled or broil
as soon as it is taken from the sea, it has a juicy, tend
taste and a flavor which defies description.

LOBSTER BOILED IN COURT BOUILLON
TIME: 20 MINUTES; SERVES 4

4 *live lobsters (2 lbs. each)*   6 *qts. water*
2 *large carrots*   6 *peppercorns*
2 *bay leaves*   ¼ *cup red wine vinegar*
2 *cloves*   1 *large onion, sliced*
2 *tbs. salt*   2 *stalks celery, with tops*

Pour water into large kettle; add salt, carrots, ba
leaves, cloves, peppercorns, wine vinegar, onion, and celer
cover; bring to boiling point over high flame; lower flame
medium; boil 10 minutes. Place lobsters in boiling brot
When broth begins to boil again, cook 10 minutes (if lobste
are less than 2 pounds each, cook only 7 minutes). Remov
lobsters from bouillon; cool at room temperature before pla
ing in refrigerator.

To serve chilled, boiled lobster, remove from refrigerator. ice lobster on back. Split from head to tail; spread open; nove dark vein running length of lobster; remove small : back of head but do not take out edible green and coral rts; crack large claws. Serve with generous portion mayon- ise or tartar sauce.

VARIATION: Use six quarts ocean water, boil 15 minutes salted water (1 tablespoon to each quart water).

OBSTER BON VIVANT

ME: 45 MINUTES; SERVES 4

live lobsters (1¼ lbs. each)	¼ cup sherry wine
cups fresh crab meat	¼ cup cream
cup bread crumbs	4 ozs. butter
lt and pepper	Paprika
mon wedges	Water cress

Clean and prepare lobsters as for broiling (pages 105-6). emove green liver and coral parts; set aside. Melt butter in aall saucepan. Place bread crumbs in large mixing bowl; end well with 2 ounces melted butter, sherry wine, cream, lt and pepper to taste; add green liver and coral parts; mix oroughly; add crab meat flakes; mix again.

Stuff lobster cavities with mixture; spread balance evenly er top; pour other 2 ounces melted butter over this; bake preheated hot oven (400° F.) 15 minutes, or until lobster eat is tender. (Be careful not to overcook, otherwise lob- er grows tough.) Serve immediately, garnished with lemon edges and water cress.

OBSTER BORDELAISE

ME: 20 MINUTES; SERVES 4 TO 6

½ lbs. fresh lobster meat	¼ cup claret wine
ozs. butter	1 small onion, minced
tbs. flour	½ small carrot, minced
tsp. salt	¼ tsp. oregano
cup rich milk	Pinch of cayenne
inch of nutmeg	12 stuffed olives, chopped
slices buttered toast	Water cress

If cooked lobster meat not available, purchase 1 live lob- ter (about 2 pounds); boil and prepare as shown on page 05.

Melt butter in top section of double boiler placed in low section half filled with boiling water. Gradually add flour melted butter, stirring constantly; add salt, cayenne, ar nutmeg.

Pour milk into small saucepan over medium flame; ad onion, carrot, and oregano; sauté gently 5 minutes. Slowl pour milk and vegetables into mixture in double boiler; st continually until very smooth and sauce begins to thicke (about 6 minutes); cook 5 minutes more; add lobster mea mix well; heat 3 minutes; add claret wine; heat 2 minute more. Serve piping hot over buttered toast placed on in dividual preheated plates; garnish with chopped olives an water cress.

VARIATION: Use *1½ pounds fresh crab flakes* instead o lobster.

LOBSTER BRANDY BLAZED
TIME: 45 MINUTES; SERVES 4

2 *lobsters (1½ lbs. each)*	1 *tbs. curry powder*
4 *scallions, or*	3 *ozs. brandy*
2 *tbs. chopped chives*	*Water cress*
1 *cup heavy cream*	*Salt*
4 *ozs. butter*	

Boil lobster as usual (page 105). Remove meat from claw and tail; cut into large cubes; set aside.

Melt 2 ounces butter in skillet over low flame; add chopped scallions; cook 2 minutes; add curry powder, stir ring constantly; gradually add cream; continue stirring; sal to taste; heat thoroughly but do not boil; set aside and keep hot over very low flame.

Melt other 2 ounces butter in separate skillet; add lobster meat; heat well and evenly by stirring constantly for 5 minutes. When hot, pour brandy over lobster; remove from heat. Quickly set lobster meat ablaze with lighted match; blaze only ½ minute.

Arrange lobster on preheated platter. Pour steaming hot cream sauce over lobster. Garnish with water cress. Serve immediately.

VARIATION: Cut time to 15 minutes by purchasing fresh lobster meat at market. *Amount of curry powder* may be varied to suit individual tastes.

LOBSTER BUTTER FRIED

TIME: 15 MINUTES; SERVES 4

1½ lbs. lobster meat	4 ozs. butter
¼ tsp. oregano	2 tbs. sherry wine
Paprika	4 sprigs fresh mint
12 stuffed olives	Salt

Purchase cooked lobster meat at market or boil live lobster (pages 144-45); cut meat into large cubes. Melt butter in frying pan over medium flame; when hot, add oregano and lobster meat; lower flame slightly; cover pan 5 minutes, allowing lobster to heat through; remove cover; continue frying lobster 5 minutes over higher flame until crispy brown on all sides. (Stir occasionally to brown evenly.) Lift lobster pieces out of butter; arrange on preheated individual plates. Quickly add sherry wine and pinch of salt to butter in pan; boil 1 minute; pour steaming hot over lobster. Garnish each serving with stuffed olives, dash of paprika, and sprig of mint. Serve immediately.

LOBSTER CANTONESE

TIME: 45 MINUTES; SERVES 4 TO 6

4 lobsters (1½ lbs. each)	½ lb. ground pork
2 eggs, well beaten	2 tbs. cornstarch
1 clove garlic, minced	4 tbs. sherry wine
1 tsp. salt	½ cup lukewarm water
¼ cup lard	⅛ tsp. white pepper

Select lobsters of equal size; sever spinal cord by inserting sharp knife between body and tail; scrub shell thoroughly under cold running water. Place lobsters in steaming basket or directly in rapidly boiling salted water; steam or boil 8 to 10 minutes; remove. When only slightly cool, break off claws; remove head. Split lobster in half lengthwise; remove dark vein; chop into serving pieces, using cleaver or very sharp knife; cut through shell and all; set aside. Separate the meat particles of the ground pork; place them in saucepan over medium flame; fry 10 minutes, stirring constantly until golden brown; add garlic, salt, and pepper. Blend cornstarch with lukewarm water; when very smooth, add to pork in saucepan; gradually stir in beaten eggs, then add sherry; cook 5 minutes over low flame, stirring constantly. Keep hot over low flame.

Heat lard in large skillet over medium flame; add lobster pieces. Pour hot sauce over lobster; heat thoroughly 5 minutes. Serve immediately with or without steamed rice.

LOBSTER AND CRAB PATTIES
TIME: 45 MINUTES; SERVES 6

1 cup lobster meat	1 egg, beaten
1 cup crab meat	1 tsp. salt
2 ozs. butter	⅛ tsp. pepper
1 tbs. flour	Pinch of nutmeg
1 cup milk	1 cup cracker crumbs
Juice of ½ lemon	6 tbs. peanut oil
Water cress	Tartar Sauce

Purchase freshly cooked lobster and crab meat at market. Remove all shell particles from crab; cut meat into small cubes. (Crab meat is usually small enough.)

Melt butter in small saucepan over low flame; add flour, salt, pepper, and nutmeg; blend well; gradually add milk; stir constantly until sauce thickens (about 5 minutes); add lemon juice; stir well; cook 3 minutes more; add lobster and crab meat; mix well; remove from heat; cool at room temperature; then chill thoroughly by placing in refrigerator 10 minutes. Remove; divide into several portions for easy handling; shape into patties; roll in cracker crumbs; dip in beaten egg, and roll again in crumbs.

Pour peanut oil into large skillet; heat; when very hot (375° F.), fry patties quickly 5 minutes, or until golden brown. Drain on absorbent paper. Garnish with water cress. Serve piping hot on preheated individual plates with generous portion Tartar Sauce (page 143).

LOBSTER NEWBURG À LA MINUTE
TIME: 20 MINUTES; SERVE 4 TO 6

1½ lbs. fresh lobster meat	1½ cups light cream
2 tbs. butter	2 egg yolks, beaten
3 tsp. flour	2 drops tabasco sauce
¼ tsp. salt	Pinch of cayenne
⅛ tsp. pepper	4 slices buttered toast
¼ tsp. dry mustard	4 sprigs parsley
4 tbs. sherry wine	

Melt butter in top section of double boiler placed in lower section half filled with boiling water; gradually add flour;

blend well; add seasonings except parsley sprigs and sherry wine; mix thoroughly; cook over medium flame 2 minutes; gradually pour in cream, stirring constantly. When well blended, remove from flame; cool 5 minutes.

Break egg yolks into large mixing bowl; beat until foamy; pour cooled sauce over egg yolks, stirring constantly. Return mixture to double boiler; add lobster meat; mix well; add sherry wine; heat 2 minutes. Serve piping hot over buttered toast; garnish each serving with parsley sprig.

VARIATION: *Cooked crab meat, crayfish, scallops, shrimp,* and *prawns; ½ lobster and ½ crab meat* makes a delectable combination. Lobster may be heated in melted butter before adding to sauce; then add to mixture after sherry and serve immediately.

LOBSTER NEWBURG AU GOURMET
TIME: 1 HOUR; SERVES 6

2 *live lobsters (2 lbs. each)*	4 *tbs. sherry wine*
6 *ozs. butter*	4 *tbs. brandy*
¼ *lb. mushrooms, sliced*	1 *cup heavy cream*
3 *tsp. flour*	2 *egg yolks, beaten*
½ *tsp. salt*	3 *drops tabasco sauce*
⅛ *tsp. pepper*	4 *slices buttered toast*
Paprika	12 *stuffed olives*
Court Bouillon (page 20)	*Water cress*

Prepare and boil lobsters in Court Bouillon. When cooled, place lobster on back, split from head to tail; spread open; remove dark vein in tail and small sac back of head but save green and coral parts; crack large claws; remove meat from body and claws; cut into large cubes; set aside.

Melt 2 ounces butter in top section of double boiler placed over lower section half filled with boiling water; gradually add flour; blend well; add salt, pepper, dash of paprika, and tabasco sauce; mix thoroughly; cook over medium flame 2 minutes; gradually pour in cream, stirring constantly. When well blended, remove from flame to cool.

Meanwhile, melt 2 ounces butter in small saucepan over medium flame; sauté mushrooms 10 minutes, or until tender; keep hot over very low flame.

Break egg yolks into large mixing bowl; beat until foamy; pour part of cooled cream sauce over egg yolks, stirring constantly. When well blended, return mixture to double boiler;

add mushrooms; mix gently. Blend green liver and coral roe; add to cream sauce; stir well. Melt 2 ounces butter in frying pan over medium flame; add lobster meat; heat well 5 minutes, stirring constantly. Add lobster to cream sauce; mix gently; add sherry wine and brandy; stir gently; heat 2 minutes. Serve piping hot over buttered toast placed on individual preheated plates. Garnish each serving with stuffed olives and water cress.

LOBSTER RAGOUT
TIME: 15 MINUTES; SERVES 4

1 lb. lobster meat	1 tbs. white wine vinegar
1/8 tsp. cayenne	2 ozs. butter
Pinch of white pepper	Salt
4 slices buttered toast	Lemon wedges
2 tbs. rich cream	

Use cooked lobster meat purchased at market, or boil lobster at home (pages 144-45). Blend in mixing bowl cayenne, pepper, cream, and vinegar; add lobster; stir well.

Melt butter in saucepan over low flame; add lobster mixture; simmer 5 minutes, or until very hot. Serve piping hot over buttered toast; garnish each serving with lemon wedges or favorite green herb.

VARIATION: Substitute 2 *tablespoons madeira wine.*

LOBSTER THERMIDOR
TIME: 1 HOUR; SERVES 4

2 live lobsters (1½ lbs. each)	4 ozs. butter, extra
	2 tbs. flour
4 qts. water	¼ tsp. dry mustard
2 tbs. salt	¼ tsp. salt
¼ cup white wine vinegar	1 pt. rich milk
2 ozs. butter	3 egg yolks, beaten
¼ lb. mushrooms, chopped	2 tbs. chopped parsley
3 tbs. chopped shallots	2 sprigs tarragon, minced
Salt and pepper	1 stalk celery, minced
4 tbs. grated Parmesan cheese	8 parsley sprigs

Insert sharp knife between body and tail of lobster to sever spinal cord. Pour water and vinegar into deep pot over high flame; add salt; when boiling rapidly; place lobsters in water, which should cover them; cook 7 minutes from time water begins to boil again. (If lobsters weigh more, cook 2 or 3 minutes more.) Remove lobsters from water; when cool, place on back and split from head to tail; spread open; remove dark vein running to end of tail; take out small sac back of head; green liver and coral roe are edible; crack large claws; remove meat carefully; cut into cubes; reserve shells.

Meanwhile, melt 2 ounces butter in large saucepan over medium flame; add mushrooms and shallots; salt and pepper to taste; sauté 5 minutes; add lobster meat; stir well; cover; keep warm over very low flame. Melt 2 ounces butter in separate saucepan over medium flame. Sift flour, salt, and mustard; gradually add to melted butter, stirring until very smooth; gradually pour in milk, stirring constantly.

Break egg yolks into large mixing bowl; beat yolks until foamy; gradually pour milk sauce over beaten eggs, stirring vigorously until well blended. Pour ½ milk sauce into lobster mixture; blend well. Add chopped parsley, tarragon, and celery to lobster mixture; stir well.

Arrange lobster shells in shallow baking dish; fill with mixture; pour remaining sauce over top; sprinkle with grated Parmesan cheese; dot with remaining 2 ounces butter; place in preheated broiler compartment 3 inches below flame for 5 minutes, or until cheese is golden brown. Arrange on preheated platter. Garnish with parsley sprigs.

VARIATION: Cut time to 30 minutes by purchasing *1 pound fresh lobster meat* at market.

LOBSTER VINAIGRETTE
TIME: 1 HOUR; SERVES 4 TO 6

2 *live lobsters (2 lbs. each)*	6 *tbs. tarragon vinegar*
4 *tbs. butter*	6. *egg yolks, beaten*
1 *tbs. chopped parsley*	½ *tsp. dry mustard*
2 *tsp. minced onion*	2 *tsp. chopped capers*
2 *tsp. minced chives*	*Salt*
Parsley sprigs	6 *slices buttered toast*

Insert sharp knife between body and tail of lobster to sever spinal cord. Pour 2 quarts water into deep pot over high flame; add 2 tablespoons salt. When boiling rapidly, place lobsters in water, which should cover them; cook 10 minutes from the time water begins to boil again. (If lobster weighs less, cook only 7 minutes.) Remove lobsters;

reserve ¾ cup water in which lobsters were boiled. When lobster is cool, place on back; split from head to tail; spread open; remove dark vein running to end of tail; take out small sac back of head; green liver and coral roe are edible; crack large claws; remove meat carefully; cut into cubes; reserve shells.

Pour lobster water and vinegar into large saucepan; add onion and chives; sauté 2 minutes; add lobster meat; heat thoroughly about 3 minutes but do not boil.

Meanwhile, break egg yolks into large mixing bowl; add mustard; beat yolks and mustard until foamy. Arrange shells on preheated fireproof shallow dish placed over low flame to keep hot. Lift hot lobster meat from liquid and fill shells with lobster. Pour hot liquid very slowly over the beaten egg yolks, stirring constantly; gradually add parsley; blend well. Return liquid to fire; cook 2 minutes, or until sauce is smooth and thick; stir continuously. When piping hot, pour over lobster meat in shells. Garnish with parsley. Serve with 1 slice buttered toast at side.

◆§ MUSSELS   SEA MUSSELS are found on the shores of the Atlantic both in Europe and America. A fresh-water species is particularly abundant in the streams of both countries.

The blue-black mussel shell is so thin that there is considerably more food in a pound of mussels than in the same amount of oysters or clams. The shell is from 2 to 2½ inches long and is pear-shaped. Mussels are marketed alive in shells. Mussel meats are available canned.

Mussels may be prepared in all the ways in which clams and oysters are cooked, and they are one of the most delicate and inexpensive of sea foods. The mussel meats are a creamy golden-yellow of such tenderness that they melt in your mouth, and the flavor is as sweet as that of the smallest clams.

MUSSELS BAKED IN RHINE WINE
TIME: 45 MINUTES; SERVES 4

4 doz. mussels, in shells	½ cup rhine wine
4 slices lean bacon	½ tsp. salt
1 tbs. grated Parmesan cheese	¼ tsp. paprika
	½ tsp. dill, crumbled
1 tsp. minced onion	

Select large, fresh mussels with shells *closed*; scrub shells well; rinse under running water. (If time allows, after scrubbing, let mussels soak 2 hours in large pot filled with water. Discard any mussels that float.)

Pour 1 inch water into large kettle; add 1 teaspoon salt; add mussels; cover; steam 3 minutes, or until shells begin to open; remove; drain. Take mussels from shells; remove dark, hairy beard. Strain broth through sieve; set broth aside and use same as clam broth, as desired.

Place mussel meats in casserole; season lightly with salt, paprika, dill, and minced onion; pour in rhine wine; sprinkle grated cheese over top; arrange bacon slices over all. Bake in preheated moderate oven (350° F.) 15 minutes, or until bacon is crisp. Serve piping hot from casserole.

VARIATION: Use *cooked shrimp* or *prawns*.

MUSSELS AU GRATIN
TIME: 45 MINUTES; SERVES 4

4 doz. mussels, in shells	Salt and pepper
4 ozs. butter	1 cup mussel broth
2 tbs. flour	2 tbs. sherry wine
1 small onion, minced	1 cup cracker crumbs
½ cup Cheddar cheese,	Water cress
crumbled	

Select large, fresh mussels with shells *closed*; scrub shells well; rinse under running water. (If time allows, let mussels soak 2 hours in large pot filled with water. Discard any mussels that float.) Pour 1 inch water into large kettle; add 1 teaspoon salt; add mussels; cover; steam 3 minutes, or until shells begin to open; remove; drain. Strain broth through fine sieve; set broth aside. Take mussels from shells; remove dark, hairy beard; set meats aside.

Melt 2 ounces butter in saucepan over medium flame; add onion; sauté gently 5 minutes, or until golden brown; gradually add flour, stirring continually. When very smooth, slowly add 1 cup mussel broth. Continue stirring until sauce is thick (about 5 minutes). Add salt, pepper, and sherry wine. Make sauce of desired thickness by adding more mussel broth if necessary. In casserole arrange alternate layers of mussels, sauce, cracker crumbs, and light sprinkling of cheese until ingredients are all used. Save sufficient crumbs and cheese for top layer. Dot top with other 2 ounces butter. Bake in preheated oven (350° F.) 15 minutes, or until top is golden brown.

MUSSELS IN SAFFRON PROVENÇAL
TIME: 30 MINUTES; SERVES 4

4 doz. mussels, in shells	½ tsp. saffron
Juice of 1 lemon	3 cups mussel broth
2 ozs. butter	4 egg yolks, beaten
2 tsp. flour	Salt
Croutons	Parsley sprigs
1 tsp. salt, extra	

Select large, fresh mussels with shells *closed*; scrub well; rinse under running water. (If time allows, let mussels soak 2 hours in large pot filled with water. Discard any mussels that float.)

Pour 1 inch water into large kettle; add 1 teaspoon salt and juice of 1 lemon; add mussels; cover; steam until shells begin to open; remove; drain. Take mussels from shells; remove dark, hairy beard. Keep mussels hot over steam.

Strain broth through fine sieve; pour 3 cups broth into small saucepan. Dissolve saffron in small amount mussel broth; add to broth in saucepan; stir well; boil 2 minutes over medium flame. Melt 2 ounces butter in separate saucepan over medium flame; stir in flour; when very smooth, dissolve this in mussel-saffron liquid; bring to boiling point, stirring constantly; remove from heat; allow to cool.

Meanwhile, break egg yolks into large mixing bowl; beat until foamy. Pour cool sauce over eggs very slowly; stir constantly until well blended; return to saucepan; place over medium flame; stir constantly until sauce thickens (about 5 minutes); season with salt to taste.

Arrange mussels on preheated platter; cover with fragrant saffron sauce. Serve steaming hot over croutons placed in preheated individual plates. Garnish each serving with sprigs of parsley or favorite green herb.

MUSSELS FISHERMAN'S STYLE
TIME: 45 MINUTES; SERVES 4

4 doz. mussels, in shells	½ cup dry sauterne
1 small onion, chopped	¼ tsp. thyme
1 bay leaf, crumbled	⅛ tsp. dill
2 tbs. minced parsley	2 ozs. butter
Pinch of cayenne	Salt and pepper

Select large, fresh mussels with shells *closed;* scrub well; rinse under running water; place in large saucepan; add onion, bay leaf, parsley, cayenne, sauterne wine, thyme, and dill; cover tightly; steam actively 2 minutes, or until shells open; remove and drain. Strain broth through fine sieve and reserve. Take meats from shells; remove dark, hairy beard; set meats aside. Pour broth into small saucepan; simmer 2 minutes; add butter; season with salt and pepper to taste; add mussels; heat to boiling point but do not boil.

Place small bowl of sauce in center of preheated plate; arrange mussel meats around bowl. Dip mussels into sauce and eat.

VARIATION: Use *soft-shell clams.*

◄§ OYSTERS   More than half the supply which reaches our retail markets comes from Chesapeake and Long Island bays. The Eastern oyster's shell is from 2 to 2½ inches long. There is also the small Olympia oyster of Puget Sound and the giant Japanese oyster of the Pacific. This bivalve mollusk grows in shallow waters, bays, sounds, and river mouths where the saltines of the water is reduced by the flow of the fresh water from the tributary streams flowing into them. The oyster has a rough irregular shell closed by a single muscle. They are marketed alive in shells, shucked, and canned. Smoked oysters are also canned.

OYSTER AND BACON ROLLS OR
ANGELS ON HORSEBACK
TIME: 20 MINUTES; SERVES 6

2 doz. large oysters, shucked	⅛ tsp. paprika
½ tsp. salt	2 tbs. parsley
⅛ tsp. pepper	Lemon wedges
12 slices bacon	

Drain oysters; remove shell particles.

Cut bacon slices in half; arrange on large mixing board. Lay each oyster in center of bacon; sprinkle with seasonings and chopped parsley; roll bacon around each oyster; fasten with toothpick. Place oysters on rack in shallow baking dish; bake in preheated hot oven (450° F.) 6 to 8 minutes, or until bacon is crisp. Serve piping hot on preheated individual plates. Garnish each serving with lemon wedges.

VARIATION: If broiled, place 3 inches below flame; broil only 1½ minutes on each side, or until bacon is crisp.

OYSTERS BROILED AU GOURMET

TIME: 20 MINUTES; SERVES 4

2 dóz. oysters on half shell · 2 tsp. prepared horse-radish
4 ozs. butter · ⅛ tsp. Worcestershire sauce
1 scallion, minced · ⅛ tsp. basil, crumbled
1 slice raw bacon, minced · Rock salt
Salt and pepper · Water cress
4 doz. oyster crabs

Select large oysters; have them opened and left in curved half shell. Purchase oyster crabs; wipe carefully with damp cloth. Place 2 oyster crabs on each oyster; set aside.

Place butter in mixing bowl; cream at room temperature with wooden spoon; blend in scallion, raw minced bacon, horse-radish, Worcestershire sauce, and basil; season delicately with very little salt and pepper.

Cover bottom of shallow baking dish with light layer rock salt; heat in preheated hot oven (400° F.) 10 minutes.

Meanwhile, place teaspoonful butter mixture over top of each oyster. When pan and salt are hot, carefully arrange filled oysters in half shell on bed of hot salt; bake 6 minutes, or until bacon sizzles, being careful not to overcook. Serve piping hot from baking pan at table. Garnish each serving with generous helping water cress.

OYSTERS BROILED ON HALF SHELL

TIME: 15 MINUTES; SERVES 4

2 doz. large oysters, in shell · 2 slices raw bacon, minced
2 cloves garlic, minced · 2 tbs. chopped parsley
Salt and pepper · Lemon wedges

Scrub oyster shells thoroughly; rinse under running water. Insert blade of thin, strong knife between edges of shells; pry open by twisting. (Or have oysters opened at market.) Discard flatter shell; oyster remains in curved shell.

Arrange oysters in shallow baking dish; sprinkle each oyster lightly with minced garlic, then parsley, and finally raw bacon; season with very little salt and pepper. Place in preheated broiler compartment 3 inches below flame; broil 3 minutes, or until bacon is slightly browned. Serve piping hot on half shell with lemon wedges.

VARIATION: Use hard-shell clams.

OYSTERS CASINO

TIME: 30 MINUTES; SERVES 4

2 doz. oysters, shucked
1 oz. butter
1 small onion, minced
½ green pepper, minced
1 stalk celery, minced
Salt and pepper

2 slices lean bacon, diced
1 pimiento, chopped
1 tsp. lemon juice
½ tsp. Worcestershire sauce
Paprika
4 slices toast

Place bacon in small skillet over low flame; fry slowly 3 minutes, or until crisp. Melt butter in separate saucepan over medium flame; add onion, green pepper, celery, salt and pepper to taste; sauté 5 minutes, or until vegetables are tender; combine with bacon in skillet; add lemon juice, pimiento, and Worcestershire sauce; mix well.

Arrange toast in shallow baking dish; place 6 oysters on each slice; cover with bacon mixture; sprinkle with paprika. Place in preheated hot broiler compartment 3 inches below flame; broil 3 minutes. Serve piping hot on preheated individual plates. Garnish each serving with radish buds and water cress, or favorite green herb garnish.

OYSTER FRITTERS AMERICAN

TIME: 30 MINUTES; SERVES 4 TO 6

1 doz. oysters, in liquor
3 eggs
Salt
1 cup rich milk

1 cup oyster liquor
1 cup flour
1 pt. peanut oil

Prepare fritter batter 2 hours before using.

Drain oysters; remove shell particles; strain liquor through fine sieve; reserve. Chop oysters; set aside.

Separate egg yolks from whites; beat each separately, the yolks until thick and light yellow, the whites until stiff.

In large mixing bowl blend egg yolks, milk, and oyster liquor; add salt to taste; fold in whites; sift in enough flour to make thin batter; add chopped oysters. Cover; place in refrigerator to chill 2 hours.

Pour oil in large skillet over high flame; heat but do not allow to smoke. Fry spoonfuls of batter (few at a time) in hot oil 3 minutes, or until golden brown. (Too many fritters in oil at one time cools oil too much.) Serve piping hot with tartar sauce.

VARIATION: Use *shucked clams in liquor*, or *2 cups cooked lobster meat, prawns, shrimp,* or *crayfish,* chopped fine with 2 cups milk. Serve with favorite cream sauce.

OYSTERS CREOLE
TIME: 20 MINUTES; SERVES 4 TO 6

2 doz. oysters, in liquor	2 tbs. chopped parsley
2 ozs. butter	1/8 tsp. oregano
1 small onion, minced	3 drops tabasco sauce
3 tbs. flour	Paprika
1/2 tsp. salt	Buttered toast
1 cup tomato juice	

Drain oysters. Melt butter in small saucepan over medium flame; add onion and oregano; sauté 5 minutes, or until onion is tender; gradually stir in flour. When blended, add salt and tomato juice; cook 5 minutes, or until thick, stirring constantly. Add oysters, parsley, and tabasco sauce; simmer gently 3 minutes, or until edges of oysters begin to curl. Serve piping hot over buttered toast placed on preheated individual plates. Sprinkle each serving with paprika. Garnish with chopped stuffed olives and water cress, or preferred green herb garnish.

VARIATION: Use *clams in liquor* instead of oysters.

OYSTER AND MUSHROOM BROIL
TIME: 30 MINUTES; SERVES 4

2 doz. oysters, shucked	2 doz. large mushrooms
4 slices lean bacon, diced	Salt and pepper
2 ozs. butter, melted	1/2 tsp. rosemary
4 slices buttered toast	Water cress

Select large oysters; have them shucked at market; remove all shell particles; set aside.

Select large mushrooms; rinse, drain, and peel; remove stalks. (Reserve for flavoring or making mushroom sauce; do not throw away.) Dip mushroom caps in melted butter; arrange on rack in shallow baking dish; broil in preheated broiling compartment 3 inches below flame 4 minutes; dust with salt and pepper. Remove from heat. Turn mushrooms over; sprinkle very lightly with rosemary. Place raw oyster in hollow of each mushroom cap; cover with diced bacon; return to broiling compartment; broil 3 minutes, or until bacon is golden brown. Serve piping hot on buttered toast

placed in preheated individual plates. Garnish each serving
with generous helping water cress.

VARIATION: Use *raw clams, shrimp,* or *prawns.*

OYSTERS ORIENTALE
TIME: 30 MINUTES; SERVES 4

2 doz. oysters, shucked
6 slices bacon
Paprika

4 firm tomatoes, sliced
12 stuffed olives
Salt and pepper

Use approximately 12 skewers. Cut bacon into 2-inch
pieces. Slice tomatoes desired thickness. Remove all shell
particles from oysters.

Arrange piece of bacon, oyster, slice of tomato, and oc-
casional olive alternately on skewers; repeat until all ingredients are used; sprinkle with very little salt and pepper
to taste.

Arrange filled skewers in shallow baking dish; place in
preheated broiler compartment 3 inches below flame; broil
3 minutes, or until tomato is heated through and bacon is
crisp. Serve piping hot on preheated individual plates. Sprinkle each serving with paprika. Garnish with water cress,
of favorite green herb.

VARIATION: Use *shucked clams, raw shrimp,* or *prawns.*

OYSTER PIE DUCHESS
TIME: 1 HOUR; SERVES 6 TO 8

2 doz. oysters, in liquor
½ lb. mushrooms
½ cup butter or margarine
¼ tsp. pepper
Pinch of cayenne
2 stalks celery

3 cups rich milk
1 cup oyster liquor
½ cup flour
¾ tsp. salt
Pinch of nutmeg
1 flaky pastry crust (page 132)

Prepare flaky pastry crust; set aside.
Drain oysters; strain liquor and save.
Wash and peel mushrooms; slice in thickness preferred.
Melt butter or margarine in deep saucepan; add mushrooms and celery; cook 3 minutes, or until mushrooms are
light brown. Gradually blend in flour, stirring until smooth;
slowly pour in milk and oyster liquor while continually stirring; bring to boiling point; stir in pepper, cayenne, salt, and
nutmeg; when well blended, add oysters. Pour into large
casserole; cover with flaky pastry, pressing its edge to the

rim of dish; cut 2 gashes in pastry, allowing steam to escape; bake in preheated hot oven (450° F.) 15 minutes, or until top is golden brown. Serve immediately in preheated plates. Garnish servings with green herbs if desired.

VARIATION: *1 dozen clams, and 1 dozen oysters* may be combined; or *2 dozen clams* without oysters may be used.

OYSTER ROAST AL FRESCO
TIME: 20 MINUTES; SERVES 12

12 doz. large oysters, in shell	*1½ lbs. butter, melted*
Salt and pepper	*Paprika*

Prepare wood or coal fire in outdoor oven. Place a sheet-iron plate or grid over heat. Scrub oysters well. On hot grid arrange oysters placed with larger half of shell face downward; roast 10 minutes, or until shells open.

Each person may remove oysters, or they may be removed and placed in preheated individual plates. Dip oyster meat in melted butter; sprinkle with paprika, salt and pepper.

VARIATION: Use *clams*; scrub shells well.

OYSTERS ROCKEFELLER
TIME: 30 MINUTES; SERVES 6

3 doz. large oysters, in shell	*½ lb. butter*
1 small onion, minced	*½ cup cracker crumbs*
2 bay leaves, crumbled	*1 tsp. Worcestershire sauce*
½ tsp. celery salt	*3 tbs. sherry wine*
⅛ tsp. cayenne	*Rock salt*
½ tsp. salt	*½ cup grated Parmesan*
6 sprigs parsley, minced	*cheese*
½ cup bread crumbs	*Lemon wedges*
1 cup minced, raw spinach	

Select large oysters; scrub thoroughly; rinse under running water. Insert blade of thin, strong knife between edges of shells; pry open by twisting. (Or have oysters shucked at market.) Discard flatter shell; oyster remains in curved shell.

In large mixing bowl combine onion, bay leaves, celery salt, cayenne, salt, minced spinach, parsley, and Worcestershire sauce; mix thoroughly.

Melt butter in small saucepan over low flame; remove from heat; combine with cracker crumbs and sherry wine; mix thoroughly; add to seasonings in bowl; mix well.

Arrange covering of rock salt over bottom of shallow baking dish; place oysters on this. Pour mixture over oysters; sprinkle with grated Parmesan cheese and bread crumbs; bake in preheated hot oven (400° F.) 10 minutes, or until golden brown. Garnish each serving with lemon wedges.

OYSTER SCALLOP OHIO

TIME: 40 MINUTES; SERVES 6

1 qt. oysters, in liquor
¼ onion, minced
3 cups cracker crumbs
¼ tsp. nutmeg
⅛ tsp. mace
Tartar Sauce (page 143)
2 cups canned corn (kernels)

¼ cup oyster liquor
¼ cup cream
¾ cup dry sauterne wine
4 ozs. butter
Lemon wedges
Salt and pepper

Drain oysters; remove shell particles; strain liquor; reserve. In mixing bowl blend corn and onion; season with salt and pepper to taste; add nutmeg and mace; mix well.

Spread ⅓ crumbs in bottom of buttered casserole; cover with corn mixture; sprinkle with ⅓ crumbs. Arrange oysters over crumbs; sprinkle lightly with pepper; top with remaining crumbs. Blend oyster liquor, cream, and wine; pour over all; dot generously with butter; bake in preheated moderate oven (350° F.) 20 minutes, or until golden brown. Serve piping hot with Tartar Sauce and lemon wedges.

OYSTERS SAUCEPAN GRILLED

TIME: 15 MINUTES; SERVES 4

2 doz. oysters, in liquor
¼ tsp. Worcestershire sauce
⅛ tsp. salt
2 cups oyster liquor
4 ozs. butter

2 tsp. lemon juice
Pinch of cayenne
4 slices toast
2 tbs. chopped parsley

Drain oysters; remove shell particles. Strain liquor through fine sieve; reserve. Melt butter in saucepan over medium flame; add oysters; stir and heat 1 minute; add oyster liquor, Worcestershire sauce, salt, lemon juice, and cayenne; heat 2 minutes. Serve piping hot over toast placed on preheated individual soup plate with generous helping of sauce. Sprinkle with chopped parsley.

VARIATION: Use small clams, in liquor.

✑ OYSTER CRAB This is only the size of a man's thumbnail, and the body surface is smooth and shiny. Oyster crabs are found in the mantle cavity of the oyster, for which they are named. Much sought after by gourmets, it should be served on buttered toast or as a garnish on a delicately flavored fillet of fish. Its flavor is so sweet and delicate and the supply at times so limited that it probably belongs in the category with hummingbirds' tongues.

OYSTER CRABS DEEP-FRIED
TIME: 10 MINUTES; SERVES 2 TO 3

4 doz. oyster crabs	½ lb. butter
Salt and pepper	Juice of 1 lemon
Tartar sauce	Buttered toast

Wipe oyster crabs carefully with damp cloth; sprinkle lightly with salt and pepper to taste.

Melt butter in frying pan over medium flame; heat but do not allow to smoke. Fry crabs quickly 2 or 3 minutes, or until golden brown. Serve piping hot on buttered toast placed on preheated individual plate. Place generous helping tartar sauce at side.

✑ PRAWNS This shrimplike crustacean ranges in length from 1 inch to 6 inches. Pale green when alive, it turns a delicate pink when cooked. Only the small body is eaten. The meat is firm and white; the flavor is sweet and juicy when carefully prepared and not overcooked.

PRAWNS BAKED MEXICANA
TIME: 30 MINUTES; SERVES 4

1 lb. fresh prawns	4 firm tomatoes
3 ozs. butter	1 cup bread crumbs
1 small onion, minced	4 tbs. rich cream
1 stalk celery, minced	⅛ tsp. mace
1 bay leaf	¼ tsp. salt
⅛ tsp. crushed red pepper seeds	4 tsp. bread crumbs, extra
Paprika	4 slices toast

Select large fresh prawns; peel raw; remove sand vein; wipe with damp cloth. Wash tomatoes; carefully cut away top core and hollow out all pulp; reserve pulp.

Melt 2 ounces butter in saucepan over medium flame; dd onion; sauté 3 minutes, or until light brown; add celery, ay leaf, crushed red pepper seeds, tomato pulp, mace, and alt; cover; simmer gently 15 minutes; add cream and suf- cient bread crumbs to make a very thick sauce; blend well; dd prawns, cut in half lengthwise; simmer 3 minutes.

Arrange tomato shells in shallow baking dish; fill with rawn mixture; cover each with 1 teaspoon bread crumbs; ot with butter; sprinkle lightly with paprika.

Bake in preheated hot oven (375° F.) 10 minutes, or ntil well browned. Arrange each filled tomato on toast.

VARIATION: Use *raw shrimp* instead of prawns.

PRAWNS NEW ORLEANS

IME: 30 MINUTES; SERVES 4

lb. fresh prawns	1 *stalk celery, minced*
ozs. butter	½ *tsp. basil*
firm tomatoes, diced	⅛ *tsp. thyme*
green pepper, minced	*Pinch of cayenne*
alt and pepper	4 *slices buttered toast*
small onion, diced	

Simmer vegetables before peeling prawns and save time. Melt butter in saucepan over medium flame; add tomatoes, reen pepper, onion, celery, basil, thyme, cayenne, salt and epper to taste; bring to boiling point; lower flame; cover; immer gently 20 minutes.

Meanwhile, peel raw prawns; remove sand vein; wipe with damp cloth; cut in half lengthwise.

When vegetables have simmered 20 minutes, add halved prawns; simmer gently 10 minutes, or until tender. Serve iping hot over buttered toast placed on preheated individual plates.

VARIATION: Use *raw shrimp* instead of prawns.

PRAWN PUFFS

TIME: 30 MINUTES; SERVES 4 TO 6

½ lb. raw prawns	½ tsp. salt
1 qt. boiling water	1 egg, well beaten
2 tsp. salt	1 cup milk
1 bay leaf	3 tsp. baking powder
Juice of 1 lemon	Tartar Sauce
4 peppercorns	1 pt. peanut oil
2 cups flour	

Select large fresh prawns; peel raw; remove sand vein.

Pour boiling water into small saucepan; add 2 teaspoon salt, peppercorns, bay leaf, lemon juice, and prawns; cover simmer 5 minutes. (Count cooking time after water return to boiling.) Remove from heat; strain stock and reserve fo use in fish sauces. Chop prawns; set aside.

In separate large mixing bowl sift flour, ½ teaspoon salt and baking powder. Blend beaten egg and milk; add choppe prawns; mix well; add to flour; mix well.

Pour peanut oil into large skillet; heat but do not allow t smoke. Drop prawn mixture by large spoonfuls into hot oil fry 3 minutes, or until golden brown. Drain on absorben paper. Serve piping hot on preheated individual plates wit Tartar Sauce (page 143) or favorite cream sauce.

VARIATION: *Cooked, chopped clams, crayfish, lobster crab flakes,* and *raw shrimp* may be used instead of prawns

PRAWNS TEXAS FRIED
TIME: 45 MINUTES; SERVES 4

2 lbs. raw prawns	½ tsp. curry powder
2 eggs beaten	⅛ tsp. salt
1 cup cracker crumbs	3 cups peanut oil
½ cup flour	Chili sauce

Select large fresh prawns; peel raw; remove sand vein wipe with damp cloth; split open lengthwise; spread apar like butterfly; salt lightly.

Sift flour, curry powder, and salt into mixing bowl; add cracker crumbs.

Dip prawns into eggs beaten until foamy, then roll in sea soned flour mixture.

Pour peanut oil into large skillet; heat but do not allow t smoke (about 350° F.); fry prawns 3 minutes, or unti golden brown.

Drain on absorbent paper. Serve on preheated individua plates with generous helping prepared chili sauce.

VARIATION: Use *raw oysters, clams,* or *shrimp.*

PRAWNS WITH HERB BUTTER
TIME: 20 MINUTES; SERVES 4

1 lb. fresh prawns	2 ozs. butter
½ cup boiling water	¼ tsp. paprika
½ tsp. salt	⅛ tsp. marjoram

bay leaf
peppercorns
½ tsp. celery seed
slices toast

Pinch of nutmeg
Juice of 1 lemon
Salt and pepper
Water cress

Select large fresh prawns; peel raw; remove sand vein; wipe with damp cloth. Pour boiling water into saucepan over medium flame; add salt, add prawns; cover; simmer gently 8 minutes, or until prawns are pink and water is absorbed.

Meanwhile, melt butter in separate saucepan; add *all* seasonings except water cress; cover; simmer gently 3 minutes. Serve hot over toast placed on preheated individual plate. Pour seasoned hot butter over prawns. Garnish each serving with water cress or favorite green herb.

VARIATION: Use *shrimp* or *scallops*.

SCALLOPS   A mollusk with two shells like the oyster and clam, but, unlike them, it swims about in the water or moves over the bottom along the sand. Its shell is rounded with a wavy, scalloped edge and a large muscle controls the movements of the shell as it propels itself. This muscle, sometimes called the "eye," is the only part of the scallop eaten here although Europeans eat the entire scallop. BAY SCALLOPS and SEA SCALLOPS, come from the two localities from which they derive their names. The flavor of the bay scallop is often much sweeter and the quality of its muscle more tender than that of the larger sea scallop, whose muscle measures approximately 1½ inches long and is about 1 inch or 1½ inches thick. But the white firm meat of each species is equally tasty when prepared with a quick, light hand.

SCALLOPS BAKED WITH MUSHROOMS
TIME: 1 HOUR; SERVES 4

1 lb. scallops
3 ozs. butter
2 cups Basic White Sauce
½ cup cracker crumbs
4 tbs. grated Cheddar cheese
½ lb. mushrooms, sliced

3 stalks celery, diced
½ small onion, grated
½ green pepper, minced
½ green pepper, minced
⅛ tsp. basil
Parsley sprigs

Wipe scallops with damp cloth; set aside. Melt 2 ounces butter in large saucepan over medium flame; add mushrooms, celery, onion, green pepper, and basil; simmer gently 10 minutes, or until celery and mushrooms are tender but not soft.

Meanwhile, prepare Basic White Sauce (page 81).

Add scallops to mushrooms; mix well; heat 5 minutes then add 2 cups Basic White Sauce; mix thoroughly.

Pour mixture into casserole; cover with layer of cracker crumbs, then layer grated cheese; dot with other ounce butter. Bake in preheated moderate oven (350° F.) 25 minutes or until golden brown. Serve piping hot from casserole at table. Garnish each serving with parsley sprig.

VARIATION: Use *raw clams, oysters,* or *lobster meat.* Heat clams or oysters only 2 minutes; bake 15 to 20 minutes.

SCALLOPS "CHAPON FIN DE BORDEAUX"
TIME: 1 HOUR; SERVES 6

2 lbs. scallops	½ lb. mushrooms, sliced
1 cup water	2 ozs. butter
1 tbs. salt	1 tbs. minced parsley
1 tomato, diced	1 cup White Sauce
1 small onion, minced	Salt and pepper
Paprika	12 parsley sprigs

If scallops are large, cut in half across grain. Pour water into saucepan over medium flame; add salt; add scallops; boil 2 minutes, or until scallops begin to shrink; remove chop scallops into small pieces but do not mince.

Place butter in saucepan over medium flame; add mushrooms; sauté 10 minutes, or until tender; add tomato, onion parsley, salt and pepper to taste; simmer gently 10 minutes add scallops; mix well; add hot White Sauce (page 81) stirring constantly.

Fill scallop shells or individual ramekins with mixture, sprinkle lightly with paprika. Place in preheated broiling compartment 3 inches below flame; broil 2 minutes, or until golden brown. Serve piping hot. Garnish with parsley.

SCALLOP CHEESE CUPS
TIME: 30 MINUTES; SERVES 6

1 lb. scallops	4 tbs. grated Cheddar cheese
1 cup water	3 tbs. flour
½ cup dry sauterne wine	1 egg yolk, beaten
2 ozs. butter	½ tsp. salt
Paprika	6 tsp. chopped chives

If scallops are large, cut in half across grain; place in saucepan over medium flame; cover with water and sauterne wine; boil 2 minutes, or until scallops begin to shrink; remove; chop fine but do not mince; reserve liquid.

In separate saucepan, over medium flame, melt butter; gradually stir in flour. When smooth, add scallop liquid, stirring constantly; add scallops, paprika, and salt; stir constantly until thick (about 5 minutes); remove from flame; gradually add beaten egg yolk; stir in 2 tablespoons grated cheese; blend well. Pour blended mixture into custard cups; sprinkle tops with balance grated cheese; place in shallow baking dish with ½ inch water in pan; place dish in preheated hot oven (400° F.) 5 minutes, or until cheese is melted and brown. Garnish each serving with 1 teaspoon chopped chives.

VARIATION: Use *oysters, clams, prawns, shrimp,* or *cooked crab* and *lobster chunks.*

SCALLOP LOBSTER KABOBS

TIME: 30 MINUTES; SERVES 6

1 lb. deep-sea scallops	4 slices bacon
2 cloves garlic, minced	½ cup dry sherry wine
2 ozs. butter, melted	2 tbs. chopped chives
Salt and pepper	Tartar Sauce
½ lb. cooked lobster chunks	

If scallops are extra large, cut in half across grain; wipe with damp cloth. Cut bacon into 2-inch pieces. Blend very little salt, pepper, and minced garlic in ½ melted butter in mixing bowl. Dip scallops and lobster chunks in seasoning.

Have 12 or more skewers ready. Fill skewers by alternating scallop, lobster, and bacon until all ingredients are used; arrange on broiler rack; place in preheated broiling compartment (350° F.) 4 inches below flame; broil 10 minutes, or until bacon is crisp and shellfish is golden brown.

Meanwhile, heat sherry in small saucepan. Remove skewers from broiler; place on preheated platter. Ignite sherry with lighted match; pour sherry over skewers; pour other ounce melted butter over all. Quickly garnish with chopped chives. Serve sizzling hot with tartar sauce.

VARIATION: Use *½ pound large green shrimp* or *1 dozen shucked clams* with this combination.

SCALLOPS OVEN-FRIED
TIME: 30 MINUTES; SERVES 4 TO 6

2 lbs. deep-sea scallops	½ tsp. thyme
2 eggs	¼ tsp. dill
2 tbs. water	1 cup cracker crumbs
Salt and pepper	2 ozs. butter, melted
Buttered toast	4 tsp. chopped chives

Wipe scallops with damp cloth. Break eggs into mixing bowl; beat until foamy; add water; season with salt and pepper to taste, thyme, and dill; mix well.

Dip scallops into egg, then in cracker crumbs. Arrange in shallow baking dish; pour melted butter over scallops; oven-fry or bake in preheated hot oven (450° F.) 20 minutes. Serve piping hot over buttered toast placed on preheated individual plates. Garnish each serving with chopped chives.

VARIATION: Use *small bay scallops* also. Oven time 10 to 15 minutes, depending upon size. Add bacon strips.

SCALLOP AND OYSTER FRY
TIME: 30 MINUTES; SERVES 4

1 lb. scallops	1 pt. peanut oil
1 doz. large oysters, shucked	Pinch of cayenne
2 eggs, beaten	Pinch of nutmeg
1 cup cracker crumbs	Salt and pepper
Tartar Sauce	1 tbs. chopped chives

If scallops are large, cut across grain to about ¾-inch thickness; immerse in salted water 3 minutes, using 1 tablespoon salt to 1 cup cold water; drain; sprinkle them and oysters lightly with salt and pepper.

Break eggs into mixing bowl; beat eggs until foamy; add pinch of cayenne and nutmeg; beat well.

Dip scallops and oysters into egg, then in cracker crumbs.

Heat peanut oil to 400° F. (hot but not smoking). Place single layer scallops in well-oiled frying basket; fry 4 minutes, or until golden brown. Place layer oysters in basket; fry 3 minutes, or until golden brown. Sprinkle each serving with chopped chives and generous helping tartar sauce.

VARIATION: Serve 2 *slices lean, broiled bacon* with each portion if desired.

SCALLOPS PAN-SAUTÉED WITH RHINE WINE

TIME: 20 MINUTES; SERVES 4

1½ lbs. scallops	Pinch of paprika
4 ozs. butter	1 cup dry bread crumbs
¼ tsp. salt	4 slices toast
⅛ tsp. pepper	4 tsp. chopped mint
3 tbs. rhine wine	

Wipe scallops with damp cloth; roll in bread crumbs.

Melt butter in skillet; season with salt, pepper, and paprika. Heat butter but do not allow to smoke. Add scallops; cook 5 minutes only over high flame, turning constantly to brown evenly; remove from butter; add rhine wine; simmer 1 minute, stirring constantly.

Arrange scallops on toast placed on preheated individual plates; pour steaming hot pan sauce over scallops. Garnish each serving with chopped fresh mint or favorite herb.

◄§ SHRIMP   Live shrimp is a pale green or gray and is semi-transparent but turns pink or reddish in cooking. Marketed fresh, frozen, frozen-peeled, and canned. Approximately 16 or 17 of the smaller shrimp are required to make a pound, but there is no waste, since the head and thorax have been removed. The JUMBO SHRIMP average 10 or 12 to a pound. Only the meat in the tail of the shrimp is eaten, and it has a firm white texture which is very sweet and juicy when properly prepared and not overcooked.

SHRIMP LOUISIANA

TIME: 45 MINUTES; SERVES 4

1½ lbs. raw shrimp	⅛ tsp. paprika
2 ozs. butter	½ tsp. salt
2 onions, chopped	⅛ tsp. pepper
2 green peppers, chopped	⅛ tsp. basil
1 clove garlic, minced	4 slices buttered toast
1 pt. fresh stewed tomatoes	

Select fresh shrimp; peel raw; remove dark sand vein from center back; wipe with damp cloth.

Melt butter in saucepan over medium flame; add onions, green peppers, garlic, paprika, salt, pepper, and basil; stir well; cover; simmer 10 minutes, or until green peppers are tender; add stewed tomatoes; cover; simmer 5 minutes; add raw shrimp; mix well; cover; simmer 10 minutes. Serve piping hot on buttered toast on preheated individual plate. Garnish with water cress or preferred green herb.

VARIATION: Use *raw prawns* or *scallops* split in half. Time for prawns same as for shrimp; simmer scallops 15 minutes.

SHRIMP AND OLIVE CASSEROLE
TIME: 30 MINUTES; SERVES 4 TO 6

1½ lbs. raw shrimp	¾ cup sliced stuffed olives
3 ozs. butter	1 cup chopped celery
3 tbs. flour	⅛ tsp. basil
1½ cups rich milk	⅛ tsp. pepper
¼ tsp. Worcestershire sauce	1 cup bread crumbs
Water cress	8 whole stuffed olives

Select fresh shrimp; peel raw; remove dark sand veins.

Melt 2 ounces butter in saucepan over medium flame; gradually add flour; blend well; slowly pour in milk, stirring constantly. When smooth, add Worcestershire sauce, celery, basil, and pepper; cook 5 minutes, stirring constantly; add shrimp; cook 2 minutes longer; add chopped olives. Place thin layer bread crumbs in casserole; alternate shrimp mixture with layers of bread crumbs until all ingredients are used. Save sufficient crumbs to cover top; dot with other ounce butter; bake in preheated hot oven (400° F.) 12 minutes, or until golden brown. Serve piping hot from casserole at table. Garnish each serving with water cress and 2 whole stuffed olives.

VARIATION: Use *raw clams, oysters,* or *prawns.*

SHRIMP TANGY BOILED
TIME: 20 MINUTES; SERVES 4

1½ lbs. raw shrimp	½ cup dry sauterne wine
1 stalk celery, with leaves	½ cup water
1 bay leaf	1 tsp. salt
4 peppercorns	1 scallion

Select fresh shrimp; peel raw; remove dark sand vein from center back; wipe with damp cloth.

Pour wine and water into saucepan over medium flame; add celery, bay leaf, peppercorns, salt, and scallion; cover; simmer gently 10 minutes; add shrimp; cover; simmer 5 minutes more. (Count cooking time after stock returns to boiling.) Remove from flame; strain stock and reserve for use in making fish sauces. Place cooked shrimp in jar; cover with stock; store in refrigerator until ready to use.

SHRIMP RAMEKINS
TIME: 45 MINUTES; SERVES 4 TO 6

1 lb. raw shrimp	2 tbs. chili sauce
3 ozs. butter	2 egg yolks, well beaten
1 tbs. flour	½ tsp. salt
1 tbs. cream	⅛ tsp. cayenne
1 cup shrimp stock	2 tsp. grated onion
Parsley sprigs	4 tbs. cracker crumbs

Select fresh shrimp; clean, boil, and prepare as for "Shrimp Tangy Boiled" (pages 170-71).

Melt butter in saucepan over medium flame; gradually stir in flour; blend well; add cream and shrimp stock slowly; continue stirring; cook 5 minutes; remove from heat; cool 5 minutes. Gradually stir in egg yolks, chili sauce, salt, cayenne, and grated onion; mix well; add shrimp; stir again.

Fill 4 to 6 ramekins with shrimp mixture; top each with 1 tablespoon crumbs; dot each with butter; place in preheated hot oven (400 F.); bake 5 minutes, or until top is brown. Serve piping hot. Garnish each ramekin with parsley sprig.

VARIATION: Use raw prawns, or cooked crab or lobster meat baked in casserole or ramekins.

SHRIMP SPICY BOILED
TIME: 20 MINUTES; SERVES 4

1½ lbs. raw shrimp	12 cloves
1 qt. water	12 whole allspice
2 tbs. lemon juice	2 tbs. chopped chives
2 tbs. wine vinegar	6 peppercorns
4 sprigs fresh thyme	1 fresh red pepper
4 sprigs parsley	1 small onion
2 tsp. salt	1 stalk celery, with leaves

Select fresh shrimp; peel raw; remove dark sand vein from center back; wipe with damp cloth.

Pour water into large saucepan over medium flame; add all seasonings; cover, simmer 15 minutes; add shrimp; cover, simmer 5 minutes more (count cooking time after liquid returns to boiling). Remove from flame; strain stock. Place cooked shrimp in jar; cover with stock; store in refrigerator until ready to use.

VARIATION: Use *prawns.*

∾§ SNAILS   These mollusks live in single well-developed spiral shells into which they can withdraw for protection. Highly esteemed as a food delicacy, especially in France, Switzerland, Italy, and Japan. Americans are learning to use these mollusks more and more. Baked in mussel shells or stuffed with anchovies, snails are a most unusual treat. The fresh snails in our retail markets rarely measure more than 1 inch or 1½ inches in diameter; but tropical snails grow to 6 inches and may weigh more than a pound.

SNAILS PROVENÇALE
TIME: 1 HOUR; SERVES 6

2 *lbs. snails*	1 *medium onion, minced*
3 *cups hot water*	8 *fillets of anchovy*
2 *tsp. salt*	2 *tbs. chopped fresh spinach*
1 *bay leaf*	2 *cloves garlic, minced*
4 *peppercorns*	4 *tbs. grated Gruyère cheese*
1 *whole clove*	2 *tbs. chopped parsley*
1 *small onion, extra*	2 *ozs. butter, extra*
2 *ozs. butter*	6 *slices toast*
½ *cup dry sauterne wine*	

Select large fresh snails; place in large deep kettle; cover with cold water. Rub with salt inside rim of kettle just below edge to prevent snails coming out of water. Soak ½ hour. Wash thoroughly in several waters; drain well. Use only snails with heads out of shells.

Pour 3 cups hot water in large kettle over medium flame; add salt, bay leaf, peppercorns, clove, onion, and snails; boil 5 minutes; remove from flame. Take snails from shells, using small oyster fork or nutpick. Cut off tip of head and small black part at end of snail; set snails aside.

In separate saucepan melt 2 ounces butter; add minced onion; sauté over medium flame 3 minutes, or until onion is golden brown; add sauterne wine, fillets of anchovy, fresh spinach, and garlic; sauté 15 minutes more; add snails, parsley, and cheese; sauté 10 minutes, or until sauce is reduced to medium thickness or desired consistency. Serve piping hot over toast placed on preheated individual plates; place dot of butter in center of each serving. If desired, garnish with favorite green herb.

SNAILS À LA SUISSE

TIME: 1½ HOURS; SERVES 4 TO 6

2 lbs. snails
3 cups hot water
2 tsp. salt
1 bay leaf
4 peppercorns
1 whole clove
1 small onion, whole
1 clove garlic, minced
¼ cup dry sauterne wine
½ onion, minced, extra
¼ lb. mushrooms, diced
3 tbs. olive oil
2 sprigs parsley, minced
⅛ tsp. rosemary
Salt and pepper
6 slices toast

Select large fresh snails; place in large deep kettle; cover with cold water. Rub with salt inside rim of kettle just below edge to prevent snails coming out of water. Soak ½ hour. Wash thoroughly in several waters; drain well. Use only snails with heads out of shells.

Pour 3 cups hot water in large pot over medium flame; add salt, bay leaf, peppercorns, clove, whole onion, and snails; boil 5 minutes; remove from flame. Take snails from shells, using small oyster fork or nutpick. Cut off tip of head and small black part at end of snail; set snails aside.

Pour 1 tablespoon olive oil in small saucepan over medium flame; add mushrooms; sauté 10 minutes. Meanwhile, pour 2 tablespoons olive oil in separate saucepan over medium flame; add garlic, minced onion, parsley, rosemary, salt and pepper to taste; sauté 5 minutes, or until onion is golden brown; add snails and sautéed mushrooms; simmer gently 45 minutes; add sauterne wine; simmer 5 minutes. Serve piping hot over toast placed on preheated individual plates. Sprinkle each serving with chopped green herb.

SNAILS STUFFED WITH ANCHOVIES

TIME: 1½ HOURS; SERVES 6

2 lbs. snails
3 cups hot water
2 tsp. salt
1 bay leaf
4 peppercorns
1 whole clove
1 small onion
1 cup dry bread crumbs
6 fillets of anchovy, minced
1 egg, beaten
2 tsp. chopped chives
2 tsp. minced parsley
4 ozs. butter
⅛ tsp. pepper
1 cup Béchamel Sauce
    (pages 81-82)
6 tsp. minced parsley, extra

Select large fresh snails; place in large kettle; cover with cold water. Rub rim of salt inside kettle just below edge to prevent snails coming out of water. Soak for ½ hour. Wash thoroughly in several waters; drain well. Use only snails with heads out of shells.

Pour 3 cups hot water in large pot over medium flame; add salt, bay leaf, peppercorns, clove, onion, and snails; boil 5 minutes; remove from flame. Take snails from shells, using small oyster fork or nutpick. Cut off tip of head and small black part at end of snail; chop snails fine; set aside. Wash shells thoroughly in boiling water; set shells upside down to drain.

In large mixing bowl blend well bread crumbs, anchovies, egg, chives, parsley, 2 ounces butter, and pepper. Fill each shell with mixture. Melt other 2 ounces butter in large frying pan over medium flame. Place filled shells, with open side down, in pan; fry 3 minutes, or until golden brown.

Place 1 teaspoon hot Béchamel Sauce on side of preheated individual plate. Garnish sauce with 1 teaspoon minced parsley. Serve piping hot snails at side of plate. To eat, remove stuffing with small oyster fork then dip in Béchamel Sauce.

VARIATION: *Chill on ice; serve with mayonnaise.*

◆§ TERRAPINS AND TURTLES   The common SNAPPING TURTLE or SNAPPER is the species most frequently sold in our retail markets, and ranges from 4 to 25 pounds. The alligator snapping turtle is usually marketed in New Orleans and Saint Louis. It often attains a weight of 200 pounds. Live snapping turtles are usually butchered immediately and the meat frozen for fall and winter use.

Other fresh-water turtles used for food are the Mississippi turtle, the Pacific pond turtle, the Mobile and Suwanee turtle, as well as the red-bellied, yellow-bellied, and chicken turtle.

The DIAMOND-BACK TERRAPIN lives in the salt marshes along the Atlantic and Gulf coasts from Florida to North Carolina. There it merges into a Northern variety found as far north as Buzzards Bay. Highly valued as food, its exotic flavor is known to gourmets the world over. If prepared turtle meat is not available, it is quite easy to dress a live turtle. Turtle fishermen say that it takes less time than to kill, pluck, and dress a chicken (*see* pages 108-9).

TERRAPIN CREAMED WITH SHERRY
TIME: 45 MINUTES; SERVES 6 TO 8

1 qt. terrapin meat, cubed	¾ cup sherry wine
¼ lb. butter	2 cups rich cream
8 hard-boiled egg yolks	Salt to taste
Pinch of cayenne	Hot croutons

Purchase prepared cooked terrapin meat, otherwise clean and dress live terrapin as shown on pages 108-9. Boil terrapin meat 20 minutes, or until tender, in Fish Stock.

Soften butter at room temperature; grate egg yolks through fine sieve; blend with softened butter. Pass this mixture through fine sieve; set mixture aside.

Pour cream into large saucepan over medium flame; add terrapin meat; stir constantly and boil 5 minutes; gradually add prepared butter-and-egg mixture; stir well; simmer gently 10 minutes; stir occasionally to prevent sticking; season with salt to taste; add pinch of cayenne; blend well; add sherry wine; heat thoroughly, stirring constantly. Serve piping hot over croutons placed in preheated individual plates. Garnish lightly with minced parsley if desired.

VARIATION: Use *madeira wine* instead of sherry.

TERRAPIN MADEIRA
TIME: 2 HOURS; SERVES 4 TO 6

2 lbs. terrapin meat	Salt and pepper
4 ozs. butter	6 sprigs parsley
Madeira Sauce (See page 85).	

Sauce should be prepared in advance to save time.

Select terrapin meat prepared in steak form; wipe with damp cloth. Melt butter in skillet over medium flame; when very hot, fry terrapin 20 minutes, or until tender and brown; season to taste with salt and pepper. Serve piping hot with generous helping Madeira Sauce.

TURTLE BOURGEOISE
TIME: 45 MINUTES; SERVES 4 TO 6

2 lbs. snapping turtle meat	1 clove garlic, minced
1 onion, minced	1 sprig thyme, minced
1 tbs. butter	1 cup water
1 tbs. flour	Salt and pepper
1 bay leaf	6 slices buttered toast
½ cup sherry wine	

Have turtle meat cut into 1-inch cubes. Melt butter in saucepan over medium flame; add onion; sauté 3 minutes, or until golden brown; gradually stir in flour; when smooth, add garlic, thyme, water, and bay leaf; blend well; add turtle meat and sherry wine, salt and pepper to taste; cover; simmer gently over medium flame ½ hour, or until turtle meat is tender. Serve piping hot over buttered toast placed on preheated individual plates.

VARIATION: Use *any variety fresh-water turtle*.

TURTLE STEAK ROSEMARY
TIME: 30 MINUTES; MARINATE 24 HOURS; SERVES 4 TO 6

2 *lbs. snapping turtle steak*	1 *tsp. rosemary*
2 *qts. water*	4 *ozs. butter*
2 *tbs. salt*	½ *cup flour*
Pepper	*Lemon wedges*

Select turtle meat prepared in steak form. Place cold water in large mixing bowl; add salt. Place turtle steaks in solution and marinate overnight. Remove turtle; wipe with damp cloth; dip in flour. Melt butter in skillet over high flame; when very hot, sear steaks quickly on both sides; sprinkle with rosemary; lower flame to medium, fry slowly 20 minutes, or until tender and golden brown. If necessary, add more butter. Sprinkle each serving very lightly with pepper if desired. Garnish with lemon wedges.

~~~~~~~~~~~~~~~~~~~~~~~~~~~~~~~~~~~~~

Salad Bowls

CALIFORNIA SHELLFISH SALAD

TIME: 30 MINUTES; SERVES 4

½ lb. fresh crab flakes	12 grapefruit sections
½ lb. lobster meat	1 avocado
½ bunch water cress	¼ cup French dressing
12 lettuce leaves	Paprika

Remove all shell particles from shellfish; set aside. Arrange lettuce and water cress on each prechilled plate. Cut avocado in crescent-shaped slices. Skin grapefruit or use canned grapefruit sections. Arrange alternate slices of avocado with grapefruit sections around edge of plate.

In separate bowl mix crab flakes and lobster meat; serve in center of each salad plate; pour French dressing lightly over salad; sprinkle with paprika. Serve very cold.

VARIATION: *Crab flakes only or lobster may be used.*

SHELLFISH COMBINATION SALAD BOWL

TIME: 45 MINUTES; SERVES 6 TO 8

½ lb. crab meat, chunks	1 avocado
½ lb. lobster meat, chunks	1 firm tomato, diced
½ lb. cooked shrimp	1 cucumber, cubed
2 tbs. fresh chopped dill	2 hard-boiled eggs, quartered
6 radishes	Water cress
Crisp lettuce leaves	French dressing

Purchase freshly cooked shellfish at market to save time (or use canned crab, lobster, and shrimp). Remove all shell particles from crab and lobster; cut shrimp in half lengthwise. In large bowl mix crab, lobster, and shrimp.

Line prechilled salad bowl with crisp lettuce leaves; add

chilled tomato, cucumber, and water cress; toss lightly; add mixed shellfish; pour in French dressing; toss lightly.

Border salad bowl with alternate slices of avocado, quartered eggs, and radishes; sprinkle lightly with chopped dill. Serve immediately.

CRAB IN AVOCADO BOATS

TIME: 15 MINUTES; CHILL 20 MINUTES; SERVES 4

½ lb. fresh crab meat	2 avocados
Juice of 1 lemon	8 stuffed green olives
3 stalks celery, chopped	Crisp lettuce leaves
½ tsp. celery salt	French dressing

Select firm, ripe avocados; cut in half lengthwise; sprinkle outside and inside with lemon juice and little salt to prevent avocado turning brown.

In large mixing bowl blend well crab flakes, celery, and celery salt. Fill avocado halves with crab mixture. Cover with wax paper and chill on ice. When ready to serve, place avocado boats on crisp lettuce leaves arranged on salad plates. Pour French dressing over crab mixture. Garnish with parsley and stuffed olives.

VARIATION: Use *cooked lobster meat* or *shrimp*.

CRAB MEAT MARINATED SUPRÊME

TIME: 30 MINUTES; MARINATE 3 HOURS; SERVES 4 TO 6

1 lb. crab meat	2 cups chopped celery
½ cup olive oil	½ cup mayonnaise
½ cup white wine vinegar	12 ripe olives
¼ tsp. tabasco sauce	1 green pepper, cut in rings
⅛ tsp. salt	Water cress
⅛ tsp. thyme	Crisp lettuce leaves

Purchase cooked crab meat in chunks; remove all shell particles; place in large mixing bowl with cover; set aside.

Blend well olive oil, wine vinegar, tabasco sauce, salt, and thyme. Pour blended liquid over crab meat chunks; cover; stand in cool but not cold place; allow to marinate 3 hours.

When ready to use, drain crab flakes; blend with chopped celery and mayonnaise sufficient to coat all the pieces.

Arrange crisp lettuce leaves on prechilled individual plates; pile generous serving in center of leaves; garnish with ripe olives, green pepper rings, and water cress. Serve very cold.

VARIATION: Use *cooked lobster meat in chunks.*

LOBSTER SALAD PLAIN

TIME: 15 MINUTES; SERVES 4

1 lb. lobster meat	1 tbs. wine vinegar
4 tbs. olive oil	8 crisp lettuce leaves
1 lemon, quartered	Salt and pepper

Blend olive oil, vinegar, salt and pepper to taste in small bowl.

Arrange lettuce leaves on prechilled salad plates. Place lobster meat in center. When ready to serve, pour blended dressing over it; garnish with lemon wedge.

VARIATION: Instead of blended dressing use *4 teaspoons mayonnaise mixed with 1 teaspoon horse-radish.*

SHRIMP AND ANCHOVY TOMATO CUPS

TIME: 30 MINUTES; SERVES 6

1 cup cooked shrimp	6 firm tomatoes
6 anchovy fillets, minced	2 stalks celery, chopped
12 stuffed green olives, chopped	6 tsp. mayonnaise
	Crisp lettuce leaves

Select firm, round tomatoes; hollow out stem ends to form round cup; place in refrigerator to chill. Meanwhile, chop cooked shrimp into small pieces; mince anchovy fillets; chop olives and celery. In mixing bowl blend shrimp, anchovies, olives, and celery. Fill tomato cups with shrimp mixture; arrange on crisp lettuce leaves; garnish each tomato cup with mayonnaise.

VARIATION: Use *1 cup cooked lobster meat, prawns, crab flakes,* or *crayfish* instead of shrimp. Serve well chilled.

SHRIMP MAYTIME SPECIAL

TIME: 30 MINUTES; SERVES 4 TO 6

1 lb. cooked shrimp	½ cucumber, diced
8 radishes, sliced	1 green pepper, cut in rings
6 stuffed green olives, sliced	12 crisp lettuce leaves
½ tsp. rosemary	Water cress
2 firm tomatoes, cubed	French dressing
1 cup chopped celery	

Prepare shrimp as shown on pages 107-8. (Or use canned shrimp.) Line prechilled salad bowl with lettuce leaves; add

olives and all chilled vegetables except pepper rings; add
chilled shrimp; toss all lightly; add French dressing; toss
lightly again. Sprinkle salad mixture lightly with finely
crushed rosemary; garnish with green pepper rings.

VARIATION: Use *any shellfish, freshly cooked or canned*

Salad Molds

LOBSTER AND CELERY FAVORITE

TIME: 30 MINUTES; CHILL 3 HOURS; SERVES 4 TO 6

½ lb. cooked lobster meat, chunks	1 tbs. gelatine
	¼ cup cold water
2 cups tomato juice	1 tbs. lemon juice
¼ tsp. salt	Water cress
⅛ tsp. cayenne	Crisp lettuce leaves
1 bay leaf	Mayonnaise
1 slice onion	1 cup chopped celery

Purchase cooked lobster meat at market to save time. (Or
boil and prepare lobster as shown on page 105.) Cut chunks
into cubes; set aside.

Pour tomato juice in small saucepan; add salt, cayenne,
bay leaf, and onion; heat over low flame; simmer gently 10
minutes; add lemon juice; strain liquid through fine sieve.

Soften gelatine in cold water; add to strained seasoned
tomato liquid; allow to cool 1 hour, or until slightly thick;
add chopped celery and lobster pieces. Pour mixture into
ring mold which has been chilled in cold water; place in
refrigerator; chill 2 hours, or until firm.

Unmold salad on crisp lettuce leaves. Garnish with water
cress. Serve with generous helping of mayonnaise or Russian
Dressing. VARIATION: Use any preferred cooked shellfish.

LOBSTER MOLD FANTASTIC

TIME: 45 MINUTES; CHILL 3 HOURS; SERVES 6 TO 8

½ lb. cooked lobster meat	1 small cucumber, diced
1 tbs. gelatine	½ cup radishes, sliced
½ cup of cold water	1 stalk celery, chopped
1 tsp. sugar	½ tsp. celery seed
¼ cup white wine vinegar	Romaine lettuce
1 cup hot water	6 stuffed green olives
6 ripe olives	Mayonnaise
1 green pepper, chopped	

Purchase cooked lobster meat in chunks to save time. (Or boil and prepare lobster as shown on page 105.)

Soften gelatine in cold water in large mixing bowl; add sugar, wine vinegar, and hot water; blend well; chill 1 hour, or until slightly thick; add green pepper, cucumber, radishes, celery, and celery seed; mix well; add lobster pieces. Pour into mold which has been chilled in cold water; chill 2 hours, or until firm. Unmold on crisp romaine lettuce leaves; garnish with ripe and stuffed green olives. Serve very cold with generous helping of mayonnaise.

VARIATION: Use any preferred cooked shellfish.

CRAYFISH TOMATO CIRCLE

TIME: 30 MINUTES; CHILL 2 HOURS; SERVES 4 TO 6

2 crayfish or spiny lobsters	⅛ tsp. pepper
¼ onion, minced	⅛ tsp. thyme
2 stalks celery, minced	1 tbs. unflavored gelatine
1 tbs. minced parsley	¼ cup cold water
2 tbs. sugar	1 tbs. lemon juice
½ tsp. salt	Fresh mint sprigs
Crisp lettuce leaves	6 tbs. mayonnaise
1 pt. tomato juice	

Purchase crayfish or spiny lobster; wash well; place in saucepan over medium flame; cover with unsalted boiling water; cook 10 minutes; remove from water; peel and cut meat into small cubes; set aside.

Pour tomato juice into saucepan over medium flame; add onion, celery, parsley, sugar, salt, pepper, and thyme; simmer gently over low flame 5 minutes. Soften gelatine in cold water; add to simmering liquid; blend well; remove from heat; chill slightly; add lemon juice. If more tangy flavor is desired, add ½ teaspoon Worcestershire sauce.

Strain liquid through colander into bowl; add crayfish pieces to liquid. Pour into circle mold which has been chilled in cold water; place in refrigerator; chill until firm.

Unmold on prechilled platter garnished with lettuce leaves and sprigs of fresh mint. Serve very cold with generous helping mayonnaise or preferred dressing.

VARIATION: Use 1 pound cooked lobster meat.

SHRIMP ICED PERFECTION

TIME: 45 MINUTES; CHILL 2 HOURS; SERVES 4 TO 6

1 lb. cooked shrimp
1 tbs. unflavored gelatine
¼ cup cold water
¼ cup lemon juice
2 cups hot tomato juice
¼ tsp. salt
¼ tsp. sugar
6 stuffed green olives, sliced

1 pimiento, chopped
½ cup shredded cabbage
½ tsp. Worcestershire sauce
Parsley sprigs
Radish buds
Crisp lettuce leaves
Mayonnaise

Purchase cooked shrimp, or boil and prepare as shown on pages 107-8. Leave shrimp whole; set aside.

Soften gelatine with cold water and lemon juice; dissolve in hot tomato juice; add salt, sugar, and Worcestershire sauce; chill 1 hour, or until slightly thick; add shrimp, green olives, pimiento, and shredded cabbage to thickened gelatine. Pour mixture into mold which has been chilled in cold water; chill in refrigerator 2 hours, or until firm.

Unmold on crisp lettuce leaves. Garnish with radish buds and parsley sprigs. Serve with generous helping of mayonnaise.

VARIATION: Use any preferred cooked shellfish.

~~~~~~

◄§ HOW TO PREPARE CANAPÉS   Prepare almost at the split second they are to be served. The flavor, the appearance, and the eating enjoyment of the most expertly and daintily designed little tidbits can be utterly wrecked when allowed to stand before serving.

Canapé spreads may be prepared in advance, but the finishing touches of actual spreading and broiling should be left till the last moment. The spreads which are to be served cold may be mixed, placed in little bowls, and chilled in the refrigerator until serving time.

When bread is used instead of toast, small discs, diamonds, or half circles of white, brown, or pumpernickel may be cut ahead of time. These are easily kept fresh by covering with a slightly dampened napkin. They will keep fresh for several hours if placed in the refrigerator. When almost ready to serve, take the bread from the refrigerator and spread the canapés.

Spreads which are to be oven-toasted or broiled may also be prepared in advance, but do not chill; allow these to stand at room temperature. If you are planning on broiling a small oyster tipped with bacon, it's so quick and easy when the oysters have been drained and the little squares of bacon neatly arranged ahead of time.

You can acquire real skill in making a great variety of mouth-watering and tempting canapés; it can be fun and easy if you remember:

1. Much time is needed; be sure to allow for it.

2. Prepare the working equipment.

3. *Canapé cutters* differently shaped, or very small cookie cutters for the breads.

4. A *pastry bag* that will squeeze out professional-looking decorations of the soft spreads.

5. Plenty of *colored toothpicks* as fasteners for rolled canapés.

6. Whenever bread is used, the daintier the shape and size the more appetizing the canapé.

7. Arrange bread shapes, crackers, or toast diamonds on broiler rack ready to be placed in broiling compartment 2 or 3 minutes before canapés are to be served. Result? Piping hot, appetizing, and tempting tidbits that sizzle while being served.

8. *Never serve a soggy canapé.*

9. *Never serve a drippy canapé.*

10. Don't be afraid to experiment with combinations.

11. Prepare both mild and highly seasoned canapés.

12. Always have plenty of gaily-colored toothpicks near the stuffed olives and pickles for easy handling; and an extra napkin or two when there are buttery canapés.

13. Always heat crackers and potato chips.

14. Always have a special favorite of your own in reserve for that unexpected guest or the unexpected appetite; or plenty of toasted crackers and cheese; or hot potato chips.

CRAB FLAKES AND RIPE OLIVES
1 cup crab flakes, minced   *6 ripe olives, minced*
½ tsp. *Worcestershire sauce*

Mix minced crab flakes with olives and Worcestershire sauce. Spread mixture on toast diamonds. Broil canapés in preheated broiling compartment 2 minutes 2 inches below flame. Serve piping hot. Approximate yield: 2 dozen canapés.

OTHER SUGGESTED COMBINATIONS: *Crab Flakes with Anchovy Fillet.* Blend 1 teaspoon lemon juice with minced

crab flakes; arrange on toast diamonds; top with ½ anchovy fillet. Follow recipe.

Crab Flakes with Grated Egg Yolk and Caper Center. Mince crab flakes; arrange on toast disks; sprinkle with grated egg yolk; place 1 caper in center. Follow recipe.

Crab Flakes with Minced Chives and Pimiento Strips. Mix crab flakes with 2 teaspoons minced chives. Arrange mixture on toast or crackers; decorate with crisscross pimiento strips. Follow recipe.

Crab Flakes with Stuffed Green Olives. Mix minced crab flakes with 6 minced olives. Arrange mixture on toast disks; top with a ring slice of stuffed green olive. Follow recipe.

VARIATION: *2 teaspoons mayonnaise may be blended with crab flakes in all these suggested combinations.*

CRAB FLAKE CANAPÉS ONE WORLD

TIME: 1 HOUR

1 cup crab flakes, minced	2 tbs. sherry wine
1 tbs. melted butter	½ cup dry bread crumbs
1 tbs. chopped chives	½ tsp. Worcestershire sauce
2½ tbs. flour	Salt and cayenne
½ cup heavy cream	2 cups peanut oil

Melt butter in saucepan over medium flame; gradually stir in flour; when very smooth, add cream, stirring constantly; cook 5 minutes, or until sauce thickens; add chopped chives and minced crab; mix well; add Worcestershire sauce, salt and cayenne to taste. Remove mixture from heat.

Spread bread crumbs on mixing board. When crab mixture is cool enough to handle, drop by teaspoonfuls into bread crumbs; shape into tiny "one-world" balls.

Pour peanut oil into kettle; heat to 400° F. Place crab balls in frying basket (1 layer at a time); fry 2 minutes only until golden brown. Drain quickly on absorbent paper. Serve immediately on colored toothpick. Approximate yield: 3 dozen.

VARIATION: *Cooked, minced lobster meat, prawns, or shrimp, also raw, minced clams, oysters, or mussels.*

LOBSTER TIDBIT

TIME: 30 MINUTES

2 cups lobster meat	4 tbs. minced fresh dill
½ cup butter, melted	½ tsp. paprika

Use freshly cooked lobster meat; cut into tidbit chunks; dip in melted butter; sprinkle with paprika; arrange in shallow baking dish; place in preheated hot broiling compartment (500° F.); broil 2 minutes only.

Remove from oven. Quickly impale each piece of lobster on colored toothpick. Dip tidbit in minced dill. Serve immediately.

VARIATION: Dip in *minced parsley or chives*. Use cooked *crab meat, split prawns or shrimps*.

MUSSEL BACON TIDBITS
TIME: 45 MINUTES

2 cups raw mussel meats	6 slices bacon
Paprika to taste	2 tsp. celery seed

Select large mussels; clean and prepare as for steaming but do not steam (pages 106-7). Take meats from shells; remove dark, hairy beards; set raw mussel meats aside.

Cut bacon into strips ½ inch wide and 2 inches long. Place one mussel meat on each strip; roll together and fasten with colored toothpick; sprinkle lightly with paprika.

Arrange rolls in shallow baking pan; place in preheated hot broiling compartment (450° F.); broil 2 minutes, or until bacon is crisp and edges of mussel begin to curl.

Remove from oven; quickly dip lightly in celery seed. Serve immediately.

VARIATION: Use *whole cooked shrimp or prawns; also crab or lobster chunks*. Broil only 2 minutes, and serve sizzling hot.

SHRIMP BUTTER CANAPÉS
TIME: 40 MINUTES

¼ lb. cooked shrimp	¼ lb. butter, softened
Salt	Cayenne pepper

Chop freshly cooked shrimp into very small pieces, then pound with pestle until mixture is creamy; add equal amount of softened butter; blend into smooth paste; add salt and cayenne to taste.

Spread shrimp butter on tiny diamonds *hot* toast moment before serving. Serve immediately.

(Shrimp butter may be prepared ahead of time and kept in tightly covered jar in refrigerator until ready to use.)

VARIATION: Use *cooked prawns* instead of shrimp.

18. Shellfish Sauces and Stuffings

~~~~~~

Cold Sauces

COCKTAIL SAUCE
TIME: 10 MINUTES; CHILL 30 MINUTES; SERVES 4

½ cup tomato catsup   1 tbs. grated horse-radish
6 tbs. lemon juice   3 drops tabasco sauce
⅛ tsp. salt   ½ tsp. celery salt

Blend all ingredients in small mixing bowl; chill in refrigerator 30 minutes or more.
Serve with clams or oysters on half shell.

COCKTAIL SAUCE SUPRÉME: See page 79.

COOKED CHILLED CUCUMBER SAUCE: See p. 79.

MAYONNAISE CAPER SAUCE: See page 143.

TARTAR SAUCE: See page 143.

Hot Sauces

BASIC WHITE SAUCE: See page 81.

BÉCHAMEL SAUCE: See pages 81-82.

CLAM SAUCE AU LAIT
TIME: 20 MINUTES; SERVES 4 TO 6

½ cup minced clams   1 cup rich milk
2 ozs. butter   Pinch of nutmeg
¼ tsp. salt   ⅛ tsp. pepper
2 tbs. flour   Pinch of paprika

Melt butter in top section double boiler placed in lower section half filled with boiling water; gradually add flour, stirring constantly. When smooth, add salt, pepper, nutmeg, and paprika; slowly pour in cold milk. Stir continually until smooth; and begins to thicken; add minced clams; heat 5 min. Serve piping hot over steamed, boiled, or baked fish.

VARIATION: Use ½ cup minced oysters, lobster, mussels, prawns, shrimp, or crayfish instead of clams. Also for richer Golden Clam Sauce, remove sauce from heat just before serving; fold in 1 well-beaten egg; stir briskly until hot sauce absorbs and cooks egg. Garnish with fresh mint or dill.

HOLLANDAISE SAUCE. See page 141.

LOBSTER CORAL SAUCE
TIME: 45 MINUTES; SERVES 4 TO 6

Shells of 2 lobsters	1 qt. chicken broth
¼ lb. butter	Juice of 1 lemon
½ onion, minced	2 egg yolks, beaten
½ carrot, minced	½ cup sherry wine
Coral of 1 or 2 lobsters	

Use the shells of lobsters which have been boiled. Pound the shells with a wooden mallet until they are pulverized; add the coral.

Place pulverized shells, coral, butter, onion, and carrot in saucepan over medium flame; cover; simmer gently 20 minutes; add chicken broth, lemon juice, and sherry wine; simmer 3 minutes, or until hot but not boiling. Remove sauce from flame; strain through fine sieve; gradually stir in beaten egg yolks; return to flame; heat carefully 2 minutes, stirring gently. Serve piping hot oven baked fish or shellfish.

VARIATION: Pulverized shell mixture may be added to Basic White Sauce (page 81) instead of using chicken broth, but omit egg yolks, simply strain seasoning and add.

NEWBURG SAUCE FOR LOBSTER NEWBURG
TIME: 10 MINUTES; SERVES 6

3 tbs. butter	4 tbs. sherry wine
3 tsp. flour	1½ cups light cream
¼ tsp. dry mustard	2 egg yolks, beaten
¼ tsp. salt	2 drops tabasco sauce
⅛ tsp. pepper	Cayenne

Melt butter in top section of double boiler placed in lower section half filled with boiling water; gradually add flour; blend well; add seasonings; cook over medium flame 2 minutes; gradually pour in cream, stirring constantly; when well blended, remove from flame; cool 5 minutes. Meanwhile, break egg yolks into large mixing bowl; beat until foamy; pour cooled sauce over egg yolks, stirring constantly.

Return mixture to top section double boiler; add sherry wine; heat 1 minute. Serve piping hot with shellfish added.

SAUCE PIQUANTE FRANÇAISE
TIME: 20 MINUTES; SERVES 4 TO 6

2 cups melted butter
1 tbs. tarragon vinegar
1 tbs. lemon juice
¼ tsp. onion salt
⅛ tsp. cayenne

2 tbs. chopped stuffed green olives
2 tbs. chopped sour gherkins
2 tbs. capers, drained

Melt butter in saucepan over low flame; add all seasonings and ingredients; mix thoroughly; heat well.

Serve hot sauce over boiled, baked, or broiled fish fillets.

VARIATION: *Flavor may be varied by using white wine vinegar instead of tarragon and ripe olives instead of green.*

Stuffings

CLAM-BREAD STUFFING
TIME: 20 MINUTES; FILLS 4-LB. FISH

1 pt. small clams, in liquor
2 ozs. butter
1 small onion, minced
½ tsp. thyme
¼ tsp. basil

2½ cups dry bread crumbs
1 egg
½ tsp. salt
⅛ tsp. pepper
Paprika

Drain clams; remove small dark mass; mince fine; set aside; save clam liquor.

Melt butter in saucepan over medium flame; add onion, thyme, basil, salt, pepper, and pinch of paprika. Sauté onion 3 minutes, or until golden brown; set aside.

Break egg into large mixing bowl; beat well; add bread crumbs and seasoned, sautéed onion; mix thoroughly; add minced clams; blend lightly and well. (If moister stuffing is desired, add small quantity clam liquor.)

For smaller fish, use ½ amounts given.

VARIATION: *Crab Meat Stuffing.* Omit clams; use 1 cup cooked crab meat flakes; follow recipe; add 2 tablespoons milk to moisten slightly.

Crayfish Stuffing. Omit clams; use 1 cup cooked crayfish flakes; follow recipe. (If moister stuffing is desired, add 2 tablespoons milk.)

Lobster Stuffing. Omit clams; use 1 cup cooked lobster meat, minced; follow recipe. (If moister stuffing is desired, add 2 tablespoons milk.)

Oyster Stuffing. Omit clams; use 1 pint oysters in liquor; follow recipe.

Prawn Stuffing. Omit clams; use 1 cup cooked prawns; minced; follow recipe. Variation for prawn stuffing: *Use raw, peeled prawns; add sufficient milk to make stuffing slightly moist.*

Shrimp Stuffing. Omit clams; use 1 cup raw, peeled, minced shrimp; follow recipe; add sufficient milk to make stuffing slightly moist.

Spiny Lobster Stuffing. Omit clams; use 1 cup cooked spiny lobster meat, minced; follow recipe; add sufficient milk to make stuffing slightly moist. *Sherry wine* may be used instead of milk.

CRAB MEAT WINE STUFFING

TIME: 20 MINUTES; FILLS 4-LB. FISH

1 *cup cooked crab meat*	¼ *tsp. salt*
2 *ozs. butter*	⅛ *tsp. pepper*
½ *small onion, minced*	1 *tbs. chopped parsley*
½ *tsp. basil*	1 *stalk celery, chopped*
⅛ *tsp. rosemary*	2 *cups cracker crumbs*
¼ *cup rhine wine*	

Melt butter in saucepan over medium flame; add onion, basil, rosemary, salt, pepper, and celery; sauté gently 5 minutes, or until onion is golden brown. (Celery need not be soft.) Remove from heat.

Place cracker crumbs in large mixing bowl; add parsley and sautéed seasonings; blend well; add crab meat; mix thoroughly. Add enough rhine wine to moisten stuffing slightly.

For smaller fish, use ½ amounts given here.

VARIATION: *Crayfish or Lobster Wine Stuffing.* Omit

crab meat; follow recipe; use 1 cup cooked crayfish or lobster meat, minced.

Prawn or Shrimp Wine Stuffing. Omit crab meat; follow recipe; use 1 cup raw, peeled, minced prawn or shrimp.

Wine Stuffing with a favorite shellfish is a delicious stuffing for all fat fish, such as *lake herring, bluefish, butterfish, mackerel,* and *porgy,* (or *scup*).

LOBSTER HERB STUFFING

TIME: 30 MINUTES FILLS 4 OR 5-LB. FISH

1 cup cooked lobster meat	½ clove garlic, minced
3 ozs. butter	½ tsp. salt
2 shallots, minced	⅛ tsp. pepper
¼ tsp. sage	Paprika
¼ tsp. thyme	1 egg, well beaten
1 stalk celery, minced	3 cups dry bread crumbs
¼ cup sherry wine	

Melt butter in saucepan over medium flame; add shallots, sage, thyme, celery, garlic, salt, pepper, and pinch of paprika; sauté 5 minutes, or until shallots are soft.

Meanwhile, mince lobster meat; place in large mixing bowl.

In separate mixing bowl mix bread crumbs and well-beaten egg; add sautéed shallots to bread crumbs. Add bread-crumb mixture to lobster meat; mix thoroughly. Add sherry wine sufficient to moisten stuffing slightly; mix well.

Use stuffing as desired. For smaller fish, use ½ amounts given here.

VARIATION: *Clam Herb Stuffing.* Omit lobster; follow recipe; use 1 cup raw, minced clams.

Crab Meat Herb Stuffing. Omit lobster; follow recipe; use 1 cup cooked crab meat.

Oyster Herb Stuffing. Omit lobster; follow recipe; use 1 cup raw, minced oyster.

Prawn or Shrimp Herb Stuffing. Omit lobster; follow recipe; use 1 cup raw, peeled, minced prawns or shrimp.

~§ Light, well-chilled, dry white wines are best with most sea foods. If you prefer a pale old sherry with *Lobster Bisque,* it's quite all right and very delicious when just slightly chilled. Many persons prefer all types of sherry served at room temperature, but I always serve it slightly chilled. Careful chilling, and not too much, will not interfere with the fruity bouquet of most sherries.

If red wines are ever served with sea food, always select those wines which are very dry and light: a *médoc,* a *rosé,* or a *sparkling burgundy.* The combination of flavors will *always be right,* however, when you serve a *white wine* with all sea food.

The following chart identifies the type, taste, color, and quality of a number of excellent white wines and suggests the temperature at which they should be served with specific courses. My favorite of them all is either an *American* or *Alsatian Riesling* with all shellfish except lobster. With this crustacean nothing is quite so delicious as a very cold, very dry *champagne.*

✑§ WINES TO SERVE WITH FISH AND SHELLFISH

TYPE OF WINE	TASTE	COLOR AND QUALITY	SERVING TEMPERATURE	WITH COURSES
BORDEAUX BLANC	Medium sweet	Straw-colored, fruity	Chilled*	All
CHABLIS	Medium dry	Pale, full-bodied	Chilled	All
CHABLIS SUPERIEUR	Very dry	Pale yellow	Chilled	All
CHAMPAGNE	Very dry	Pale, sparkling	Cold*	Lobster
GRAVES	Crisp dry	Pale, fruity	Chilled	All
HAUT BARZAC	Sweet	Golden, fragrant	Well chilled*	All
HAUT SAUTERNE	Sweet	Pale, full-bodied	Well chilled	All
MADEIRA, DRY	Dry	Golden, full-bodied	Chilled	Canapés, and cocktails
MOSELLE	Medium dry	Straw-colored, light-bodied	Chilled	All
RHINE (ALSATIAN)	Dry	Straw-colored, fruity	Chilled	All
RHINE (AMERICAN)	Dry	Pale, light-bodied	Chilled	All
RIESLING (ALSATIAN)	Dry	Straw-colored, fruity	Chilled*	All
RIESLING (AMERICAN)	Dry	Pale, light-bodied	Chilled	All
SAUTERNE	Medium dry	Golden, full-bodied	Chilled	All
SAUTERNE, DRY	Dry	Golden, fruity	Chilled	All

SHERRY, EXTRA DRY	Dry	Pale, fruity	Chilled	Bisques, soups, chowders, and stews
SHERRY, GOLDEN	Medium dry	Golden, full-bodied	Room temperature	All
SHERRY, OLD	Dry	Pale, full-bodied	Room temperature	Canapés and cocktails
SPARKLING MOSELLE	Medium dry	Pale, light-bodied	Cold*	All
SPARKLING SAUTERNE	Medium dry	Golden, light-bodied	Cold	All
WHITE BURGUNDY	Medium dry	Golden, full-bodied	Well chilled*	All
WHITE CHIANTI	Medium dry	Pale, light-bodied	Chilled*	All
WHITE PORT	Sweet	Pale, fragrant	Room temperature	Canapés and cocktails

* Chilled—55° F.
** Cold—35° F.
*** Well chilled—50° F.

20. Standard Measurements

~~~~~~

DRY

1 tbs. (salt)	1 oz.
1 tbs. (flour)	¼ oz.
2 tbs. (butter)	1 oz.
4 tbs. (flour)	1 oz.
16 tbs. (flour)	1 cup
1 cup (flour)	4 ozs.
2 cups (sugar)	1 lb.
16 ozs.	1 lb.
1 lb.	453 grams
2 lbs., 3 ozs.	1 kilogram

LIQUID

1 tsp.	25 drops
3 tsp.	1 tbs.
2 tbs.	1 oz.
2 tbs.	½ wineglass
4 tbs.	¼ cup
4 tbs.	1 gill
1 cup	½ pt.
4 gills	1 pt.
16 ozs.	1 pt.
1 pt.	1 lb.
2 pts.	1 qt.
4 qts.	1 gal.
1 cup	¼ liter
2 cups	½ liter
4 cups	1 liter

All measurements are level; based on standard measuring spoons and cups.

❧ INDEX ❧